ART AND THE SOCIAL ORDER

By

D. W. GOTSHALK

THE UNIVERSITY OF CHICAGO PRESS
CHICAGO · ILLINOIS

701
G683A
Cop. 1

THE UNIVERSITY OF CHICAGO PRESS, CHICAGO 37
Cambridge University Press, London, N.W. 1, England
W. J. Gage & Co., Limited, Toronto 2B, Canada

Copyright 1947 by The University of Chicago. All rights reserved
Published 1947. Composed and printed by THE UNIVERSITY
OF CHICAGO PRESS, Chicago, Illinois, U.S.A.

To

NAOMI

Who Also Made the Journey

ACKNOWLEDGMENTS

For permission to quote from the book or books mentioned in parentheses immediately after their names, the author wishes to thank the following publishing companies: George Allen and Unwin, Limited (*Foundations of Aesthetics* by C. K. Ogden, I. A. Richards, and J. Wood); D. Appleton–Century Company, Incorporated (*Beauty and Human Nature* by A. R. Chandler, copyright 1934 by the publishers; *The Beginnings of Art* by Ernst Grosse, Eng. trans.); Jonathan Cape, Limited, and Peter Smith, Publisher (*The Craft of Fiction* by Percy Lubbock); Chatto and Windus (*Art* by Clive Bell); Coward-McCann, Incorporated (*Great Pictures of Europe* by Thomas Munro); Thomas Y. Crowell Company (*Aesthetic Analysis* by D. W. Prall); Doubleday and Company, Incorporated, and the Hogarth Press (*Hogarth Essays* by Roger Fry and others); Harcourt, Brace and Company, Incorporated (*The Materials of the Artist* by Max Doerner; *Beauty: An Interpretation of Art and the Imaginative Life* by Helen H. Parkhurst); Harcourt, Brace and Company, and Methuen and Company, Limited (*The Sacred Wood* by T. S. Eliot); Harcourt, Brace and Company, and Faber and Faber, Limited (*Art Now* by Herbert Read); Harper and Brothers (*The Olive Tree* by Aldous Huxley); Houghton Mifflin Company (*Ten O'Clock* by James McNeill Whistler; *The Road to Xanadu* by J. L. Lowes; *The Spirit of Modern Philosophy* by Josiah Royce); J. B. Lippincott Company (*A Century of Hero Worship* by Eric Bentley, copyright 1944 by the author); Little, Brown and Company and the Atlantic Monthly Press (*The Unforgotten Years* by Logan P. Smith); Liveright Publishing Corporation (*A General Introduction to Psychoanalysis* by Sigmund Freud; *A B C of Aesthetics* by Leo Stein); the Macmillan Company (*The Limitations of Music* by Eric Blom; *How To Enjoy Pictures* by J. Littlejohns); W. W. Norton and Company, Incorporated (*Discovering Poetry* by Elizabeth Drew, copyright 1937 by the publishers; *Science and Poetry* by I. A. Richards, copyright

viii ACKNOWLEDGMENTS

1926 by the publishers); Oxford University Press (*The Italian Painters of the Renaissance* by Bernard Berenson; *The Art and Craft of Drawing* by Vernon Blake; *XXth Century Sculptors* and *Some Modern Sculptors* by S. Casson); Princeton University Press (*The Arts and the Art of Criticism* by T. M. Greene; *The Intent of the Critic*, ed. Donald Stauffer); G. P. Putnam's Sons (*On Being an Architect* by W. Lescaze); Random House, Incorporated (*Beloved Friend* by C. D. Bowen and Barbara van Mech); the Rice Institute Committee on Publications (*The Breviary of Aesthetic* by B. Croce); Rinehart and Company, Incorporated (*The Sculptor's Way* by Brenda Putnam, copyright 1939 by the author); Charles Scribner's Sons (*Representation and Form* by William Abell; *Reason in Art* by George Santayana); Simon and Schuster, Incorporated (*Modern Art* by Thomas Craven, copyright 1934 and 1940 by the author); and Stechert-Hafner, Incorporated (*Form Problems of the Gothic* by W. Worringer).

I am indebted to the *British Journal of Psychology*, F. C. Bartlett, editor, for permission to quote from E. Bullough's article, "Psychical Distance as a Factor in Art and an Aesthetic Principle" in Volume V (1913); to the *Encyclopaedia Britannica*, Walter Yust, editor, for permission to quote from B. Croce's article "Aesthetics" in the 1942 edition; and to the *Nation*, for permission to use the passages cited from articles by J. W. Krutch, Thomas Mann, and Herbert Read and from the review by Louise Bogan. Finally, I wish to thank the editors of the *Journal of Philosophy* for permission to use material from my article "A Relational Theory of Fine Art" (June, 1941); and the editors of the *Antioch Review* for a similar permission regarding the article "Art in Modern Society" (winter, 1946).

The Research Board of the University of Illinois, Dean R. D. Carmichael, chairman, granted me sabbatical leave to study in Europe and begin this book and, several years later, a half-time research appointment to complete it. I wish to express my very great gratitude to these men for their generous assistance. I am very grateful also to the Committee on Publications of the American Philosophical Association, especially to Dean Glenn R. Morrow, of the University of Pennsylvania, chairman, for reading my book with approval and making helpful suggestions and recommendations. On several occasions the Saturday Evening Club of the University of Illinois invited me to present selections from this work, and I profited greatly from the discussions at these meetings. To Professor Arthur E. Murphy, of Cornell University, I am indebted for sound practical advice and important general criticisms. To my colleague, Professor Max H. Fisch, I am grateful for innumerable stylistic improvements. On a grant from the University Research Board, Miss Lucille Ellis prepared the final typescript, and to her and the Board I wish to record my thanks for this service. Most of all, I wish to acknowledge my debt to my wife, whose companionship, help, and very great forbearance have been invaluable.

D. W. G.

Urbana, Illinois
1947

FOREWORD

Pʜɪʟᴏsᴏᴘʜʏ is usually regarded as a difficult study. Yet philosophy is merely life, its circumstances and purposes, generalized and organized into vision. Its subject is the most common material of human experience. Possibly the difficulty of philosophy is its generality. Day-to-day living is in terms of particular persons, situations, claims, and counterclaims. It invades the level of generality only spasmodically and fugitively. To follow a philosophical discourse requires a transposition of attention from ordinary levels. One must think of "perception" instead of the view from the southwest bedroom and of "dissonance" instead of the awful racket emanating from the neighbor's kitchen.

This book is an invitation to a philosophical discussion of fine art. The problems that it considers are typically general. Instead of the particular nature and implications of Beethoven's *Fifth Symphony* or Joyce's *Ulysses*, it discusses the general nature and implications of fine art. Particular instances are cited mainly to illustrate or verify theories which are broad and generic in scope. In recent times such theories of art have been particularly numerous. Indeed, when this book was first undertaken, the most interesting fact to the author was the great variety of rival philosophical theories challenging critical thought. Especially interesting were the many "nihilist" theories ("art is play," "art is escape," "art is conscious self-deception," etc.) that had come to prominence in the late nineteenth and early twentieth centuries in the wake of the evolution hypothesis and the Industrial Revolution. These theories seemed to have a surprising congruence with the spirit of the current middle-class capitalist society, for in this society, founded on technologies derived from the sciences, the arts were rapidly becoming mere entertainment devices or were receding more and more toward the periphery of human interest and social life. Where should the arts stand in a dynamic social order founded on scientific intelligence and oriented toward the best social good? Had the arts passed their heyday, as Hegel claimed? Were the arts nearing their demise, as Spengler insisted? Long ago Socrates had suggested that fine art is a third-rate human enterprise and should have only incidental place in a social order founded on reason and scientifically trained intelligence. Was this the view coming into actualization in our society? Was this the only possibility of the arts in our times?

Interesting as this social question was, it plainly presupposed an even more fundamental philosophical question. What is art? What is the general nature and purpose of the artistic transaction? Socrates' view of art as a third-rate human enterprise clearly stemmed from his theory of art as imitation; and the apparently diminishing position of the arts in recent Western society obviously rested upon certain general widespread assumptions regarding the nature and purpose of art that the play, escape, and other "nihilist" theories were formulating explicitly. The general social question forced one back to the even more fundamental philosophical question of the generic nature of art, which itself brought one face to face again with the great variety of theory challenging attention in recent philosophical thought.

The aim of this book is to consider the general social question and the basic theoretical question necessary to resolve it. Two problems are discussed: What is art? What is the importance of the arts for social life, especially in the twentieth century? The first problem is given immediate and extended attention, since, if it can be answered satisfactorily, the implications of the arts for social life can be stated with a maximum of ease, clarity, completeness, and certitude. To facilitate an understanding of the answer to this problem, which is contained in Parts I and II of this book, let me briefly summarize the aim, content, and standpoint of these earlier parts.

The definition of art proposed for analysis is relatively simple. Fine art is the creation of objects for aesthetic experience. The analytic development of this definition is relatively novel. The novelty springs from the standpoint from which the analytic development is undertaken. This is the relational standpoint. It finds the clue to the distinctive nature of art not in some process or object or feature of these entering the artistic transaction but in the triadic pattern of creation-object-apprehension implied in the proposed definition of art. In recent speculation the usual procedure has been different. It has been to select some element within the triadic pattern and to offer it as embodying the distinctive meaning of art. This element might be in the creative process (e.g., play) or in the public object, the work of art (e.g., significant form, the expression of feeling or insight) or among the functions of the apprehending process (e.g., escape)—the play, escape, and other nihilist theories taking on a dominantly genetic or functional coloring according to the evolutionary or pragmatic emphasis of their advocates. The result has been to proliferate the great variety of recent theories of art just mentioned, of which there might have been many more, since a very large number of factors occur within the triadic pattern of fine art.

In contrast, the relational theory cuts below this surface variety and seeks to restudy the artistic transaction in the light of the underlying unity that makes this variety relevant and important. It rests upon the principle of interrelation of process-object-process imbedded in the artistic transaction, and it develops a general theory of art with this principle as its clue. The result is a relatively fresh conception of the artistic venture, more inclusive than any provided by the multitude of recent partial theories, as the text, I believe, will show. Besides novelty of approach, the analysis develops certain novelties of detail. Aesthetic experience and artistic creation are interpreted differently, as is the work of art or public object which is conceived as a four-dimensional relational structure. The main claim, however, is not that the interpretations given are picturesquely "different" or "new" but that they are more comprehensive of, and more adequate to, all the facts of art than are the prevailing views. Incidentally, the relational standpoint is applied to art's total nature—art in its broad human ramifications—as well as to the distinctive nature of art. In this connection, fine art is conceived as a unique triadic pattern internally related to a larger pattern constituted by a physical and social environment or milieu.

We may say, then, that the aim and content of Parts I and II are an analytic structural interpretation of the artistic transaction. The members of this transaction—the creative process, the work of art or public object, the aesthetic experience—are interpreted in relation to one another and derive their meaning as terms in the definition of art from their interconnection in a single whole. No a priori merit is ascribed to the relational standpoint employed throughout. The standpoint is used as a hypothesis. Its function is merely to implement analysis, and its merit consists solely of its capacity to bring together the great variety of relevant empirical detail and verified theory about art into a realistic, balanced, inclusive, and illuminating view.

We shall begin with an analysis of the aesthetic experience. As we shall see, this experience is in some ways the most important factor of all for understanding the distinctive nature of art from the relational standpoint.

CONTENTS

PART I

THE BASIC PROCESSES

I

THE AESTHETIC EXPERIENCE

WHAT is aesthetic experience? Our interest here is not in the meaning of words but in the nature of a process that will be central and crucial for the artistic enterprise as we shall interpret it. In this sense aesthetic experience, I believe, is simply intrinsic perception, or attention to an object or a field preeminently for the apprehension of the full intrinsic perceptual being and value of the object or field. This is the experience at its highest level. The experience, however, may occur at many levels. A minor instance would be the perception of a sense quality—a timbre, a texture, a brilliant flash of pink in the sky—for its striking intrinsic character. Such tiny ripples of aesthetic experience repeatedly break through the hard crust of everyday routine, adding variety and gaiety to ordinary existence. A major instance would be the extensive attention that one might give to the intrinsic features of a powerful artistic creation or of a sublime expanse of wild nature, simply for a full perception of them. Or, at the edge of a great city, one may come upon an immense park spread out below one, and the vista—the great space, the pattern of trees and paths and low hills, the leisurely movement of the people, the clear air, the light-blue sky—may seem a marvelous picture of sumptuous peace after the crowds and clatter and rank odors of the great city. The wholehearted attention to this vast panorama pre-eminently for the sake of the apprehension of what it offers to perception—the colors, the easy movements, the loose rhythms, the spatial sweep, the light, the air, above all, the deep sumptuous peace—would be a large-scale instance of aesthetic experience, according to the view proposed here.

3

Besides describing innumerable actual experiences, this characterization conforms to the original meaning of the term "aesthetic." This term is derived from the Greek *aisthesis*, meaning "perception." Intrinsic perception is simply perception given major scope, depth, and dignity. In modern times, however, thanks to the influence of eighteenth-century writers such as A. G. Baumgarten (1714–62), the term "aesthetic" became the equivalent of the term "beautiful," and numerous modern theories of aesthetic experience have been efforts to describe the experience of the beautiful. This modern limitation of the term "aesthetic" was entirely arbitrary, as a glance at the original meaning of the term shows. Moreover, if the term "beautiful" is used in the ordinary sense in which it excludes the gloomy, the heartrending, the grotesque, the crude, the droll, the morbid, and the searing, there is at least one reason for rejecting the limitation of the aesthetic to the beautiful in the present inquiry. The gloomy, the heartrending, the grotesque, and the like, as Tolstoy has pointed out, occur in what are indubitable works of fine art. There is bitter as well as sweet art, the difficult as well as the charming. Thus the limitation of the aesthetic to the beautiful in the ordinary sense would make the term hopelessly inadequate at the start for any comprehensive characterization of the kind of experience brought to fulfilment by the arts. It is to avoid this disadvantage, which is entirely unnecessary, that we reject the limitation of the term "aesthetic" originating in the eighteenth century, although our account of the aesthetic experience includes as a subtype the experience of the beautiful in the ordinary sense.

The aesthetic experience has been described by us as a process, and a process involves activity. In what sense does activity enter into the aesthetic experience? Certain types of activity can be ruled out at once. To gaze across a landscape and daydream about home and mother is no more aesthetic than to gaze across a landscape in order to calculate how much time it might take you to walk to a certain point or to determine whether you are color blind. Aesthetic attention is, above all, object-centered attention, and it ceases the moment attention wanders from the object into tangential reverie or to concerns about one's self. The attitude of ordinary reverie, in particular, is anything but aesthetic. Ordinarily, there is no effort or intent to expand perception. Effort is relaxed, attention is haphazard and indiscriminate, and the experience as a whole is anaesthetic, serving to dull, rather than to enlarge and intensify, perceptual consciousness.

Aesthetic experience, however, has sometimes been described as detached from all practical action and as involving a certain psychical distancing. This feature of the experience received some notice from Aristotle, Aquinas, and Kant; but to the student of recent thought the name of the British psychologist, Edward Bullough, will probably come first to mind. Bullough's theory of psychical distance seems most unique and successful as a description of the negative side of the aesthetic experience, and its emphasis here upon putting at a distance nonaesthetic interests is certainly correct.[1] Yet, even in regard to the negative side of the aesthetic experience, the theory is not altogether satisfactory. Thus Bullough speaks of "putting the phenomenon, so to speak, out of gear with our practical actual self." But, clearly, this is not true in every sense. For example, in viewing a work of fine art aesthetically, it is simply not true in numerous cases that elements of our practical, actual self do not operate, or even that they do not act on the phenomenon. One turns a painting to the source of light, one walks around a statue or a building, one changes the volume of the music coming from the radio or phonograph, one reads a poem aloud. In a sense the phenomena here remain decidedly in gear with our active actual self, and overt muscular behavior of many types comes into play during the experience. An experience of a phenomenon is aesthetic, I believe, not by virtue of the inhibition of all action and the consequent separation of the active actual self from the phenomenon, for this often does not take place, but by virtue of the control and subordination of action to the amplification of intrinsic per-

[1] E. Bullough, "Psychical Distance as a Factor in Art and an Aesthetic Principle," *British Journal of Psychology*, V (1913), 87–118. On its positive side, aesthetic experience is described as "interpreting even our 'subjective' affections . . . . as characteristics of the phenomenon." Here Bullough's theory is not essentially different from the empathy theory, of which we shall say something later on.

ception, which actually does take place. This subordination of overt action to the amplification of intrinsic perception is a fundamental feature of the negative side of the aesthetic experience, and its explicit recognition is required, along with putting at a distance nonaesthetic interests, in any adequate description even of this side of the process.

We may say at once, then, without attempting at this point any complete answer to the above question about activity in the aesthetic experience, that this experience involves at least active interested attention to its object and various muscular and bodily actions subordinated to the aesthetic interest in the object and that these overt actions may have a large role. It remains true however, as Bullough and others have contended, that there is a basic difference between aesthetic experience and practical activity. This difference, however, is not, I believe, in the presence and absence of overt action but in the position occupied by perception. In so-called "practical" activity, perception is a means to a metaperceptual end. When one drinks a glass of milk, avoids an onrushing automobile, or helps a friend with a distressing personal problem, perception is merely a means to the drinking, the avoiding, or the helping. It is harnessed to these metaperceptual ends and is reduced to a cryptic, economical recording of qualities and events significant for these ends. And if flickers of aesthetic experience occur during the actions, they are incidental and are crushed like the tip of a lighted cigarette if the requirements of the metaperceptual ends demand. In aesthetic experience the opposite is the case. Primarily, perception of the field is the end; and actions, such as moving the head, swaying the body, humming to one's self as one listens to music, are cut to serve perception, to make it more clear and precise, more ample and subtle. Far from being the prime concern of the experience, these actions pass almost unnoticed by the percipient in the absorption of rapt aesthetic experience, and they are eliminated entirely whenever they are useless or obstructive to successful aesthetic response. What is primary in so-called "practical" activity is incidental and secondary in aesthetic experience, just as self-terminal perception, which is the internal principle of the aesthetic response, is incidental and secondary in the so-called "practical" activities of life.

II. COGNITIVE THEORIES: THE ROLE OF KNOWLEDGE

Observation in science—the delicate perceptual activity of the pure research worker—has sometimes been described in terms similar to some that we have used in describing aesthetic experience, e.g., as free from the narrowing urgencies of so-called "practical" action and as the opposite of daydreaming. How does such perceptual activity differ from the aesthetic response as we have described it?

The difference between the two is genuine, I believe, and may be stated as follows: Both activities employ perception. But scientific observation, like so-called "practical" activity, employs perception as a means to a further end, in its case the derivation or verification of a description or an explanation of features of observed situations. Knowledge is the end—grounded and tested information—and perception is incidental to this. Thus a chemist applies a Bunsen burner, an electric current, or a drop of acid to a new compound to discover the temperature at which the compound will disintegrate. As a scientist, his end is to determine the temperature of disintegration of the compound and to formulate a statement of it that will survive criticism from scientific experts. His perception is a means to this end. Now aesthetic experience reverses this pattern of scientific observation as fully as it does that of so-called "practical" activity. Knowledge, like action, is a means, and aesthetic experience employs knowledge, sometimes large stores of it, to light up points within the perceptual field and to help to establish a full and amplified perception of all that is perceptible there. But the perception is the end. Suppose, for example, the chemist should alter his compound to create a more resplendent perceptual field. Suppose, further, that he ceased to busy himself with measuring the thermal behavior of his compound and gave the whole power of his mind to perception and let his entire consciousness, as Schopenhauer says, be filled with a quiet apprehension of all the aspects of the object—the colors, the shapes, the patterns—actually present to his perception. Then our chemist would have ceased to be engaged with the compound as a scientist and would have become engaged, however briefly, in an aesthetic response.

Basically, the difference between aesthetic experience and scientific observation, according to this view, is a difference of purpose, aim, direction, or immanent plan. The two move in opposite directions and with opposite aims or immanent plans.

Cognitive theories of aesthetic experience, however, which describe knowledge as its end, have not been lacking since Plato described the aim of art as the purveying of third-rate information. Indeed, cognitive theories have considerable vogue at the present time, being held in some form by such diverse thinkers as Bergson, Croce, Roger Fry, D. W. Prall, S. C. Pepper, T. M. Greene, and Leo Stein, among others. Such theories, I believe, unwittingly jeopardize the status of art and the aesthetic response as major modes of human activity. They set art and aesthetic experience in manifest rivalry with science, since they ascribe to art, aesthetic experience, and science the same generic aim. Such a view opens the floodgates to those who, like recent nihilists, would dispraise the arts, since in the attainment of knowledge (the aim of science) few today at least will be persuaded, despite the attacks of the anti-intellectuals, that science has an equal, much less a superior, either in the arts or in the aesthetic response.

Cognitive theorists have not been unaware of the danger of their procedure and have sought to avoid it by assigning to science a certain area of objects, reserving another area for art and aesthetic experience. But this position does not seem tenable. Typical of it are the following assertions: Science deals with the space-time structure of the world; art and aesthetic experience with the qualitative stuff or surface. Science deals with causes and effects; art and aesthetic experience with things in isolation, independent of their causes or effects. Science is concerned with facts; art and aesthetic experience with values. Science deals with the abstract and universal; art and aesthetic experience with the concrete and individual. In most of these contrasts "science" means either physical science or an inquiry modeled on it, and this suggests a direction in which a partial difference of object matter between science and art or aesthetic experience might be found. Microscopic physics deals with the subperceptual—electrons, protons, electromagnetic waves; but it is not possible to manipulate artistically, or to have an aesthetic experience of, the subperceptual or the superperceptual, but only the middle-sized entities which fall within the field of perception itself.

Apart from this, however, there seems to be no difference in object matter between art or aesthetic experience and science in its full scope. Thus, to compare aesthetic experience in particular and science: in apprehending the three-dimensional rhythms of masses in deep space or the pattern of succession in the notes of a flute passage, aesthetic experience deals with the space and time structure of things, while, in the study of sound by the physicist and in the analysis of color by the psychologist, science deals with the qualitative stuff or surface of the world. In appreciating a sequence of musical tones as the projection of a certain violinist or pianist, aesthetic experience deals with a cause-effect structure, while, in treating (say) a gas in a certain chamber or area as a closed system and analyzable independent of its causal setting, science gets about as close as man ever does to dealing with things in isolation and without reference to antecedents or consequents. In the perception of the grass of a field or a storm over the ocean, aesthetic experience certainly deals with facts, while, in analyzing the preferences exhibited in animal and human behavior and in summarizing the uniformities among these preferences, psychology and social science are certainly dealing with evaluations and values. As to the abstract and universal, in the appreciation of an elliptical contour in a sky or of a general trait of character in a dramatic agent or in a portrait, aesthetic experience deals with the abstract and the universal, while the material entities and situations examined by science are always particular and concrete, individual and unique, and some sciences—notably geography, geology, and psychology in case studies—aim largely at a knowledge of the individual and the concrete, e.g., a particular region of the earth's surface or subsurface or the par-

ticular character and history of the individual person subjected
to psychological study.

It must be admitted that there is a difference between science
and aesthetic experience in the treatment of these object matters.
But this difference is exactly what one would expect if one supposed the two activities merely to have different aims—tested
knowledge and intrinsic perception. Moreover, these different
aims give the qualitative, the "isolated," the concrete, the particular, and the values of things whatever superiority they have
as materials for aesthetic experience, even as they give the space
and time dimensions, the cause-effect structure, the universal,
the abstract, and the matter-of-fact whatever superiority they
have as materials for science. The superiority for aesthetic experience of the qualitative, the isolated, the concrete, the particular, and the values of things, for example, arises from the
fact that, as psychologically more immediate and full-bodied for
most people, they offer a more substantial and inviting field for
the expansion of intrinsic perception which is the achievement
of the aesthetic aim. This superiority, however, is purely relative. Indeed, in the appreciation of works of fine art, numerous
people find most excitement and satisfaction in the intrinsic perception of abstract spatial organization (architecture, sculpture,
painting), represented causal sequence (drama), matter-of-fact
characterizations (novel), abstract and universal expressive traits
(portraiture, music). In sum, there is nothing within the range
of perception, universal or particular, spatiotemporal or qualitative, causal or isolated, fact or value, which may not prove superior material for aesthetic experience or, for that matter, appropriate material for scientific analysis; and this is probably the
only unqualified general truth that can be asserted about the object matter of either activity.

Cognitive theories themselves contain, of course, a certain
amount of truth about art and the aesthetic response. Cognitive
elements, for example, operate throughout the aesthetic response. Even in the simplest cases, such as beholding a simple
color combination in the sky, the aesthetic experience involves
the operation of a mass of funded knowledge making possible

the recognition of the sorts of colors, lines, shapes, and volumes being perceived. Such effortless recognition of the obvious is necessary to put the perception in rapport with the content of the object and permit the perception to rise without intellectual interruptions to the full aesthetic level. More complicated aesthetic experiences, particularly of works of fine art, often use both larger ranges of funded knowledge and incidental intellectual analyses. The appreciation of a painting by Watteau is aided by applying both one's general powers of art analysis and one's particular knowledge of the Flemish and Venetian traditions in painting and of early modern French civilization, to help one to see more fully precisely what is before one on the canvas. A page of Dante becomes much more vivid if one's experience of it is aided by knowledge of the Italian language and history, Greek and medieval science and philosophy, and an analytical apprehension of metrical form.[2] All such knowledge and analytic attention are not only useful preliminaries but helpful factors in aesthetic experience, provided that they do not become the center of the experience but are used as means to clarify and to enrich the apprehension of what is offered perception by the object.

In general, this is also the place of "truth" in works of fine art, in music, in literature, and in the graphic arts, not to make the aesthetic experience a rival of science in a different field but to draw out and excite the cognitive powers so that the aesthetic experience moves on more than the minimum psychical level and intrinsic perception is correspondingly enhanced. Truth is a helpful factor, not the end. Truth is an amplification of the aesthetic response by addition of a stimulation to the experient and an intrinsic content to the object. In works of literature the cognitive element is sometimes so predominant that these works are taken as philosophical tracts or as documents of psychological and social situations and are discussed as such. Literature, particularly prose literature, is the borderland where art is mixed most freely with "science" and "philosophy" and where attention is most prone to shift from intrinsic perception of the particular work be-

[2] Cf. H. N. Lee, *Perception and Aesthetic Value* (New York: Prentice-Hall Book Co., 1938), p. 134.

fore one to primary preoccupation with general ideas and their verification in the facts of psychological and social experience. And literary artists have, of course, used "ideas" primarily for metaperceptual ends and with indifference to intrinsic enrichment, often to the detriment of their works as aesthetic objects. In works of the graphic arts the thought is less likely to come to the center and more likely to remain an element contributing incidentally and properly to the intrinsic perceptual response. "This comparative Dimness and Untraceableness of the thoughts," writes Ruskin, "is not a *fault* in the thoughts, at such a time. It is, on the contrary, a necessary condition of their subordination to the pleasure of Sight. If the thoughts were more distinct we should not *see* so well, and beginning to think, we must comparatively cease to see."[3]

Besides a useful preparation for, and a factor in, the aesthetic experience, knowledge also results from the aesthetic response. In witnessing a characteristic play of Shakespeare, for example, one may learn a good deal incidentally about Elizabethan conceptions, manners, and taste. Probably no aesthetic experience of intensity, from gazing at a vast American prairie to exploring a complicated work of fine art, fails to leave some residual imprint on thought. Our chief point in this discussion has been merely that the primary aim of the aesthetic experience is not to engage the cognitive powers and leave an imprint on thought. Its primary aim is the elaboration of intrinsic perception. But, since perception contains cognitive elements, the elaboration of intrinsic perception will engage cognitive powers and leave an imprint on thought. Indeed, one of the chief themes of this book is that the full elaboration of intrinsic perception, especially in the experience of works of fine art, results in all sorts of surprising important consequences. This is not because the aesthetic experience is not intrinsic perception but precisely because it is and because intrinsic perception, vigorously exercised, inevitably has such consequences, as we shall see.

[3] John Ruskin, *Modern Painters*, III (3d ed.; New York: John Wiley & Son, 1868), 288. Italics and capitals in original.

III. EMPATHY

Besides scientific observation, there are other types of perceptual activity similar to, yet distinguishable from, aesthetic experience, e.g., that of the partisan spectator at an athletic contest. To be sure, an athletic contest can be taken aesthetically, since anything perceptible can. To take it aesthetically, a person would view the conflict, the surprise, the suspense, the skill, the fury of the contest, for their intrinsic perceptual appeal. The "show" would be the thing. This is hardly the attitude of the partisan spectator. Much more than a show, an athletic contest is for him a struggle for victory, and he is interested primarily in the winning of that victory. He wants his side to win, he cheers for it, and, like a hunter who scarcely notices the scenery in chasing the fox, he follows the play and watches the score chiefly for the bearing of each on the losing or the winning. Perhaps there is no spectator, at least at a contest between able opponents, who is so rabidly partisan that his experience does not contain moments of aesthetic perception, when, forgetting everything else, he is lost momentarily in viewing some maneuver or incident for its sheer intrinsic appeal. But for the partisan such moments are not the chief thing. The winning is. Indeed, the usual partisan spectator will pass over, or even rejoice in, almost unbelievably sloppy playing by his side or by its opponent, provided that it helps his side to win.

Nor is this interest in the result or in victory confined to sports spectators of the rabidly partisan type. An athletic contest between mediocre players which has a great stake, such as a championship, will usually bring out a far greater crowd than a match between much abler opponents in which nothing at all is at stake; and, although a great many in the crowd may not be partisans interested in a particular side's winning, the overwhelming majority usually are very much interested in seeing who does win; and this interest in seeing the winning of the victory with its attendant honors rather than an interest in seeing in its perfection a faultless perceptual whole is the decisive factor in determining their attendance. Equally nonaesthetic interests govern, I believe, the attitude of the usual spectator of murder trials, public executions, city fires, mob demonstrations, etc. Doubtless an aesthetic interest may operate here; indeed, in a few instances, it may be dominant. But the usual dominant interest of the inveterate "fan" of such occasions, I think, is something different —the satisfaction of morbid curiosity, of sadistic impulses, of the itch for excitement, and the like rather than the having for its own sake of a rich, flawless, and marvelously well-ordered perceptual experience of an object.

The discussion of athletic contests brings up the theory of *Einfühlung* or empathy, which has been offered as an account of the aesthetic experience. In simplest terms, empathy in its current meaning is the perception of an object in terms of its movement or its tendency to movement, actual or supposed. The object may actually be static and inert and only suggest tendency or movement, as a statue such as a Michelangelo "Bound Slave"; or it may actually be dynamic and alive, as a ballet dancer. In either case the spectator perceives the object in terms of its tendencies and movements or its suggestions of tendencies and movements, and, in consequence, the object is experienced in a new light. The figure depicted by Michelangelo, instead of being inert and static, seems sinking in exhausting struggle; and the ballet dancer, instead of being one more object passing in space, seems radiant with inner impulse and grace, joyous energy, and sparkling life. Empathy, however, may occur not merely in perceiving statues and ballet dancers but also in witnessing athletic contests in rabidly partisan fashion. Moreover, it may occur here not as an interruption of partisan perception, as the aesthetic experience is according to our view, but as an organic factor of such perception. The very zeal to witness the victory of his favorite athlete may lead a partisan to perceive the athlete vividly in terms of his actual and suggested tendencies and movements, and this empathic perception may be so vigorous, indeed, that at the end of the contest the spectator, not to mention his neighbors, is utterly exhausted, even more so than the athlete.

It must be said at once that, whatever its defects as a theory of the aesthetic response, the empathy theory makes important contributions to an adequate understanding of the positive side of the aesthetic experience. The empathy theory, first of all, brings into prominence the factors of imagination and feeling. In empathy the tendencies and movements, actual or supposed, on which the perception of the object is based are not merely noted cognitively but also performed imaginatively by the percipient in terms of the object. They are "felt" in the object. This type of imaginative and affective appreciation of the content of an object is generally true of the best aesthetic experience, as an instrument of apprehending most vividly what is there for intrinsic perception. Empathy also brings into prominence another characteristic of the full-scale aesthetic response, previously mentioned, viz., object centrality. This is basic in empathy. It is also basic in aesthetic experience. In the aesthetic experience the great concern is to let all that is present in the object appear to the self in the fullest and most vivid manner. The object consequently becomes the guide, and the self submits to its lead, allowing his powers to run into all the grooves of the object to their fullest capacity. This submissive union of the self with the object, the aesthetic unison, is undertaken, however, for the sake of a more intimate and lively perceptual appreciation of the actualities and suggestions, the settled content and overtones, of the object, not for the sake of distorting the object by imposition of subjective fancy. Transformation by the object, not transformation of the object, is the chief thing. "The aesthetic unison means the transformation of the self in terms of the object, and sentimentality means the transformation of the object in terms of the self."[4] Through transformation by the object in the aesthetic unison, the self is able to attain in his own being the fullest possible apprehension of the object's intrinsic perceptual value and being, which is the aim of the aesthetic experience.

This characteristic of object centrality enables one to distinguish aesthetic experience from so-called "sensual" experience, e.g., eating and drinking. Some philosophers, Kant and Münsterberg, for example, have sought to distinguish these two types of

[4] Leo Stein, *A B C of Aesthetics* (New York: Boni and Liveright, 1927), p. 106.

experience by saying that the aesthetic experience contains a claim of universal validity that is absent from sensual experience. The aesthetic experient feels that his pleasure is universally valid and ought to be shared by all; the sensualist does not. But this seems highly dubious. Often, indeed, it is the enthusiast for a new food or drink who seems to feel that his enthusiasm is universally valid and ought to be shared by all, while the enthusiast for a new poem or picture frequently refuses to levy such an unqualified imperative on other people. In any case it is unnecessary to invoke such a highly controversial property as universal validity to distinguish the aesthetic from the sensual experience. Object centrality is sufficient. Sensual experience is organism-centered. When the sensualist drinks whiskey or eats a huge meal, his interest is in the bodily feelings arising, in the vigorous warmth or soft coolness in the throat and the frame. Organism centrality is painfully apparent in the violent sensualist, the ravenous feeder, the lascivious lover, the drug addict. Of course, one may have an aesthetic experience of the objects of sensual enjoyment. A person tasting whiskey who appreciated its gustatory properties as qualities intrinsic to the whiskey, objectified and resident there, would be having a minor aesthetic experience. But the unregenerate sensualist does not taste in this exquisite fashion. He tastes and eats and drinks as a tired summer hiker cools his feet in a stream or as a farmer, chilled to the bone in winter, warms his hands at a fire, not to perceive the object more completely but to have certain sensations in the organism. His experience is organism-centered, and, like tangential reverie and other types of experience wherein the object itself is not the major terminus of the experience but a means, sensual experience moves in a direction contrary to that of the aesthetic experience.

Returning to empathy, much aesthetic experience can be enriched by empathy, especially the intrinsic perception of static objects—zigzag and spiral lines, the spreading forms of plants and trees, statuary, the rhythmic shapes and sweeping lines of architecture. But the empathy theory by itself seems a very inadequate theory of aesthetic experience. Empathy seems to be more an instrument for vividly apprehending the motor properties and suggestions of objects, a mere mechanism of attention adaptable to many pursuits, not only the aesthetic but also those that are exact contraries of the aesthetic, e.g., partisan perception. Moreover, even when used for aesthetic ends, empathy is limited. There are aesthetic experiences into which, as some proponents of empathy, such as Vernon Lee, seem to grant, empathy does not enter. In coming suddenly and briefly upon a glorious sweet scent or a rich blue color, perception may be so captivated by the sheer sensory quality, the sheer sweetness or blueness intrinsic to the perceptual field, as not to go beyond it to the "motor" properties of the object. Thus much empathy is nonaesthetic, some aesthetic experiences are nonempathetic, and empathy itself is never more than an element in a total aesthetic response, one method of vivifying the content of an object for the fuller intrinsic perception of it.[5]

IV. ANALYSIS OF PERCEPTION

Aesthetic experience, then, is intrinsic perception or attention directed simply toward the full apprehension of the intrinsic perceptual being and value of the object of perception. What more precisely does "perception" mean in this theory of aesthetic experience? So far we have mentioned that perception involves intellectual or cognitive factors and sensation, imagination, and feeling. How are we to view these factors more systematically as elements of a single complex activity?

As understood in our account of the aesthetic process, perception is a complex operation with two major aspects, a "mechanical" and a "telic" aspect. The mechanical aspect consists of the powers of apprehension which operate in the perceptual act. In ordinary alert perception these powers, at a minimum, are three. The first is sensation, or the awareness of objects in their sensory features: their colors, pitches, timbres, textures, masses, bulks, weights, etc. The second is intuition in the Kantian, not in the Crocean, sense, primarily the awareness of objects in their spatial and temporal order and arrangement. The third is intellect, in minimum cases the usually effortless and variously muted inter-

[5] Cf. C. J. Ducasse, *Philosophy of Art* (New York: Dial Press, 1929), chap. x.

pretation both of the type of the object being perceived and of
the type of its detail, such as its sensory and spatiotemporal
features. Suppose, for example, that I am perceiving a blue vase.
Sensations, sight and touch chiefly, disclose the object as exhibiting color, texture, solidity, etc. Intuition discloses it as
exhibiting spatial position and arrangement. Intellect interprets
its color as turquoise blue, its texture as smooth glaze texture,
its spatial pattern as Chinese, and the total object as an imitation
oriental vase. It is true, of course, that, even in very alert ordinary perception, different persons often perceive objects differently. But this is due to differences in a common perceptual equipment, particularly differences in the capacity of their sense or-
gans and in the character of the symbols acquired from the
past and available for interpreting entities. If such persons do
perceive any object at all in a given perceptual act, however, they
will sense something, intuit something, and automatically recognize or deliberately judge what they sense and intuit to be
something, i.e., they will interpret it. Sensation, intuition, and
intellect, in some form, will enter into their act of perceiving an
object, although the form taken may exhibit individual differences.

Ordinary alert perception of objects usually contains, I believe, more than these three minimum mechanical factors. The
chief additional factors, I think, are feeling and imagination.
Suppose, for example, that the vase mentioned above is standing
on the top and squarely in the center of a small table at which I
wish to write a letter. Then, upon entering the room where the
table is located, intent upon writing, I might perceive the vase
not only as an individually shaped blue object of a certain sort
but also as a ''nuisance'' or as an annoying obstacle. Clearly, I
would be perceiving the vase with feeling, with annoyance, and
the feeling quality ''annoying'' would be a property of the object as perceived. But I would also be perceiving the vase with
imagination. By ''imagination'' is meant here the ability to connect the absent with the present or, more precisely, the ability
to apprehend as if present in an object for perception something
only suggested but not literally present. Thus the vase is not lit-

erally an obstacle to my writing as I enter the room and see it on the table. It would literally be such an obstacle only when, upon my trying to write at the table, the vase actually cramped my activity. Accordingly, for me to perceive the vase as an obstacle to my writing when I first enter the room, as I do, is to apprehend as if present in the object for perception something not literally present but only suggested or indicated. Such is imagination in perception.

Feeling and imagination, I believe, operate very considerably in all alert everyday perception. The operation of imagination here usually has a practical orientation and is locked in a total practical sequence as in the case of the vase just cited; and very often it consists simply of apprehending as if present in an object the feeling quality of a practical implication of the object, as when a farmer at harvest time sees a storm cloud as "terrible" or a lost aviator sees an airfield toward which he descends as a "relief" from his woes. In aesthetic experience, feeling and imagination are freed from the narrowness of a specific practical connection and are more ample and more fertile, as, indeed, all the perceptive powers are. The role of imagination in alert aesthetic perception is to give the fullest possible body to the suggestions of the object so that these suggestions are as apparent and as vivid for perception as are the actualities of the object themselves. Taking advantage of this operation of imagination in aesthetic perception, works of fine art are able to condense great ranges of experience within a small range of actuality, making available by vivid suggestion an infinite detail of qualities and relations, events and things, within the comparatively tiny span of a canvas or statue, a musical or poetical composition, a dance or a building.

Imagination with feeling is indeed very active all through alert aesthetic perception of works of fine art. Simple examples are a person hearing music as sad or gay or gentle or boisterous or melancholy; seeing a sculptured Apollo as fleshy, soft, self-confident, relaxed; perceiving an architectural form as light, serene, soaring, sharp as a needle; feeling a poem to be robust and bursting with rough animal spirits. All these are instances of perceiving with feeling. The objects are perceived as possessing vivid feeling qualities—sad, gay, self-confident, etc. All these perceptions, however, are also instances of perceiving with imagination. In all of them, something is perceived as if it were actually present in the object of perception, although literally it is only suggested and not actually there. Music is not literally sad or gay or gentle; only sentient creatures or creatures with feelings, such as human beings, could be that. Sculptured stone is not literally fleshy, soft, self-confident; only creatures who have flesh and spirit could be that. But imagination can seize suggestions of these traits in appropriately constructed objects and, drawing upon memory or funded experience, give these suggestions a vivid intrinsic appearance in these objects. Captivated by this fact, some thinkers have described aesthetic experience and art, too, as all imagination, as moving solely on a plane of suggestion or nonactuality, just as other thinkers, captivated more by the feeling qualities imagined than by the imagination of them, have made equally sweeping claims for feeling. Both views are exaggerations, as I think our whole argument shows. There is more to aesthetic experience, and to art also, than that. Yet it is true that, without imagination and feeling, aesthetic experience at least would be reduced to an apprehension of only the barest actualities; a world of suggestions and all the feelings entwined by experience around these suggestions would be missed from objects; objects, consequently, would be appreciated as much less than they fully are; and works of fine art, in particular, would lose the property of containing so much in so little which makes them so fascinating to aesthetic interest.

As far as the mechanical aspect of alert perception is concerned —and aesthetic experience is simply alert perception allowed intrinsic scope—sensation might be described as a core around which intuition and intellect and feeling and imagination operate to complete the perceptual apprehension of the object; and the five powers together with memory might be described as a complex apparatus for revealing the object, for opening up its being, its actualities, and its suggestions, to a telic consciousness, so that the object becomes fully available for some end, aesthetic or nonaesthetic. Incidentally, in this account of the mechanical aspect of perception, no mention has been made of reflexes; of neural, glandular, and cortical processes; of muscular tensions and relaxations and the other physiological factors of perception. This is because our concern here is primarily with perception as an experience of objects not with perception as an intra-organic phenomenon. In an account of perception less limited than ours in aim, the relevant physiological factors would, of course, receive due recognition.[6]

The telic aspect of perception is, in a sense, more fundamental than the mechanical aspect. In general, this aspect consists of those telic factors of the percipient—the cravings, needs, interests, purposes, aims, drives, desires, conations, impulses, strivings—that figure in the perceptual response. Usually, in a given case, some telic factor is central, as the desire to write a letter may be said to be central in the case of the perception of the vase cited above. But usually this telic factor is a co-ordinator of a number of lesser telic factors, e.g., in this case, of such lesser telic factors as the desire to use the table holding the vase for the writing, the desire to see whether the table can be so used, the impulse to remove the vase, etc. Moreover, the co-ordinating factor itself is often a subordinate of larger telic factors, e.g., the desire to obtain, by writing the letter, a certain amount of money, the desire to buy a house with the money, etc. The telic factor governing alert everyday perception, in other words, ordinarily stands somewhere between a slight directional impulse

[6] Modern philosophical analysis of perception as an experience of objects often reduces it to the three minimal psychological factors—sensation, intuition, and intellection—or to the apprehension of "actuality," the "given." This analysis is oriented toward supplying an epistemological basis for science and is provisionally adequate in this context. But the analysis is clearly incomplete. In its interest in observing actuality, scientific observation ignores the feeling qualities and imaginative suggestions of objects or it does so until the "actualities" or the "given" of the field is clearly perceived. But these qualities and suggestions remain within the perceptual field, and any account of perception as an experience of objects that is adequate to all types of perception, including, in the end, the scientific, must make provision for the apprehension of these. To abstract from these qualities and suggestions and to perceive things in their bare actuality is a relatively recondite and basically artificial way of perceiving things; and this would have to be noted in any adequate account of perception in science.

and the total system of interests and impulses which is sometimes described, and not altogether inappropriately, as the "personality" or the central element of the "self" of the percipient.

In alert perception—practical or scientific, partisan or aesthetic—the telic aspect is more fundamental in a number of respects. First, this aspect differentiates the total process, determining what type of perception it is—practical or scientific, partisan or aesthetic. As we have seen, it is the purpose, aim, or immanent plan and direction of the activity that distinguishes aesthetic perception from scientific, practical, and partisan perception. Second, the telic aspect unifies and controls the mechanical factors. It focuses these factors on a certain objective area and coordinates their diverse efforts as phases of a single directional process. If a person is interested in seeing a certain horse run a race and if this is his momentarily dominant interest, then the total possible field of perception is cut to the areas occupied by the horse, its rival horses, and the shifting scenes of the race; and sensing, intuiting, feeling, judging, anticipating, and imagining are employed as co-ordinate and mutually supplementary means of implementing the interest in seeing the horse run the race. These mechanical factors are not merely subordinated to this interest but are integrated by it into a unified directional process.

Third, the telic aspect "energizes" the whole perception, the strength of the purpose, interest, or need determining whether one perceives with vigor or apathy, with care or indifference. Fourth, the telic aspect supplies a principle of value to the perception, the degree of adequacy to the purpose, the interest, or the need determining the worth of the perceptive process as a perception. Thus, if the above-mentioned person interested in seeing a certain horse run a race sees the running excellently, his perceptive process would have great worth as a perceptive process, even if the horse should lose the race. Of course, if the person were mainly interested in seeing the horse win and then the horse lost, the total experience might be painful, and the value of the perceptive process per se would be diminished for the person in the degree that the main purpose of the perception, which was not gratified, dominated over such subordinate purposes as the desire merely to see the race adequately. Finally, the telic aspect is the point of contact between the object and the whole system of interests possessed by the "self." It is the point at which the object first vividly impinges on the background of personality and becomes connected with that wider set of telic factors with which the given telic factor is ordinarily connected.

The mechanical aspect of perception, then, serves as a complex machinery for experiencing the perceptual field in its actualities and suggestions. But the telic aspect—the purpose, aim, interest, desire, motive, or need central in the perception—focuses and directs the machinery and supplies a principle of differentiation, a principle of invigoration, a principle of evaluation, and the contact point between the object and the wider structure of interests constituting the background of the self.

In summing up this analysis of perception, we may say that, within the orbit of alert perception as here understood, sensation, intuition, feeling, imagination and intellect, impulse, purpose, conation, desire, aim, preference and interest operate, not to mention neural, muscular, glandular, and other physiological factors, as well as the background of memory and knowledge, of character and personality. Thus it would be no exaggeration to say that alert perception brings into action, in one form or another, the total being of the percipient, except that in all alert perception, save the aesthetic, the expansion of the percipient on the level of perception usually is sharply curtailed in the interest of some ulterior end. In aesthetic perception alone no such restriction prevails, the governing purpose or end being simply the perception itself. In consequence, the sensory, intuitive, imaginative, emotional, and intellectual generators, variously muffled in nonaesthetic perception; the telic and physiological factors; and the backgrounds of memory, knowledge, personality, and character are opened up and allowed a new freedom. They become free to attain their own ends, to develop themselves as fully as possible on the level of perception, in terms of the opportunities for intrinsic perception offered by the object.

V. CONDITIONS AND USES OF AESTHETIC EXPERIENCE

It remains to say something, in the light of the foregoing analysis of perception, about some of the favorable subjective conditions and some of the major uses of aesthetic perception, particularly at its best.

We have said that aesthetic experience is an effort on the perceptual level to mold the subject in accordance with the features of an object. In this connection, one of the major favorable subjective conditions of the aesthetic response is a certain abandonment of the will and a relaxed submission to the object. The sense of "letting the object carry us away" is characteristic of the experience here; and, where this does not occur, extra effort is necessary to bend the subject to the object and to sustain attention against distraction. This letting the object carry us away itself rests upon certain requirements. For example, as Helen Parkhurst says, "we need a low threshold of responsiveness, fancy, large vitality, depth of emotion and wideness of experience. We need to be enamoured of all the basic elements of existence—with space and time, matter and motion. We should be able to respond vividly to silence as well as to sound, to darkness no less than light. We should possess appreciation for rare cadences and for exquisite line, for symmetries and balance and the provocations of blended rhythm and the arhythmic."[7] To be sure, responsiveness can be so spontaneous and so gushingly enthusiastic that one may be blind to the larger characteristics or the subtler flaws of an object. One may be too emotional and too childlike in the aesthetic experience, especially of works of fine art. Accordingly, fusion is usually best when tempered with some critical detachment, except where one is on absolutely familiar and absolutely solid ground. Stated precisely, then, the first major favorable subjective condition of aesthetic experience at its best is a certain combination of responsiveness and reserve, of eager submission and sensitive discrimination, of going out into the object and keeping detached from the object, of fusion and reflection. The immanent critical vein normal to the aesthetic

[7] Helen H. Parkhurst, *Beauty: An Interpretation of Art and the Imaginative Life* (New York: Harcourt, Brace & Co., 1930), p. 288.

process as a telic or end-seeking process is then not overwhelmed, as in the case of the sentimentalist, by a flood of feeling which the object does not adequately justify.

As a supplement of this first major condition, a second condition should be mentioned—a mood of freshness and energy at the moment of the aesthetic response. This condition, again, is particularly important in the experience of works of fine art. The greatest works of art, those most rich in aesthetic values, require by their inherent nature a high tension and a keyed-up attitude for their apprehension. At the moment of experience one must have a freshness and a reserve of vitality to match the challenge and demands of the complex object. Much aesthetic experience lacks this freshness of vitality. It is indolent, halfhearted, half-thinking, the product of weariness and indifference rather than of energy and earnestness. The casual gallery visitor, the sleepy music listener, the restless reader of fiction and poetry, are familiar to everyone and, in moments of dulness, laziness, anxiety, or fatigue, may be joined by anyone. The mood for the best aesthetic response is a delicate condition easily disturbed by shifting physiological and psychological factors; and even a person as exquisitely prepared and equipped as you please may lack it in the duller or the distraught moments of his experience.

As for the major uses of the aesthetic response, the most immediate is the wealth of terminal good that it provides. Ordinarily, the human being prizes living, but much more he prizes being fully instead of half alive. Now the aesthetic experience at its best offers an opportunity for this. It engages the whole self on the level of perception, all the typical powers and resources of body and mind; and at its best—for example, in an adequate appreciation of a very fine work of art—it engages this self in a way to bring these powers and resources into free and full-orbed and intrinsically rewarding activity, unimpeded by the pressures of ulterior ends. Some people live as if anything without a cash value for a future moment of living were luxury and folly. This is epitomized by the conception of the spiritual life as living for a materialistic happiness in a future world. In its extreme form, such a conception is an obvious fallacy. Indeed, a life in which each moment was devoted merely to living for a future moment would be an obvious waste of time. It is the moments which possess intrinsic substance and terminal value that make living worth having, and the other moments are important to the extent to which they promise such substance and value or lead to the existence of moments which do. To these moments of intrinsic value the aesthetic experience is a direct addition. If we define the spiritual life as a life lived for the spirit of the living, for the intrinsic substance and value of the living itself and the heightening of the self which goes with this, the aesthetic experience with its concern for intrinsic fulness of object experience is plainly a part of the spiritual life. Indeed, as offering one of the simpler ways of bringing intrinsic substance and value into all living and as raising one of the more primitive responses of the organism—perception—to an activity providing a wealth of intrinsic good, the aesthetic experience might be described as one of the primary moments of the spiritual life.

The uses of aesthetic experience, however, are not exhausted by its addition to spiritual living. Like many things of intrinsic value, aesthetic experience also possesses instrumental values. It may serve as refreshment, as escape, as pastime, as emotional release. Perhaps more important than these uses, however, are two other instrumental values which attach particularly to aesthetic experience at its best.

First, aesthetic experience can be a means of self-growth, in general as well as in specific ways. Aesthetic experience, for example, fosters in the self, as Leo Stein has pointed out, an affection for appreciation and contemplation as against possessiveness.[8] It deflects the self from its powerful natural impulse to seize and exploit, into habits of response, which enlarge its range and liberalize its attitudes. Again, aesthetic experience may bring home to a person some realization of his general scale of preferences and values, e.g., that he is attracted to large, ornate, sumptuous things or, more deeply, to fine, delicate, unostentatious things. As to the specific ways in which the aesthetic response can be a means of self-growth, these consist of the specific

[8] *Op. cit.*, pp. 257 ff.

suasions and influences to which it subjects the self. These operate to some extent in connection with so-called "natural" objects, where even the incidental free appreciation of specific
scenes and surroundings, as in childhood, may color and shape
deeply the subsequent motions of the soul. But potentially of
even more importance here are the aesthetic experiences of works
of fine art. In such experiences the self is subjected to the suasion
and influence not merely of an external object but of a whole system of values wrought into an object by the artist's self. The self
is led in directions cherished by the artist's self, and its system of
values is acted upon by a body of content grounded in the artist's
system of values. This point—the nurture of the self intrinsic to
the aesthetic experience of art—in its general as well as in its specific aspects will receive much more attention in our later discussions when we come to drawing out the implications of our view
of art for social life.

Second, aesthetic experience can be of incalculably great use as
a preparation for the creation of works of fine art. One may think
here of Walt Whitman listening to the sea on the Long Island
coast, as he "tried and tried to seize the meaning which the voice
of the ocean was always whispering in his ears." He was "listening in a kind of torment of attention to that great voice—some
voice—in what words could he best describe it?

> Some voice, in huge monotonous rage, of freedom-lover pent,
> Some vast heart, like a planet's, chain'd and chaffing in the
>   breakers.

"This notion of receptivity to experience, and of complete surrender to it, combined with a patient effort to grasp its deepest
meaning and to embody that meaning in significant words—this
account of the old man's poetic method, as he told it one summer
evening, was deeply impressive."[9] Aesthetic experience can be
used to quarry from both the physical and the social environment
endless "terms" and suggestions for artistic creation. Rodin
watching his models, Cézanne glowering at the landscape in
Provence, Beethoven listening in the forests near Vienna, and

[9] Logan P. Smith, *The Unforgotten Years* (Boston: Little, Brown & Co., 1939), pp. 104–5.

Inigo Jones observing the architectural monuments of Italy are perhaps more famous than Whitman listening to the sea on the Long Island coast.

Here, of course, we have passed from a consideration of aesthetic experience in itself to a consideration of it in relation to the creative process of fine art. And in this connection a new point, I think, will become clear. Not only is aesthetic experience valuable for gaining perceptions subsequently useful in creation; but it is also the point toward which the creative impulses of the artist move in fashioning his creation. The peculiar aim of the fine artist's creative process is to fashion an object completely satisfying to his aesthetic aspirations. That is, the peculiar aim is to create an object that, by its nature, transforms the creative artist into an intrinsically satisfied perceptual agent.

II

FINE ART

IN ITS broadest sense, art is the skilful use of instruments and materials to produce objects of value. Primitive man, manipulating clay into the form of a jug, produced an object of utility to himself. Such work is an example of handicraft or industrial art. Frequently, primitive man also shaped his jug with an eye to proportion and decorated it with figures and surface patterns. He thereby made the jug more interesting to perception than it would have been as a mere utility. This early solicitude for perception, however strong it may have been and however mixed with religious, utilitarian, and other interests, is, I believe, the distant beginning of fine art.[1]

Speaking generally, fine art is the production by man of objects intrinsically interesting to perceive; and any object so skilfully produced by man that it has intrinsic perceptual interest has fineness of art. Jugs and dresses and automobiles often have such intrinsic perceptual interest in a marked degree and hence have fineness of art. The special class of objects called "works of fine art"—paintings, musical compositions, and the like—are distinguished from jugs, dresses, automobiles, and utilities generally by the centrality or eminence of their intrinsic perceptual appeal. An automobile constructed simply to fascinate the eye and serving no other purpose, theoretical or practical—e.g., transportation, demonstration, etc.—ordinarily would be considered

---

[1] Regarding primitive ornamentation, Ernst Grosse writes: "While the choice of an ornamental motive may be determined by a religious interest, its execution and its combination with other similar or dissimilar motives into a design are carried out under the influence of aesthetic requirements" (*The Beginnings of Art*, Eng. trans. [New York: D. Appleton & Co., 1900], p. 24; cf. also S. Langer, *Philosophy in a New Key* [Cambridge, Mass.: Harvard University Press, 1942], pp. 251-52).

a very queer automobile. But a canvas painted and displayed simply to be observed for its intrinsic perceptual qualities would not ordinarily be considered queer for that reason, although it might be considered queer for some other reason. When finely shaped or decorated jugs have ceased to serve as utilities and are placed on museum shelves, they are sometimes said to "become" works of fine art. But all that has happened is that, with the disappearance of their utilitarian function, the aesthetic function of the jugs has been given peculiar prominence. So-called works of fine art are distinguished from other human products not by any art quality that other types of humanly created objects universally lack but by the centrality or eminence in their existence of their intrinsic perceptual appeal. As creations of human beings who possess many interests, so-called works of fine art usually have many properties and satisfy many interests. But they stand or fall as works of fine art not on the basis of these properties but on the basis of their excellence in the aesthetic experience.

These sentences outline the general theory of fine art for which we shall argue and seek to bring support in the following discussion. But perhaps at the outset one point should be made especially clear. As a rule, the impulse to fine art in the artist, like single telic factors generally, is only one of a number of purposes operating in his concrete activity. Some artists compose for fame, some for personal pleasure, some to save themselves from debt, some to save others from hell-fire. The Greeks wrote dramas to win prizes, and Haydn wrote music to entertain the Esterhazys. Most artists are teachers, moralists, businessmen, philosophers, entertainers, sensualists, psychopaths—some or all of these. But if they are artists—and this is the important point here—they are also persons who strive to construct something splendid to perceive, if only for their own perceiving, or who exercise powers which achieve constructions in this direction. This is not their total nature, but it is their distinctive nature as artists. Similarly, with so-called works of art: ordinarily, they are multifunctional, connected with many different activities and interests of human beings. Works of fine art make money, edify, educate—or, at least, some of them do. Works of fine art serve as memorials, decorations, shelters, religious icons, or historical documents. But if they are works of fine art, they are also objects intended to be superior or focal in the aesthetic process, or they are human creations that occupy or are capable of occupying by convention a position similar to such objects. This also is not their total nature, but it is their distinctive nature as works of art, among the manifold creations of human activity.

The construction of objects for aesthetic experience, then, will be the distinguishing property of fine art, according to our account; and human activities approach fine art in the degree that this type of construction is central or eminent in them. This property enables us at once to distinguish fine art from such different pursuits as the utilitarian, the religious, the historical, the moral, and the commemorative, in all of which aesthetic excellence and artistic fineness may occur. Central to these pursuits in their characteristic instances, at least, is a different property, e.g., to make an instrument of "action" (utilitarian), to communicate with God (religious), to describe events for the record (historical), and the like, not primarily to construct objects for their intrinsic perceptual appeal. The centrality of the intrinsically perceptual type of construction also enables us to distinguish fine art from the sciences. In general, science is the construction of conceptual systems, either descriptive, as in the empirical sciences, or abstractly "tautological," as in the formal sciences, mathematics, etc. Characteristically, science strives to build structures embodying knowledge either of an object matter lying in some sense beyond these structures or of the implications of the initial premises on which the structures are reared. These conceptual systems or knowledge structures may have great beauty or elegance; and those who confuse fine art with the creation of beauty may contend that the sciences are indistinguishable from fine art or that some single science, such as mathematics, is.[2] But, centrally, science is a quite different enterprise, in which the perceptual is at least secondary and incidental to the attainment of cognitions either objectively de-

[2] G. H. Hardy, *A Mathematician's Apology* (Cambridge: At the University Press, 1940), pp. 25 ff.

scriptive or merely coherently reflective of bases postulated in advance. Science is primarily an intellectual, not a perceptual, construction; and the aesthetic is marginal to an operation focally different in its basic nature and plan.

II. ART AND NATURE: THE IMITATION THEORY

It may be objected, however, that, if fine art is the construction of intrinsically interesting perceptual systems, it is not clear why such an activity should ever have come into existence. "Nature" produces in untold profusion objects of great intrinsic perceptual interest: the seas, the mountains, the plains, the sky, and the forms of plants and animals, which alone are almost infinite in variety and extent. There is no need for a special effort on the part of man in order to have an inexhaustible supply of objects of intrinsic perceptual interest. In reply, we may point out that nature produces in untold profusion objects of great "practical" usefulness—air, water, soil, minerals. Yet nature's profusion of utilities has not rendered useless the industrial arts. Nor does nature's undeniable abundance of fine aesthetic objects lack limitations and imperfections which render imperative the operation of the fine arts.

The scenes of nature are shifting and impermanent, changing with the seasons, passing away with the years, and all nature, except the environment of daily life, is remote and difficult of access for most men. Besides, even the best scenes of nature are uneven in quality. Some of the most attractive have lines or shapes or colors or masses which the human artist would rub out, and some lack lines or shapes or colors or masses which the human artist would insert, if he were composing them for intrinsic perception. Moreover, nature has made very incomplete use of many perceptual resources, e.g., sound. The roar of the ocean against the cliff, the babble of the brook, and the drone of the waterfall have their perceptual fascination. But even the simpler melodies of human invention are absent from the tonal creations of nature, not to mention the grander reaches of great music and great poetry. Impressive as it is, nature's sonorous might is only a fraction of the immense perceptual possibilities in the realm of sound; and its grandeurs for the eye as well as for the ear—a raging storm at sea, for instance—are often so entwined with disturbing physical and biological circumstances that their adequate intrinsic perception is difficult at best, and often impossible.

Moreover, the representation of human life and character and personality, the expression of human purpose and feeling and spirit, which are so fragmentary and confused in everyday experience and so complete and clear in the best of poetry, prose, fiction, dance, drama,[3] drawing, painting, and sculpture, would be nonexistent for aesthetic perception if nature were the sole source of aesthetic objects. Nor would the products of everyday human effort, particularly of the industrial arts, be altogether what they are without the play of the impulse to fine art. Indeed, the impulse to fine art, co-ordinated with the utilitarian aim, achieves here one of the grandest types of aesthetic objects, of which nature produces practically no originals, namely, the great creations of architecture. Thus, despite the profusion of superb aesthetic objects in nature, despite the fact that nature often produces with ease what man can achieve, if at all, only by the greatest effort, nature has immense limitations and defects as a source of aesthetic objects. If the rationale of fine art is what we have said it is, viz., the production of aesthetic objects, there is every reason why fine art should have occurred on the scale on which it actually has occurred, or at least no reason in the productivity of nature for believing that fine art would not have occurred on the scale that it has.

This discussion of art and nature puts us in a position to consider critically the theory in Plato's *Republic*, that fine art is the imitation of nature. Socrates included human nature in "nature"; but, as customarily interpreted, the general view of art is unchanged by this, namely, that art is the copying of the preartistic. The supreme triumph of the artist is to paint a pic-

---

[3] Although they differ from the "legitimate" or staged drama in a number of very important specific ways, opera and the usual full-length motion picture are really types of drama—musical and screened drama—and should be understood as included under all the more general references to drama in this volume.

ture of a tree or a bed with such similitude that it is mistaken for an actual tree or bed or to imitate the sound of a waterfall or the actions of a tyrant so exactly that the imitation is taken for an actual waterfall or tyrant.

Now, if what we have just been saying is correct—that nature is aesthetically deficient and that the justification of art in relation to nature lies in its aesthetic transcendence of nature, in its overcoming of nature's aesthetic limitations and defects—this theory that the purpose of fine art is the copying of nature, is about as wrong as a theory could be. At a minimum, the theory is wholly gratuitous. It supplies the fine arts with a *raison d'être* which, if they could use it, they do not need. Plato or Socrates drew the correct conclusion from the theory. If fine art is imitation, why art? The original must always be so much superior. No painting of a tree can ever completely resemble an actual tree containing all its bright lights or low lights. No imitation of a waterfall by a human actor can ever reproduce at such length and in such details the sounds of any sizable waterfall. If fine art is mere imitation of nature, it is inescapably second or third rate and has scant excuse for being.

But the truth seems to be that the imitation theory of the *Republic*, at least as ordinarily interpreted, has scant excuse for being. The pleasures of accurate transcription of nature are minor perceptual effects which the resources of fine art in some cases can achieve. But in major arts, such as music and architecture, accurate copying of the particulars of nature, except in incidental details, such as a bird call or a floral motif, scarcely exists and is rarely attempted. And even in the seemingly photographic arts, such as painting, what is usually aimed at is a selection and recomposition or accentuation of aspects of nature, not abject copying. Nature is a dictionary of terms and suggestions which serves as a point of departure for the composition of the artist, not a manuscript which he transcribes servilely. The imitation theory of the *Republic* applies with some exactness to the sound effects and the ingenuous antics of certain entertainers of the modern screen and radio. They offer imitations. But the fine arts as a whole are really a movement in the very opposite direction. Not to copy but to augment the aesthetic wealth of nature—this has been immemorially their aim; and imitation or strict copying fits so little what the arts try to do or actually do do that, as a theory of art, the imitation theory of the *Republic* has the thinnest possible empirical basis or justification.[4]

III. SOME RECENT GENETIC AND FUNCTIONAL THEORIES

In recent times there have been four main types of theories of art: genetic, formal, expressionist, and functional. In social implications at least, recent genetic and functional theories are the most similar to the Platonic. Compared with these, however, the theory of the *Republic*, with its transparent intellectual bias, is almost pleasingly naïve. The theory of the *Republic* assumes that the aim of art really is to promulgate scientific and philosophical truths and that the artist, possessing neither, tries by emotionalized imitations to give the impression, useful and successful with children, that he possesses both. Most recent genetic and functionalist theories hold a more sophisticated view of the origin and function of fine art. In some cases they contend with Plato that the business of fine art is to create an imitation world. But the motive and function of art is not to fool unsuspecting people into thinking that this is the real world. The artist knows, and everyone knows, that it is an imitation. The motive and function of art, rather, is to give playful scope to energies not used up or required in the struggle for existence or to make available a realm of illusions with which one can deceive one's self consciously for the sake of the pleasure and the sense of freedom and power obtainable by such conscious self-deception. Art is play, art is escape, art is conscious self-deception.

Now there is no denying a truth in such views. Often art is undertaken to drain off superfluous energy or to make the sting and welter of private troubles recede into the background or to give an enlarged sense of freedom and power, which is pleasant.

[4] C. J. Ducasse, *Philosophy of Art* (New York: Dial Press, 1929), p. 73. See the defense of the theory of the *Republic* by R. G. Collingwood, "Plato's Philosophy of Art," *Mind*, XXXIV (1925), 154–72. Collingwood admits, however, that the standard of art for Plato is resemblance to nature: "The picture of a bed is judged by its relation to the perceptible bed" (p. 158). And this is, of course, what we have criticized in the theory.

And, in its functioning, art performs such services to innumerable percipients. But the question is whether these motives and functions constitute the distinctive nature of fine art. And this seems very dubious indeed. Many activities besides fine art often arise from the impulses to play, to escape, to conscious self-deception; and usually they serve these functions for most people far more effectively than do the fine arts. Sports, reveries, hobbies, taking drugs, drinking hard liquor, are a few of such activities. The impulse to play, to escape, and to conscious self-deception, is not particularly distinctive of the fine arts. Moreover, there seems to be no high correlation between the degree of play, escape, and conscious self-deception and the degree of fineness in the arts. A person may be a very poor pianist—even admit the fact—yet attain a great deal of recreation and playful relaxation and escape from trouble, even an enlarged sense of freedom and power, from his pianistic activity. On the other hand, a very able pianist may find the achievement of perfection on his instrument exhausting and overtaxing, not play but the hardest kind of hard work; and he may find less escape from the troubles of life and less opportunity for conscious self-deception in the achievement of this perfection than he would find in strumming the latest popular tune at a happy cocktail party.

Instances of such noncorrelation could be multiplied indefinitely. The production of a work of great popular appeal, such as a huge sentimental novel, may work off endless superfluous energy and provide escape and conscious self-deception on a great scale, both for its producer and for others. Yet as fine art it may be found to be derivative and third rate and bristling with basic flaws when examined more closely than people who seek play and escape and deception from the arts are likely to examine it. The impulses to play, to escape, and to conscious self-deception usually are much more opulently fulfilled in the arts by meretricious works of broad appeal than by sober and original productions, which achieve the more difficult and fundamental perfections. At least such inferior works are often very superior in these respects, both for their creator and for others, so that a correlation of fineness of art with these motives and roles seems plainly inadmissible.

Similar criticisms also apply, I believe, to those recent genetic and functional theories which assert that the motive or function of fine art is wish-fulfilment, dominance over others, or, to quote Freud, to win "honor, power, riches, fame, and the love of women."[5] Doubtless fine art can, and often does, spring from these impulses and serve these ends. But other types of human activity do so even more abundantly than fine art; and works of art may be very distinguished in these respects and yet be third rate as fine art not merely in the view of an impartial and informed outsider but even in the sober judgment of their own creator, as "popular" artists sometimes freely confess.

It is worth noting that all these recent genetic and functional theories interpret fine art not only in terms of some motive or function amply discharged outside the arts and not closely correlated with the fineness of art itself but also in terms unmistakably implying that fine art is rooted in frustration and maladjustment. That is, these theories are related to a certain type of more general sociogenetic hypothesis. They imply, e.g., that the artist has energy without a life-need which requires its expenditure, or troubles from which he seeks to escape, or an exaggerated ego which requires abnormal gratification, or an inability to face "reality" and win honor, power, riches, fame, and women in straightforward he-man fashion. The artist is a balked or defective type of individual. And so are the people who enthusiastically share his work with him. Thus the nihilist conclusion reached in the *Republic* is even more inexorably an implication of these recent genetic and functional theories, namely, that in a natural, healthy, virile, rational society, wherein everyone is "normal" and properly adjusted, fine art would have scant excuse for being and would be excluded as a major enterprise for channeling the energies of adult people.

There is, however, a human impulse of a very primordial sort which is overlooked by all such genetic and functional theories.

[5] Sigmund Freud, *A General Introduction to Psychoanalysis*, authorized trans. (New York: Boni & Liveright, 1921), p. 327.

The year-old babe who turns his head away from an overbright light thrown into his eyes or who yowls and tosses when he needs dry pants already exhibits this impulse in very rudimentary form, namely, the impulse to have a perceptually satisfying environment. Now this is certainly an "original," natural, virile, healthy, "rational" impulse—this impulse to adjust the environment to our perceptual satisfaction by action instead of passively accepting the environment. This impulse flowers in its purest and fullest form in the fine arts. Moreover, although this impulse operates extensively outside the fine arts, it approaches the rationale or central purpose of extra-artistic pursuits only as these pursuits themselves approach the nature of a fine art. In an ordinary pursuit commonly recognized as rather remote from a fine art—e.g., the selling of coal or hardware—the appeals to perception in advertising and displays and in yard and office appearances are important but inflexibly subordinated to the "practical" ends of the pursuit. The central *raison d'être* of such business is practical "service" to the buyer and profit to the seller, not primarily perceptual satisfaction. But, as the needs and requirements of perception become more central in a so-called "practical" pursuit, such as decorating the walls of a home, the pursuit is recognized as coming closer to the province and business of a fine artist. This correlation of intrinsic perception with art is even closer inside the fine arts themselves. A work of fine art may or may not have won for its creator great fame and power and innumerable women, it may or may not have worked off vast amounts of superfluous energy or provided escape and conscious self-deception on a great scale. But if, face to face with it in perception, we find it to have unsurpassed excellence in what it offers intrinsic perception, then, regardless of how it has fared in the other respects, it will invariably receive the palm in fineness of art.

IV. SOME RECENT FORM AND EXPRESSION THEORIES

A work of art might be described as a four-dimensional object. It possesses a material in terms of which it is generated, a form, an expression, and multiple functions. Genetic and func-

tional philosophies seek to erect a theory of art by orienting
their interpretation from a genetic or functional feature. It seems
obvious that one might equally well attempt to formulate a
theory of art by using some formal or expressive factor as the
basis of one's interpretation. In recent times, indeed, this procedure has had considerable vogue and has resulted in numerous
form and expression theories. Typical of the form theories are
the following: Fine art is the construction of significant form; *Bell*
fine art is the creation of plastic form; fine art is the delineation
of characteristic form; fine art is the delineation of type form;
fine art is the achievement of organic form. Typical of the ex- *Santayana*
pression theories are the following: Fine art is the objectification *Tolstoy*
of pleasure; fine art is the expression of feelings; fine art is the —*Marston*
expression of personality; fine art is the expression of a vital insight into reality; fine art is the portrayal of unadorned facts;
fine art is the expression of the physicosocial milieu.

With most of these theories there are certain minor difficulties
which center around their key terms, "significant form," "vital
insight," etc. We shall deal with such difficulties, in so far as
they are important for our analysis, when we attempt a detailed
discussion of form and expression. But the more fundamental
difficulty with these theories seems to me something different.
When a clear and unambiguous meaning has been attached to the
key terms of these theories, all the theories seem to be true. Every
one of them seems to describe something done superbly well by
some instances of fine art, and some of them, such as the feeling
theory, seem to describe something generally characteristic of all
major instances of fine art. If this is correct, as I think it is, then
either all these theories are one and the same theory, which is
plainly not so, or all of them are fragments, varying in size, of a
more comprehensive theory, according to which fine art can do,
at times or generally, all that these theories say it does do. This
is, I believe, the case, and the relational theory which we are
proposing, I submit, is a theory sufficiently comprehensive to
embrace and permit the several truths of these form and expression theories.

Fine art, we might reformulate this theory to say, is this shaping of a four-dimensional object—material and form, expression and function—in the direction of intrinsic perceptual interest. Now such a theory permits fine art to be described and to be truly, if only partially, described in terms of any *de facto* form or expression of intrinsic perceptual interest developed by it. Significant form, plastic form, organic form, and the like; the expression of feeling, vital insight, personality, etc., are forms and expressions of this type. Hence, not only can this relational theory accept the *de facto* truth of these form and expression theories, but it can also interrelate these truths as diverse fragments of a more comprehensive theory. Significant form, plastic form, organic form, the expression of feeling, vital insight, and personality become simply diverse, intrinsically interesting, perceptual characteristics which fine art molds into objects in pursuing what the relational theory envisages as its peculiar and proper business. The truth of the form and expression theories consists of describing correctly various specific aims of fine art on the level of form and expression, and the assertions of these theories become so many diverse aspects of the comprehensive view embodied in the relational theory.

It may be objected that this explanation is false to the actual aims of artists. Actually, an artist does not aim to construct a four-dimensional object of intrinsic perceptual appeal. He aims to construct a significant form, he aims to express a feeling perfectly. This is his actual aim, and this is what fine art is from the standpoint of the creative artist. In a sense, we have no quarrel with this objection. Let us suppose, indeed, that artists do entertain such specific aims as those just mentioned. Does it follow that these specific aims cannot be interpreted as aspects of a wider aim? In composing a tone poem, a musician may actually seek primarily to build a work in which each phrase seems to him necessary to express a totality of feeling in him or germinal to his themes. This may be said to be his specific aim. But may he not be described equally well as seeking to build an object which possesses a certain intrinsic perceptual characteristic, viz., a totality of expressed feeling? This seems to be exactly what he is seeking to do, stated in more general language.

Similar restatements seem to me possible in all other cases. An artist may actually aim to create a significant form in a painting or to express a vital insight in a poem. But in each case he can be described equally well to be aiming to create a certain intrinsic perceptual characteristic in an object, in the one case a certain form, in the other case the expression of a certain insight. The relational theory does not deny the existence of specific and diversely formulated aims in artists. Its claim is merely that all such aims *qua* artistic can be translated into statements about intrinsic perceptual characteristics and, consequently, that the truth of the form and expression theories which are severally stated in terms of these specific and diversely formulated aims can be embraced within the theory which simply states that fine art is the shaping of objects (upon analysis, four-dimensional objects) in the direction of intrinsic perceptual interest.

V. THE CROCEAN SYNTHESIS

Form and expression theories of art have been prominent not only in recent times but throughout the entire postmedieval period of Western civilization. The classicism of the seventeenth and eighteenth centuries gave centrality to the principle of form, especially to form that was methodical, clear, and distinct, as elegant and polished as a mathematical demonstration. The romanticism of the late eighteenth and nineteenth and early twentieth centuries gave centrality to the principle of expression, especially to the spontaneous overflow of powerful feeling. In recent times both classicism and romanticism have been felt to be unsatisfactory, and frequent attempts have been made to mediate between them. Not the least distinguished of these attempts has been the very influential theory of art developed by the contemporary Italian philosopher, Benedetto Croce.

Croce's theory is that art is intuition. Intuition is feeling given form, an aspiration inclosed within the circle of a representation. Intuition is an equilibrium of expressive and formal factors. Thus a judicious synthesis of the claims of romanticism and classicism seems effected. Closer inspection, however, casts considerable doubt on the success of the Crocean synthesis. For example, according to Croce, fine art is completely independent of collaboration from the physical world. Intuition is entirely subjective, a self-inclosed moment of pure spirit. Moreover, its subsequent embodiment in physical materials is an extrinsic formality, adding nothing essential. Besides sponsoring this deep-seated subjectivism, the Crocean synthesis isolates fine art within the subject. According to Croce, fine art is essentially independent of the utilitarian, moral, social, and even intellectual sides of the spirit, and its significance can never be utilitarian, moral, social, or intellectual. Subjectivism combined with spiritual isolationism confirms one's fuller impression that Croce's philosophy of fine art is essentially romantic. This is particularly apparent in the version given in the *Breviary*. There it is argued explicitly that what gives form to art is feeling. The classic factor is derived from the romantic. "What gives coherence and unity to the intuition is feeling: the intuition is really such because it represents a feeling, and can only appear from and upon that." The primary factor of fine art is "the passions," and the works of the great masters "are the eternal flower that springs from their passions."[6] Thus the emphasis in Croce's philosophy of art here is placed exactly where the romantics placed it, viz., on feeling; and Croce's intuitionism, instead of being a broad and judicious synthesis of the two great modern or postmedieval traditions in the philosophy of fine art, here shows itself to be merely one more specimen of romanticism.

The philosophy of Croce, as I have said, conceives fine art as properly existing in a moral and social vacuum. Fine art in the strictest sense has no utilitarian, no moral, no social, significance, only the purely aesthetic significance of expressing for inward vision the surges of lyrical feeling. This theory of fine art parallels rather strikingly the recoil of many sensitive artists from the clamorous industrial and commercial bourgeois civilization which was coming so overwhelmingly to the fore in the

---

[6] Benedetto Croce, *The Breviary of Aesthetic* ("Rice Institute Pamphlets," Vol. II, No. 4 [Houston: Rice Institute, 1915]), p. 247.

West shortly before Croce first wrote.[7] This recoil resulted in
outstanding artists, from the impressionists and postimpression-
ists and symbolists of the nineteenth century to the "expres-
sionists" and imagists and dadaists and vorticists and surrealists
and stream-of-consciousness artists, among many others, of the
twentieth century, finding the substance and the justification of
their work in subjective vision and in private or abstract experience. These artists retreated from society into the ivory tower of
their individualist consciousness. Like the so-called "realists"
of the period, from Flaubert and Dickens onward, with their
often unconcealed hatred of what they portrayed, like the re-
vivalists of the times with their messianic flights to the medieval, the pre-Raphaelite, the baroque, and other distant aesthetic
lands, these artists radically separated themselves from the
rampantly middle-class society of the day and in some cases accentuated to the ultimate point the strain of subjectivism in the
more robust romanticism of the earlier nineteenth century. The
philosophy of art of Croce is, I think, a later-day correlate or
parallel in the theoretical sphere of this trend in the artistic
sphere; and in this sense also it belongs to the main stream of
romanticism which has extended from the end of the eighteenth
century to recent times.[8]

[7] In 1900, *Fundamental Theses of An Aesthetic* was read at the Accademia Pontaniana of
Naples during the sessions of February 18 and May 6, and printed in Vol. XXX of its
Acts. This memoir is the nucleus of the theoretical part of the *Aesthetic* (Eng. trans. by
Douglas Ainslie [1st ed.; London: Macmillan & Co., Ltd., 1909; 2d ed., 1922]).

[8] Frank P. Chambers, *A History of Taste* [New York: Columbia University Press, 1932],
pp. 262–63. On so-called "modernist" poetry as the tail end of romanticism see Randall
Jarrell, "The End of the Line," *Nation*, CLIV, No. 8 (February 21, 1942), 222 ff. In the
article, "Aesthetics," *Encyclopaedia Britannica* (1942), Vol. I, Croce protests against the
excessive romanticism of much recent art. "The problem for aesthetics to-day," he writes,
"is the reassertion and defence of the classical as against romanticism" (p. 269). Certainly,
Croce's aesthetics nowhere implies that an ill-formed utterance of "affective elements" is
the essence of art. Form is a fundamental of all intuition. In its *Breviary* version, however,
Croce's aesthetics makes feeling even more fundamental than form. This places the accent
exactly where romanticism always has placed it. Moreover, in both the *Aesthetic* and the
Breviary Croce insists on the autonomy of the artistic and its independence of the social;
and this rather than romanticism in general was the specific basis of the correlation just
made between Croce's aesthetics and certain developments in recent art.

As to the truth of the Crocean theory of art, we may say, first of all, that, taken merely to mean that fine art is the expression of feeling in a form or representation dictated by the feeling, the theory is plainly only another example of an expression theory. As such, it has the partial truth which we have seen is possessed by expression theories and would be fitted into our own account of fine art in the manner in which we have indicated that the other expression theories can be fitted. The peculiar subjectivism of the Crocean theory—that fine art is properly a transaction solely within the mind of the artist and is effected without collaboration from the resources of the physical world—seems largely false; but I shall postpone critical discussion of it until we consider in detail the creative process, when the merits and defects of this subjectivism can be described most conveniently. As to Croce's isolationism, his theory that fine art properly has an aesthetic but no utilitarian, no moral, or, more generally, no "social" significance, this also seems largely false. The differential aim of fine art, we may agree, is the aesthetic, not the utilitarian, the moral, or the social in the usual sense. But this does not rule out the possibility, often actualized in practice, of vigorous and fundamental collaboration in art between the aesthetic and nonaesthetic, e.g., the building by artists of aesthetic structures that have great utilitarian, moral, or social significance, in addition to the aesthetic. Nor does it rule out the possibility that the aesthetic *qua* aesthetic and independent of extrinsic collaboration may also have social significance. This second point alone, if true, would be sufficient, I believe, to refute the doctrine of isolationism. Let me therefore state one aspect of it that I think is at least as true as anything in our entire previous argument.

The distinctive aim of fine art, we have said, is to construct objects feeding intrinsic perception, when "intrinsic perception" is understood to mean the attentive submission of the subject to the object for the sake of the appreciation of the whole complex of being and value offered by the object to the subject on the level of perception. Now, just because works of fine art feed intrinsic perception, even the "purest" works or those most bare of moral and social content, such as the most abstract painting and sculpture and music, engage a vast complex of powers, such as sensation, intuition, feeling, imagination, intellect, impulse, and conation and lead out, by the system of values imbedded in them, the interests of the percipient, exerting a suasion positive or negative, gentle or violent, over the interests and the scale of values of this percipient. But the powers of a person, especially his feelings and imagination and, no less, his interests and scale of values, are the basis of his social outlook, of his vision of what is fine in human life and character and conduct; and this vision in varying degrees leaves its mark upon his moral and social actions. Thus the immediate aim of fine art is to feed intrinsic perception, but its actual consequence is to influence the capacities and resources of a person which are determinants of social behavior. In this sense fine art and social life are not two sealed and separated moments of the spirit, as the isolationist doctrine implies, but internally, properly, and profoundly related.

VI. FINE ART AND BEAUTY

There is a further question raised by Croce's theory of art that might be advantageously considered at this point. Is fine art the creation of beauty? Croce claims that it is, that art or intuition is expression and that "beauty" and "expression" are synonyms. On the other hand, others who also define art as expression, notably Véron and Ducasse, claim that fine art is not the creation of beauty; and they are joined by some theorists who define art as the construction of form—Clive Bell, for example.

The dispute between these writers seems basically linguistic. If the term "beauty" is used in the conventional sense, as it is not by Croce, it seems correct to say that, on the level of expression at least, fine art is not the creation of beauty. As Tolstoy has pointed out, works of art on the expressive level are often gloomy, heartrending, satiric, droll, bitter—the opposite of beautiful in the conventional sense. Yet these works are unquestionably works of fine art. On the other hand, if the term "beauty" is used in the rather unusual sense of successful expression, as it is by Croce, it seems correct to say that fine art aims

at the creation of beauty on the level of expression. The successful expression of the gloomy, the heartrending, the satiric, the
droll, and the bitter, which the works that Tolstoy cites achieve,
becomes by definition the creation of beauty; and the objections
brought against equating fine art on the level of expression with
the creation of beauty, such as the Tolstoyan, are eliminated by
definition.

On earlier pages we rejected the identification of aesthetic experience with the perception of the conventionally beautiful
partly because the Tolstoyan argument that fine art is often the
expression of the conventionally nonbeautiful seemed to us correct, so far as it went. This argument still seems to us correct,
so that on the linguistic question here under consideration it
seems least confusing for us to follow Tolstoy and say that fine
art is not the creation of the beautiful in the conventional sense.
There is, however, another question raised in this connection
which is not simply linguistic. Why does the conventionally
nonbeautiful exist in works of fine art? Why are there not only
works that are sweet, gracious, charming, pretty, decorative—
beautiful in the conventional sense—but also works that are bitter, scalding, gloomy, searing, heartrending—nonbeautiful in
the conventional sense? Some people have tried to explain the
nonbeautiful in fine art as due to incompetence; and in some
cases, especially ugliness of formal arrangement, this explanation seems correct. In these cases the view that fine art is the creation of the conventionally beautiful remains defensible, the de-
viations being interpreted as failures in artistic competence. But
so many very competent works of fine art possess dark and difficult qualities that this explanation carries only a short distance.
The bitter, the heartrending, and the conventionally nonbeautiful exist so plentifully in works which are, indeed, not merely
competent but often superb in formal arrangement and general
artistic skill that these qualities demand an explanation in positive terms rather than in terms of some defect.

If our theory of fine art is true, then for artists and for people
generally there must be some value as intrinsic perceptual characteristics in those conventionally nonbeautiful contents of art

which are a result of something other than artistic incompetence. I believe this to be the case.

For the artist the molding of such conventionally nonbeautiful contents into his work is frequently a source of deep and invigorating satisfaction. To be sure, it may sometimes be the satisfaction of a vindictive, spiteful, or petty impulse or the indulgence of a coarse or sinister propensity. But more often in the greater artists it is the achievement of a healthful purgation. By molding these perceptual properties into his work the artist gives the states that they symbolize a seeming detachment from himself and an independence of existence, which brings him relief from the distress that these states inspire so long as they remain merely subjective. The tranquillity brought to artists by converting their subjective tortures into objective perceptual characteristics has been described by a long list of writers from Goethe, Schopenhauer, Nietzsche, and the Romantic school of philosophers and artists generally to the most recent psychoanalytic critics and autobiographical novelists. In his analysis of ancient tragedy Aristotle, of course, long ago formulated the principle of purgation from the standpoint of the spectator.

Besides medicinal value, the molding of these conventionally nonbeautiful contents into his work may have for the artist the value of a great technical challenge. The artist *qua* artist wishes to succeed in making these characteristics perceptually vivid, forceful, and interesting. As an artist, this is his more immediate business. Now pretty pieces which appeal to agreeable sentiment usually require only conventional skill to be made passably effective. It is "hard to miss" with sweetness and light, and the major technical challenges of fine art are usually not evoked by such themes. But bitterness and gall are other matters. With them it is easy to be bombastic, melodramatic, offensive, and ridiculous. Works embodying these qualities require all the tact and ingenuity, all the careful thought and inventiveness, of the artist if they are to have eloquence without flatulence, magnificence without exaggeration. To be sure, there are master-works employing dulcet themes, the works of the Correggios and the Della Robbias, the Mendelssohns and the Offenbachs. But fine art would be infinitely poorer as a technical spectacle without the creations of those artists who have sounded the murky depths and with such men as Skopias, Euripides, Dante, Michelangelo, El Greco, Goya, Beethoven, Dostoevski, to mention only a few, struck from the list.

From the standpoint of the percipient, the presence of conventionally nonbeautiful contents in works of art is customarily a perceptual gain in several respects. First of all, it is usually a gain in emotional range. Works of sunny and cheerful mien, full of grace or fluff, open up only a few of the emotional possibilities of perception. Darker works which touch life nearer the bone, which present the more contorted and tragic and tempestuous aspects of existence, elicit new and powerful ranges of feeling and expand immeasurably the emotional scope of perception. Of course, the bitter, the gloomy and the unpleasant may repel, and certainly the more savage examples of the conventionally nonbeautiful in fine art—a late Michelangelo fresco or a Stravinsky suite—usually do not win the instant general enthusiasm accorded a Raphael Madonna or a Strauss waltz. But for those not repelled, the emotional effect here may be very intense. Moreover, the great mass of tragic and difficult art has received surprisingly wide popular acclaim, and the enlargement of emotional range afforded by this type of fine art has been anything but esoteric.

The presence of conventionally nonbeautiful contents in works of fine art is also ordinarily a gain in intellectual range for perception. It opens up a large area of subject matter which otherwise would be excluded from the arts. This darker subject matter has been acclaimed by some as the area of "truth." For seemingly excellent biological reasons, human beings tend to forget the more painful moments of the past, when defect and error have raised their heads; and works of fine art that make similar omissions seem to many persons to be equally evasions of "reality." On the other hand, dark images expressing effectively the pain and bitterness of human existence seem to such people to radiate unmistakable truth. Instead of lulling us into forgetfulness, as does sweet and pretty art, they give us a graphic and immensely vivid realization of some of the latent withering forces of human life. Whether this is a revelation of "the truth," "the higher truth," or merely "a truth," we need not decide. But it certainly is an enlargement of intellectual range for perception over what is opened up by graceful and dulcet art. Just as the dissonant adds variety and amplitude in any single work of fine art, so dissonant art itself adds variety and amplitude to the intellectual and emotional appeals of fine art as a whole. In addition, since such art has often resulted in novel formal and technical achievements of a high order, it has also been a gain in intuitive and imaginative range for intrinsic perception.

Our point is not that purgation and technical challenge for the artist and multiple augmentation of intrinsic perception for the percipient give a complete explanation of the presence in art of the conventionally nonbeautiful contents here under discussion. Certainly, nonaesthetic interest in the lurid and terrifying, usefulness for didactic purposes, and tradition and habit have had an influence and are part of any total explanation. But the reasons given do describe merits which these conventionally nonbeautiful contents in art have or can have as intrinsic perceptual characteristics and indicate that there is an intelligible basis for their existence in fine art on a theory which holds that fine art is the molding of objects in the direction of intrinsic perceptual interest.

VII. FINE ART AND VALUE

Art in its most general sense, we have said, is skill used to produce objects of value, and fine art is the shaping of four-dimensional objects in the direction of intrinsic perceptual interest or value. What more precisely is meant by "value" as a property of objects, such as works of fine art, or of dimensions of these, and what is the relevance of "value" as an objective property to perception and the artistic activity?

As a property of an object or of a dimension of an object, I believe that value is, first of all, the adequacy of the object or dimension to a telic factor of a subject, e.g., to a requirement, an interest, or a need of a person. An object or a dimension that has such adequacy to a subject has value for the subject as one of its properties. But value as an objective property has a second meaning—the adequacy of an object or a dimension to a telic factor, a need or requirement, of another object or dimension. An object or a dimension that has such adequacy to another object or dimension has value for this object or dimension as one of its properties. This distinction between the value of an object or dimension for a subject and the value of an object or dimension for another object or dimension has many ramifications in general value theory, into which we shall not enter here. Suffice it to say that, in regard to works of fine art, it is the distinction between terminal and instrumental values, or dimensional and interdimensional values, which will be illustrated in some detail in the four chapters to be devoted to the discussion of the public object (Part II).

As a possession of objects, then, value is the adequacy of objects or of dimensions of objects to telic factors, such as requirements, interests, or needs. This is objective value, independent of its modifications upon integration with other values, i.e., it is objective value in the generic sense. The relevance of value in this sense to perception and fine art is not difficult to see. Perception is a mode of exploration. Primarily, it is a process of exploration at the service of organic needs. From the earliest days, when the child explores for breast or bottle, to the last desperate gaze for help of the dying man, perception is an exploration of the adequacies of things to organic needs. Thanks to this congenital function, perception becomes a sort of watchtower of values. It becomes a process of awareness before which stand all the vivid values of the world of existence. All things in their valuableness become spread before it, including the valuableness of these things as objects of perception's own activities. Accordingly, perception finds that a certain eloquent mode of sound or speech, laden with metaperceptual values, is agreeable to listen to and that a certain radiant sight, laden with metaperceptual values, is "easy on the eyes" or visually easy to perceive. Being a basic organic function, perception has needs that are part of the total needs of the organism, and perception becomes aware of the perceptual values in things of metaperceptual value as it explores these things for their adequacies to the total needs of the organism.

Fine art capitalizes on this complex nature of perception. Primarily, it aims to provide objects of intrinsic perceptual appeal. It aims to construct systems which give full and organized opportunity for a liberated use of all the powers of perception. But to draw out perception into an activity in which all its powers are satisfactorily engaged, fine art must imbed in its systems suggestions of metaperceptual values, such as those which the objects that engage perception ordinarily have. One intrinsic power of perception is the power to discern and explore the metaperceptual; and only if fine art gives scope to this, will it bring the panoply of powers of perception into full action and provide an object entirely satisfactory to perception's own intrinsic needs. Thus a drama dealing with love, intrigue, hatred, crime, vengeance, and death is shaped by the great dramatist into a complexly organized spectacle in which the need to perceive with ease and order, with intellectual keenness and imaginative excitement, is amply gratified. But, just because it is so shaped and perception is what it is, the drama inevitably becomes a spectacle in which the percipient's interest in love, intrigue, hatred, crime, vengeance, and death are also touched and molded in manifold directions. Only so could the drama fully interest perception in which the power to discern and explore the metaperceptual is a part of the primitive nature of its being. Thus, owing to the nature of perception, works of art inevitably play upon the larger interests in the very process of seeking to fulfil perception's own intrinsic needs.

An important qualification, fairly obvious from previous discussions, is necessary, however, to keep our account clear. Fine art is not the creation of objects to indulge metaperceptual interests. If a person is interested in crime and becomes engrossed in a crime drama to gratify vicariously an impulse to perform a crime, he is not taking the drama as a work of art, and his attitude is not the aesthetic attitude. The aim of art is not vicarious wish-fulfilment. A drama is taken as art only when the intrinsic perception of the object is central and when every interest of the percipient, including the interest in crime, is subordinated to, or a part of, the interest in full intrinsic perception. But within this limitation fine art may run the gamut of all possible values and extend to all possible interests. It may touch, as in music, upon an interest in the most abstract qualities: sprightliness, verve, melancholy, gaiety, speed, resolution, calm, insouciance; or it may touch, as in portrait painting, upon an interest in the most concrete individuals: Philip IV, Aretino, Sir John Suckling, Innocent X, Napoleon. Clearly, this connection of the arts on the perceptual level with the whole gamut of human interests and values is a fact of the utmost importance, suggesting immediately the tremendous power, actual and potential, in the fine arts for the life of the people they reach.

Purists have sometimes attempted to separate the intrinsic perceptual interests and the metaperceptual interests touched in the experience of art, to denote one type as "artistic" interests and the other type as "life"-interests and to contend that for art the second type is irrelevant. Art has nothing to do with "life." The obvious fallacy in this view is that in the proper experience of art the metaperceptual interests are elicited as vehicles of the intrinsic perceptual interest. The two are not outside each other, but one is a servant of the other. And works of art are constructed so that the "life"-interests may remain in proper subordination. The assassination of Caesar on the stage is not the assassination of Caesar in historic life, and interest in this assassination does not operate as it might in the presence of an assassination in historic life. On the stage the assassination is suggested only, it is not "real." And the interest in it is for its part in an acted drama or perceptual spectacle. It is an interest not in its character as a "real" assassination but in its character as an addition to the perceptual field. At least, it is so if the interest is properly released. Accordingly, the classification of such an interest as a "life"-interest irrelevant to art is false to the position that it occupies in the experience of art. Here it serves intrinsic perception, and so do "life"-interests in the aesthetic experience of art generally. These interests are aroused, expanded, and illumined in the experience of art. But all this is incidental to achieving a fuller intrinsic perception of what is contained in the work of art as a perceptual spectacle. Similarly, in works of art themselves, the metaperceptual serves perception, making the field of perception richer and more complete in intrinsic interest, while in "real" life perception serves the metaperceptual, at least it does so in the typical or ordinary instances of so-called "life"-activities.

III

THE CREATIVE PROCESS

IN MANY respects the creative process in the arts is indistinguishable from innumerable other types of creative activity. It
consists of a series of interactions between an agent and a material.
The agent is seeking to shape the material in certain ways for
certain purposes. He is a center of impulse, of striving, of tendency toward ends; and he possesses causal powers that implement
the realization of these ends and a nature, environmentally nurtured, that colors the form of the realization. The material, for
its part, is in certain ways resistant and in other ways plastic to
the efforts of the agent. It has its own nature, its own possibilities, its own limitations, its resident self-determinacy. All
this, however, is true of many other creative situations: e.g.,
agricultural experimentation or technological invention. They
consist of an agent or set of agents in interaction with a material,
each endowed with such general characteristics as those just
enumerated. What, then, is peculiar in the case of the fine arts?
There seem to me to be two major peculiarities.

First, the material of the arts, generally speaking, is material
of great intrinsic perceptual interest. The great poet's words are
not the flat stereotypes of a business letter. The sculptor's stone
is not the lustreless shale of a river bed. The dancer's body is not
the ungainly and ill-co-ordinated organism of the ordinary ten-
year-old schoolgirl. The musician's tones are not the screeching
noises of a city street, and the architect's blocks are not the ill-
shaped boulders of a vacant lot. In the overwhelming majority
of cases the material of each art exhibits, or under transformation
is easily capable of exhibiting, vivid intrinsic values for perception. It is alive with all the possibilities of great art. The second

peculiarity concerns the artist himself. "The artist is not distinguished either by the quality or the amount of his feeling, but by the intensity and comprehensiveness of his unifying perception."[1] "Genius, considered in itself, is but superior perceptive power, coming from exaggerated excitability and elasticity in the nervous centres."[2] More precisely, the peculiarity of the artist is an extraordinarily keen interest in, and power to assimilate phases of, the perceptual world—sounds, colors, lines, motions, the perceptible oddities of people—together with the capacity to create diverse perceptual systems which extend his original interest and power and satisfy in a superior way the deeply innate craving for novel and internally complete intrinsic perceptions.

The key terms of the creative process in the arts, then, are a certain kind of agent and a certain type of material. Nevertheless, it seems impossible to give an adequate description of this creative process merely by depicting the overt interactions between the agent and the material. The agent, for example, has a complex inner consciousness, in which a great deal often occurs before overt interaction with the material takes place. In part, the development of all human consciousness consists of the acquisition of an elaborate set of symbols or imagery representative of the physicosocial world and the reintegration of these symbols as a preparation for overt "action." This is especially true in the case of the artist. Indeed, it has been so true here that some thinkers, such as Croce, have reduced the creative process of the artist to the mere subjective reintegration of symbols. Leonardo's creation of the "Last Supper," according to this view, consisted not in the overt act of painting but in that "arranging" of the colors, lines, shapes, and figures on the wall at Santa Maria delle Grazie that took place during the hours in which the artist merely gazed studiously upon the surface to be painted. The creation was this purely "spiritual" process of

[1] Leo Stein, *A B C of Aesthetics* (New York: Boni & Liveright, 1927), p. 206.

[2] Eugène Véron, *Aesthetics*, trans. W. H. Armstrong (London: Chapman & Hall, 1879), p. 73; cf. also George Santayana, *Reason in Art* (New York: Charles Scribner's Sons, 1905), p. 181.

manipulating the imagined colors, lines, shapes, and figures. The physical act of painting which followed was an act of caution to preserve the creation, adding nothing of aesthetic consequence.

Such a view, if taken as a complete account of the creative process in art, seems very unsatisfactory. It omits too many things. It forgets that the so-called "spiritual" acts even of a Leonardo depend on prior and concomitant physical occurrences. These so-called "spiritual" acts depend both upon the multitude of past interactions between Leonardo and the physical world which supplied the elements of the imagined colors, lines, shapes, and figures employed in the imaginary arranging and upon the physical acts of Leonardo's eyes and brain and organism in contemplating the physical wall at Santa Maria. Far from being purely spiritual, the processes attributed to Leonardo would have collapsed completely if the elements therein derived from past physical interactions had been removed or if the current physical interactions had been deleted. Throughout his account Croce ignores the creative potential lodged in the physical.

Croce's account also forgets the psychological and social context in which the visionary processes that he describes usually operate. From earliest days the artist—even a Leonardo—is trained in the handling of physical tools and in the mastering of a physical medium. As a consequence, his creative visions are habitually taken as ideas for the manipulation of his physical tools and medium. They are visions of new combinations in which to connect pigments, tones, masses, bodily movements—literal physical public materials. They are plans for physical action, agenda for "objective" products, not finalities. In most cases it is utterly false to the psychology and sociology of creation to describe the premanual visionary processes as terminals of the creative act. They are, rather, its inciting incidents.

Finally, the Crocean view forgets that, owing to this fact, the usual subjective visions preceding physical manipulation and alleged by Croce to be complete creations are often, even with the greatest artists, aesthetically incomplete visions. Often they contain the germ of a whole work and even most of the detail when the work is brief. But invariably they are simplified, generalized, fragmentary, or inadequately articulated versions, lacking the detailed fulness of the final creation. This fulness comes, if at all, only after overt operations on the physical material have been undertaken. Moreover, these overt operations not only produce previously ignored or unsummoned details but often open up new perspectives, evoke new inspirations, suggest manifold revisions, and, together with the physical material, add immeasurably to the artistic creation over what it was originally as subjective vision. Indeed, the organically complete and definitive inner visions which Croce contends are the essence of art and intuition are often attained for the first time by the greatest artists only after actual physical materials and numerous overt physical manipulations have been brought into play. That is, these manipulations and physical materials are frequently the very gateway to the creation of a work of fine art even in the rather odd sense of the term used by Croce.[3]

On the whole, Croce's view of artistic creation seems unrealistic in its omission of physical, psychological, and social factors, which are of the greatest importance for an accurate understanding of the process as it actually occurs in innumerable cases. The view is characteristically Crocean in the separation of art from its physical sources and social roots and in the romantic subjectivism pervading it. Our main point in discussing it, however, is that, despite its errors, the Crocean view is not without an important element of truth. The visionary process, the subjective shaping, which Croce mistakes for the whole and misdescribes as purely spiritual, is a far from negligible segment of the creative enterprise. Often the artist's freshest and keenest energies go into it, and often the most crucial and fundamental determinants of his final work make their first appearance in it. I propose, therefore, to begin our analysis of the creative process with an account of this subjective phase and then to deal with the overt manipulations of physical material that, sometimes preceding the subjective phase, are the usual way of completing the crea-

[3] S. Alexander, *Art and the Material* (Manchester: Manchester University Press, 1925), p. 29. Of course, there are exceptions; cf. Ralph Linton, "Primitive Art," *Kenyon Review*, III, No. 1 (winter, 1941), p. 34 f.

tive process in the arts. It will be understood throughout this earlier discussion that, in our view, the subjective phase is only a segment of a larger process and that artistic creation in its full form involves this larger process with its context and not merely subjective creation.

II. THE SUBJECTIVE PHASE

Besides the instance of Leonardo at Santa Maria, there are other famous examples of the visionary manipulation of symbols. "Kubla Khan" is said to have been dreamed as it is, then written down. Mozart is quoted as writing: "My ideas come as they will, I don't know how, all in a stream. If I like them I keep them in my head, and people say that I often hum them over to myself. Well, if I can hold on to them, they begin to join on to one another, as if they were bits that a pastry cook should joint together in his pantry. And now my soul gets heated, and if nothing disturbs me the piece grows larger and brighter until, however long it is, it is all finished at once in my mind, so that I can see it at a glance as if it were a pretty picture or a pleasing person. Then I don't hear the notes one after another, as they are hereafter to be played, but it is as if in my fancy they were all at once. And that *is* a revel [*das ist nun ein Schmaus*]. While I'm inventing, it all seems to me like a fine vivid dream, but that hearing it all at once [when the invention is done], that's the best. When I have once so heard I forget not again, and perhaps this is the best gift that God has granted me."[4]

Inner creation, such as this, presupposes, as I have suggested in the case of Leonardo, antecedent experience. Such creation may occur suddenly and most unexpectedly. But it does not arise from nothing. It springs from a soil usually prepared by technical training and always stocked with symbols acquired from interactions with artistic material and with a physicosocial world. Even the six-year-old musical prodigy bursts into creative invention only after antecedent social and musical observation and

[4] Josiah Royce, *The Spirit of Modern Philosophy* (Boston: Houghton Mifflin Co., 1892), p. 457. This letter has been suspected of being apocryphal, but, apocryphal or not, it describes a process which might have occurred, and so illustrates a real possibility in artistic creation.

experience. "We know that one of the conditions most favorable to invention is . . . . accumulated experience, knowledge."[5] "To become an artist the most highly gifted must go through a long course of hard practice and experiment."[6] Testimony of this sort from all quarters is almost endless.[7] A well-known detailed treatise on the acquisition of symbols from antecedent interactions is Lowes's *Road to Xanadu*, in which words and phrases in *The Rime of the Ancient Mariner* and "Kubla Khan" are traced to books of travel and adventure that Coleridge had been reading before composing the poems. "A work of pure imagination," Lowes remarks, "is not something fabricated by a *tour de force* from nothing, and suspended, without anchorage in fact, in the impalpable ether of a visionary world. No conception could run more sharply counter to the truth." Supposedly a mere vision, *The Rime of the Ancient Mariner* is steeped in the factual lore of the day. "It has swept within its assimilating influence a bewildering diversity of facts in which contemporary interest was active. The facts are forgotten, and the poem stays." But the acquisition of the "facts" was a precondition both of the poem and of the vision which it embodies.[8]

The capacity to be keenly affected by the perceptual world, to gather "facts," and to lay up memories convertible into a great symbolic repertory is usually called "sensitivity." The power to reintegrate this repertory, to construct from it images of novel perceptual systems, to shape "the facts into the fabric of a vision,"[9] is usually called "imagination," creative as distinct from reproductive imagination. Sensitivity and creative imagination are the basic powers of the subjective phase of creation.

[5] Th. Ribot, *Essai sur l'imagination créatrice* (Paris: Félix Alcan, 1900), p. 135.

[6] J. Littlejohns, *How To Enjoy Pictures* (New York: Macmillan Co., 1927), p. 6.

[7] Cf. R. H. Wilenski, *French Painting* (Boston: Hale, Cushman & Flint, Inc., 1931), p. 118; Brenda Putnam, *The Sculptor's Way* (New York: Rinehart & Co., 1939), p. 28; Elsa Lanchester, "Charles Laughton and I," *Atlantic Monthly*, CLXI (February, 1938), 167; W. S. Maugham, *The Summing Up* (New York: Doubleday Co., 1938), p. 95; Max Schoen, *Art and Beauty* (New York: Macmillan Co., 1932), pp. 54–55; Elizabeth Drew, *Discovering Poetry* (New York: W. W. Norton & Co., Inc., 1937), p. 26.

[8] John L. Lowes, *The Road to Xanadu* (Boston: Houghton Mifflin Co., 1927), p. 241.

[9] *Ibid.*, p. 241.

Sensitivity in artists is usually uneven. Some artists are extraordinarily sensitive to words or tones but not to lines or colors.
Others are extraordinarily sensitive to lines and colors but not to
words or tones. Still others are extraordinarily sensitive to the
motives and basic characteristics of human beings but not to
tones or colors. This unevenness of sensitivity conditions imagination, explaining in part the different directions that imagination takes and why there are different arts—an art of words, an
art of tones, an art of colors, etc. Nor is this unevenness of sensitivity altogether regrettable in other respects. If artists were extraordinarily affected by all the perceptual facets of the physical
and social world, they would probably be suffocated by experience, overwhelmed by its sheer massiveness. In any case artists
need merely sensitivity enough to provide their powers of symbolic reorganization with an unusually ample and fertile field
for action, and great depth of sensitivity in one direction only is
ordinarily sufficient to do this.

Sensitivity is the point of contact between the inner consciousness of the artist and the outer world. It is almost public. More
inward and secretive is the other basic power of the subjective
phase—creative imagination. Imagination, as it operates in
aesthetic appreciation, we have defined as the power to connect
the absent with the present. It is a process of synthesis of the
"not-given" with the "given." Creative imagination, as it
operates in subjective symbolic manipulations, is also a process
of synthesis. It might be defined as the power to connect a multiplicity of assimilated items into a novel synthetical unity.
At its weakest, where imagination is what Coleridge called
"fancy," this unity is like an aggregate in which the items have
some superficial interrelevance that gives them the appearance of
going effectively together, as when a person compares the frost
to icing on a cake or a child draws an ensemble in which a candle
and a doll stand as high as a house. Such facile combinations are
often momentarily startling and pleasing, but they are not particularly rewarding to closer scrutiny. On the other hand, as its
best, where imagination is what Coleridge meant by the term,
the unity created is like an organism in which the parts have a

complex, mutually sustaining interrelevance that gives the whole a dense and durable set of values, as when the poet compares the frost to a white assassin or a painter arranges the colors and shapes of the objects in a small picture so as to create subtly contrasting or parallel rhythms within a unified realistic design. In forms larger than metaphor or miniature patterns, the elements of highly imaginative wholes mutually enhance one another in more complex, and often in seemingly miraculous, ways. These combinations not only suggest the daring and audacity romantically associated with genius but sometimes also exhibit a wealth of connections so rich as to reach indefinitely beyond the grasp of the keenest analytic attention. They suggest the inexhaustible and the infinite in the manner of Kant's Aesthetical Ideas.[10] In all cases, however, creative imagination is the power to connect a diversity into a novel synthetical unity, the rank accorded the result being ultimately a function of the wealth of perceptual value that is found in the unified diversity.

Sensitivity, then, is the material principle of the symbolic or subjective phase of creation, and imagination is the form principle; and, at its best, imagination weaves the symbols derived from sensitivity into designs of great suggestiveness and power. Yet other factors besides these two inner capacities enter into the subjective manipulatory process. Abstractly, sensitivity is pure receptivity, the power to record indiscriminately anything impinging on the organism, while, abstractly, creative imagination is pure madness, the power to combine anything with anything.[11] Both require control principles, governance, and guidance for the emergence of the results which they help attain. What are the subjective control factors which modify sensitivity in its acquisitive role and govern imagination in its formal shaping?

First and foremost is the personality of the artist. By "personality of the artist" I do not mean merely his superficial whims and striking mannerisms, although these are a part and, with

[10] I. Kant, *Critique of Judgement*, trans. Bernard (2d ed.; London: Macmillan & Co., Ltd., 1914), pp. 201 ff.

[11] I. A. Richards, *Coleridge on Imagination* (London: Kegan Paul, Trench, Trubner & Co., Ltd., 1934), pp. 74, 172.

minor artists, a great part of its meaning. More basic than these is the artist's fund of inborn drives and needs as these have been released and transformed by environment and education into a system of purposes and aspirations manifesting a set of standards or a "scale of values." Personality is a fruition of heredity modified by environment, but its essence is the fruition emerging from the heredity and expressed in relation to the environment. Its essence is the system of inclinations and aspirations of the artist underlying his mannerisms and manifesting through his actions and mannerisms a scale of values.

Personality in the sense of the basic underlying value inclinations and aspirations of the artist is a fundamental control factor of the subjective creative process. It exerts a control over sensitivity and the symbolic material acquired through sensitivity. In part, sensitivity and the material it acquires are a function of native endowment and training, i.e., of the mechanical agility of the receptor mechanism. In part, however, they are a function of the underlying value inclinations and aspirations of the artist. These value inclinations and aspirations tend to determine the paths into which the receptor powers are directed, the zest with which they respond, and the items that interest the artist in these paths. Moreover, these value inclinations and aspirations generally determine the selections for symbolic use, "instinctive" and reflective, that the artist makes from the total acquisitions of his receptor mechanism. Indeed, personality so determines these selections or, with imagination, so modifies them that certain material items in a work—tone clusters, lines, words, shapes, and so on—sometimes immediately and unmistakably signalize a particular artist, independent of the larger form of the work. Hearing or seeing these, we realize at once that the work is by Debussy, Cézanne, Poe, Pope, Delacroix, Rodin, Michelangelo, and so on.

Personality equally controls imagination, the great forming power. The personality of the artist regulates the act of unification in such a way that the created product exhibits a characteristic system of accents and emphases which leads one to associate it with the artist and even with his age. Sometimes in given works this system of accents and emphases is incompletely definitive of the creator. Apprentice and imitation work, work in some type of form or material ably used by other artists, or work of short span often illustrates incompletely definitive creations. But the more vigorously creative a work is, the more definitely personal do its accents and emphases usually become. Even in music—the art in which the condition of personal indeterminacy is likely to be most pronounced because the materials and forms of music have been highly conventionalized and the expressive substance of the art is so general and "abstract"—the modifications by personality are frequently crystal clear. Certain music by Wagner is as different in its accentual system from certain music by Haydn as the two men or their two epochs are. The one is surging, ponderous, ruthlessly declarative, endlessly persistent, while the other is mechanically elegant and graciously artificial, its sprightliness and melancholy and playful surprises confined within fixed bounds as if restricted a priori to certain clear and unalterable limits. And this is a statement not merely of certain accentual qualities of the pieces of music but also of certain personal qualities of Wagner and Haydn and of certain widespread qualities of the surging bourgeois nineteenth century and of the courtly eighteenth-century mid-Continental Europe.

The personality of the artist also affects the aesthetic "depth" of a creation. Everyone is familiar with the fact that violin tones sound mellow or thin according to the nature of the sound chamber over which the strings are stretched. Now personality in the subjective phase of creation has a role similar to the sound chamber or resonator in tone production. It serves as an amplifier or denudator of undertones and overtones of value. The result is an imaginative structure that is aesthetically subtle and rich or arid and commonplace. Two artists of equally facile sensitivity and imagination go to work on the same subject, producing results utterly different not only in vocabulary and accent but in expressive depth. They may paint before the same model, one producing a "fancy" magazine-cover painting and the other a landmark in pictorial art. The greater wealth of expressive values in the one work reflects a greater depth of value penetration of its creator. It is a product of his "realizations" of the subject and springs from the system of value inclinations and aspirations that he brings to the interpretation of the subject. Thus personality is influential in supplying not only a peculiar idiom and accentual structure to a symbolic system but also an expressive wealth and richness or an expressive bareness and poverty. It may, indeed, mark a difference as wide as that between glitter and gold. Two works may brilliantly bespeak in vocabulary and syntax the unmistakable characteristics of two artists. Yet they may be the opposite in expressive density, one meretricious and thin, the other solid and mellow-toned.

Personality, then, is a basic control factor in the subjective creative process, modifying sensitivity and imagination, and the symbolic material, the form and the expression. Usually these modifications are "underground" events, occurring without the artist's explicit will or awareness at the time. But, as we shall see in the next section, there is no fixed rule on this point. Besides personality, there are other control factors in the subjective process. Some of these are fortuitous conditions: a spell of very good or of very bad health, a temporary lazy streak or a sudden disposition for hard work, personal good fortune or a great misfortune, a period of inner peace or of inner tumult. Sometimes these "scratches" on the surface of the artist's existence impair or enhance creation considerably. Sometimes you would never know from the created product that they had existed at all. More uniform and usually more profound in their effects are two other control factors, the "subject" of a work and its functional end. Both frequently control the selection of material and the shaping of the form as vigorously as personality. The subject of the "Last Supper" certainly exercised control over Leonardo's choice of colors, lines, and shapes and even more control over his arrangement of these materials into a form suitable to articulate the dramatic moment that was the subject. In general, a subject has certain broad or typic characteristics that allow a certain latitude to its treatment, e.g., a material, formal, and expressive range for personality. But the artist must keep within the broad generic bounds of these characteristics if his work is to be at all a recognizable treatment of the subject.

The other control factor here—the functional end of the work —may be simple or complex. In either case it is usually an explicit type of control factor. At its simplest it is subjectively aesthetic, i.e., the functional end of the work is simply that of satisfying the artist's private aesthetic interest. Here the selection of the material and the shaping process have maximum freedom, being governed from above solely by a purpose which the work can fulfil independently of all explicit extrinsic considerations. Usually, however, the functional end of a work is much more complex than this. Most works of art have come into existence not merely to discharge a private end but also to perform a public function, as a statue to fit a public square, a painting to decorate a church, a piece of music to fit a certain concert program. Shakespeare, writing his plays, presumably sought not merely to articulate a vision satisfying to his own private perception but to write plays fitting the requirements of his theater, the needs of his players, and the demands of his audience. The functional end of his plays was very complex, and, for him to create successfully under the circumstances, his symbols and forms had to be governed to some extent by each element of this functional complex. The imagination of the professional artist particularly, far from a free and roving fancy, is usually regulated by a number of explicit functional considerations, social in origin and character, which powerfully modify his materials as well as his forms, just as this imagination is regulated and the materials and forms modified by a number of the most obscure personal traits, reaching back into the heredity and the earliest environment of the artist.

III. THE ROLE OF CONSCIOUSNESS

This discussion of "subject" and functional control raises the more general question of the place of critical consciousness in creation. Sometimes the working of imagination in inner creation is described as "unconscious," in the sense of being without critical control. This description may apply to imagination in dream compositions such as "Kubla Khan" is said to have been, but, unless qualified, to little else. Mozart is surely as near to a great "unconscious" artist as might be found, if the letter previously quoted is believed to be authentic. Yet Mozart says there that he keeps his first musical ideas "if I like them." That is, an evaluative or critical judgment mingles with the surges of his imagination at the very outset of creation. At least some such critical control is, I believe, usually present in creation. To describe creation as pure spontaneity is a romantic exaggeration. Even the freest doodling of a surrealist, one suspects, is maintained under the aegis of conscious approval of its "unconsciousness."

Tschaikovsky writes: "Usually the seed of a future musical creation germinates instantaneously and most unexpectedly. If the soil is eager, if there is a disposition to work, that seed takes root with amazing power and speed, appears above ground as a little stalk which puts forth leaves and branches and finally, flowers. . . . . Words are vain to tell you the boundless joy that comes over me when a new idea is conceived and begins to take definite shape. One forgets everything; one is a madman, trembling and quivering in every organ, with scarcely time to outline the sketches, so rapidly does one idea pursue another." . . . .[12] The critical or evaluative control in creation will range from such mere "eagerness of the soil" and boundless approval existing on the margin of the process to all degrees of tempering analytical reflection existing nearer the center. Usually, indeed, the initial surges of imagination described by Tschaikovsky supply an incomplete whole—the sketch of a piece, or a fragment.[13] Conscious critical construction and guidance are needed to develop this sketch into a full and perfect work or to extend the happy fragment to completion. And sometimes this deliberate construction and guidance must play the major role in creation, e.g., when inspiration is thin or the *raison d'être* of a work is wholly external,

[12] C. D. Bowen and Barbara von Mech, *Beloved Friend* (New York: Random House, Inc., 1937), p. 206.

[13] Ribot (*op. cit.*, p. 49) declares categorically that inspiration "never delivers a completed work."

as in some commissions. Nor does the play of vigorous critical mentality over a piece necessarily mean that the piece will be inferior. Often just the opposite. All depends on the artist's critical mentality. Even Tschaikovsky, although far from the perfect illustration of high-powered critical mentality among artists, asserts that very often a commissioned piece which requires considerable artifice "turns out quite successfully, while pieces invented wholly on my own inspiration are sometimes less successful for various incidental reasons."[14] Critical intellect is a creative liability only in certain cases—for example, where it is used as a substitute for imagination instead of as a guide, regulator, and amplifier of imagination. Inferior artists have used the critical power in this way and have brought it into disrepute as a creative factor, whereas what is inferior in such artists is their imaginative power and their inappropriate use of critical power. Critical power may be a blight, as the romantics believed, where the original and spontaneous imaginings of an artist are aesthetically weak and the temptation to replace the unconscious with the conscious is, as a consequence, relatively strong. This tendency to an inappropriate use of the conscious and the unconscious is present in all the arts. "There is a good deal, in the writing of poetry, which must be conscious and deliberate," T. S. Eliot declares. "In fact, the bad poet is usually unconscious where he ought to be conscious, and conscious where he ought to be unconscious."[15]

Generally speaking, then, the creative process involves both the unconscious and the conscious and is, at its best, a combination of genius and taste. At its best it involves genius, the deeply personalized underground power to reintegrate into an original and resonant vision items which have been absorbed by sensitivity from the currents of the artist's experience. But at its best it also involves a sense of what is required and a sense of what is fitting for a work, i.e., a standard of taste. The proportion of the conscious to the unconscious often varies greatly from artist to artist. The conscious as well as the unconscious may be very

[14] Bowen and Von Mech, *op. cit.*, p. 247.

[15] T. S. Eliot, *The Sacred Wood* (London: Methuen & Co., Ltd., 1920), p. 52.

elaborate, as in a great literary artist, a Dante or a Milton. Or the conscious may be merely marginal, as in a nonliterary artist, a painter or a musician, a Cézanne or a Mozart. In nonliterary artists, however, the conscious is often present in a surprising degree; and, upon occasion, a Cézanne or a Mozart can be very vocal indeed regarding the critical aims of his craft. The modern self-styled "unconscious" artist who prides himself on spurning the conscious intellect as a falsifier tries to escape the conscious altogether. But his creative procedure is built upon his intellectually based anti-intellectualist credo. He lets his unconscious roam as the tenets of this credo dictate, producing formless works in a romantic manner and regulating his procedures, ironically enough, by his passionate psychological theories.[16] No matter how much he may wish it, the artist cannot be a helpless and hapless child, wholly at the mercy of the wayward wind of impulse, without abandoning all he has learned and all he has come to believe about the aims and ends of his craft. The solution would seem to lie not in foresaking reason but in developing taste, so that it is able to assist to the maximum in releasing or augmenting the values imbedded in the imaginative vision for the occasion, inner or outer, that has called the vision into being.

Such, then, is the role of critical consciousness in the subjective phase of creation. Its part may be focal where inspiration slips. But its part is always vital as the mentor of the imaginative vision, approving the vision where it seems to fit, and trying to improve it where it seems to fail to fit, the responsibilities of the artist's craft.

The subjective phase of creation, as I have already mentioned, is usually an inconclusive episode. At best, it is the projection of an image of a work of art, an "idea" of the actuality but not the actuality customarily desiderated. Usually also it is internally incomplete. Even in the case of Mozart, in whom the subjective phase is of considerable scope, the symbolic system is clearly more like a notational summary useful for the production of music

---

[16] D. H. Lawrence is an obvious example (Aldous Huxley, *The Olive Tree* [New York: Harper & Bros., 1937], pp. 215–16). Surrealists are among the most self-conscious of current instances.

than like music itself. For one thing, the whole temporal dimension of music is absent, as in a musical score: "I do not hear the notes one after the other, as they are hereafter to be played." Nor is this incompleteness mysterious. From the beginning of his training, the artist is oriented toward "objective" creation. He is educated in the public materials and tools of his craft for production in terms of these tools and materials. The subjective phase is a mere step on the way, an inner spark for creating the public blaze. It is enormously fascinating, but it has usually no terminal status. In consequence, the subjective phase tends simply toward the production of major essentials, or "sketches" in Tschaikovsky's phrase. The projection in idea of such essentials or sketches is sufficient to release or reinvigorate the forces of objective production for fruitful effort and thus to discharge the incidental role in creation that the subjective phase usually plays.

IV. THE OBJECTIVE PHASE

In its most obvious aspect the objective phase of creation is simply the manipulation by the artist of actual physical materials. In the subjective phase the physical materials are represented by images mirroring their nature. These symbols are the "stuff" of subjective creation. In the objective phase the materials are present in proper person and themselves become a major explicit factor in the process of creation.

There is a certain broad parallelism between the artist and the materials. As a sensitive and imaginative being, the artist is at once passive and active, subject to innumerable influences and self-determinate within these influences. Artistic material is also plastic and self-determinate. It is open to innumerable manipulations, yet it has a nature determinate of what emerges in it under these manipulations. Clay is not wood, nor is wood tone or pigment. Each has its own nature, and one can do with clay or wood or tone or pigment only what its peculiar nature permits. Each artistic material has its possibilities and limitations; and, in the subjective phase, the symbols representing the material are usually manipulated with considerable antecedent knowledge of these peculiar possibilities and limitations. Were this not the case, the subjective phase would be useless, like an irrelevant daydream, in the total process of creation.

It is possible to ignore and easy to exaggerate the role of the material principle in the creative process. The material principle is ignored by thinkers who describe creation as a purely spiritual process, an essay in pure inner plasticity governed solely by lyrical feeling and independent of technique. The material principle is exaggerated by thinkers who conceive art as a pure manual skill, a set of recipes for handling materials and for getting certain "effects." Both attitudes toward the material principle tend toward unfortunate results in practice. A subjective process purely lyrical and technically undisciplined, carried beyond the shortest span, usually becomes inchoate, spastic, weedy, and productive of roaming, cumbersome works that are appallingly diffuse and uninteresting. A manual skill that is merely technically expert, adroit, or slick usually turns out elaborate inanities, dainty trifles, or academic solemnities. In practice, the material principle of the creative process usually can be neither worshiped nor ignored without damage to the creative result; and wisdom would therefore seem to lie in giving the principle the fullest recognition without forgetting that it is only one important factor in the total creative venture.

The material principle is important in a number of fundamental ways. First, it accounts for the presence of certain material, aesthetic properties in the creative process and product. Each artistic material, as I have said, has its own nature, and, as a result of this, each artistic material has its own intrinsic perceptual characteristics. Even words—the least physical of artistic material—have peculiarities of physical appearance and sound and of feeling quality and sense, so that no one would mistake words for marble, wrought iron, or clay. They have different intrinsic properties, and even classes of words have different intrinsic properties: French and English, biblical English and contemporary American English. Now the works into which such materials are woven exhibit certain intrinsic qualities that are due to the sheer material. They look and sound and act on one differently. The sound and feeling qualities, the physical appearance and sense of French words cannot be exactly duplicated in American, biblical, or any orthodox form of English, any more than they can be given in the tones of a keyboard. And these clear differences of a material are not mere abstract properties but aesthetic differences, since they appear in the field of intrinsic perception. Compare two identical sculptural designs, one in plaster and one in marble. There is an adamant aesthetic diversity here in the sheer material, so much so that a person who admires a statue in fine marble may find a plaster duplicate of it repulsive or uninteresting. To some extent these material aesthetic diversities exist in the subjective phase of creation. They appear there as differences in the physical media imagined and as a function of these media. In the subjective phase, however, these material qualities usually have a certain physical insubstantiality and dimness. However vivid and forceful they may be there, they rarely have the exact vivacity and force of actual existence. This requires objective creation; and the incorporation of these qualities in the richness of their physical immediacy into works of fine art is sometimes a major motive of the objective phase of creation.

Second, the material principle of art accounts for the growth and use of technique in the creative process. Since each material is different, different methods of handling it must be developed. You cannot organize words with a chisel or tones with a paint brush. Each material requires special technical processes. In the objective phase of creation, artistic technique might be described as the power to handle material in conformity with the inspiration of the artist and the functional aims of his work. It is muscle in the service of vision. But, in its totality, technique is not only the way an artist's muscle works but also the way his mind works. It is the way in which he imagines things, as well as the craft that he expends on objective material to embody these imaginings. This inner method of imagining is formed under the discipline of interaction with physical material and is subject to constant correction from conscious craftsmanship, guided by functional aims. Nevertheless, it operates in the subjective phase of creation as a factor in shaping the vision there, illustrating once again the inadequacy of the "idealistic" conception of art as a purely spiritual process, transcending technical considerations.

The initial reference of technique, however, is to the objective phase of creation and to the explicit handling of physical materials. Certainly, in ordinary thought, technique is external method and, at its minimum, very external indeed. Finger exercises on the piano, accurate drawing of natural objects, practice modeling in clay, copying the Greek architectural orders, and writing a Miltonic sonnet are usually called "exercises in technique." Their ostensible purpose is the learning of facility in handling the materials of a craft, the acquiring of a standardized vocabulary and of ways of attaining certain standardized effects. Usually barren in themselves, such exercises, so far as creation is concerned, are generally useful preliminaries, just as it is a useful preliminary for a child to learn the conventionalized idioms of his mother-tongue if he intends to speak his mind in it. In the master-artist, however, technique is a much more complex and individualized system of procedures. In the objective phase of creation it is all the ways which the artist has found to translate his unique imaginative vision into materials and to achieve the effects desired in terms of these materials. Usually emerging from standardized methods acquired from the past, his technique departs from these methods as much as the vision which it aims to manifest departs from past visions. Thus variability from artist to artist, even from work to work of the same artist, rather than standardization is a salient characteristic of creative technique.

This variability extends not merely to the manifold details of the created product but even to some of the most general properties of the creative process. For instance, some artists create effortlessly, as the birds sing, while for others creation is infinite toil and sweat. "Writing is just like childbirth," says Tolstoy; "until the fruit is ripe it does not come, and when it does, it comes with pain and labor."[17] Again, some artists create in a single furious effort, upon which they are never able to improve; others make numerous efforts, revise and revise, and finally achieve what seems to them a perfect creation. Compare the fol-

[17] Cf. Schoen, *op. cit.*, pp. 71–72.

lowing descriptions of the methods of the painters Van Gogh and Whistler: "His [Van Gogh's] practice was to paint the whole canvas at one sitting, even if it killed him, and he was never able to improve upon his initial effort. That was the strength and the weakness of his art."[18] "His [Whistler's] method, as I observed it, was first of all to arrange his subject with incredible pains and care, so that every detail was to his liking, and to paint it with infinite touches and retouches; and then, when it seemed finished and perfect in execution, to stand back, gaze at it, and cry 'Ha!' and rush at it in a kind of fury and paint the whole thing out. It was like an actor rehearsing a part over and over again till he gets it perfect; the final performance, which may take a minute, has been preceded by many hours of rehearsal. This was the case, I think, even with Whistler's life-sized portraits. The actual painting of each, as we now see it, was performed in the briefest of periods, but these had been preceded by an almost infinite number of rehearsals."[19] Again, some artists run out of inspiration quickly and must labor endlessly to complete what began so easily and so perfectly, while other artists have enormously copious inspirations—they must cut and cut in accordance with Santayana's dictum "Thou must reject," and some of the most gleaming fish of the imagination become lost in the remorseless logic governing effective technique.[20] In the discussion of artistic form in Part II below, something more will be said about technique. The chief point here is that artistic technique springs up in connection with artistic materials. Its growth and use in creation are accounted for primarily by the material principle. And, as creative method rather than as mere recapitulation of art learning displayed for its own sake, technique is the artist's characteristic way in subjective and objective creation of shaping his material to realize his vision within the framework of the functional aims and other controls of artistic creation.

[18] Thomas Craven, *Modern Art* (New York: Simon & Schuster, 1934, 1940), p. 147.

[19] Logan P. Smith, *Unforgotten Years* (Boston: Little, Brown & Co., 1939), pp. 207–8.

[20] As an illustration of this contrast, compare A. E. Housman, *The Name and Nature of Poetry* (New York: Macmillan Co., 1933), esp. pp. 48 ff., with Thomas Wolfe, *The Story of a Novel* (New York: Charles Scribner's Sons, 1936).

Third, the material principle accounts for numerous changes in the course of the creative process from which emerge certain formal and expressive aesthetic qualities in the created product. "As your carving progresses," the sculptor R. A. Baillie writes, "the stone itself will suggest improvements over your first sketch. If you are sensitive to its messages, you will modify certain details as you work—leaving a bold plane where your sketch indicated a round or broken surface, and eliminating many unnecessary holes and details of fur or feathers. This is undoubtedly the way Michelangelo worked, as we see when we compare his rough wax sketches with the large marbles. And many times the very limits of his block forced him to revise an attitude, a turn of head or thrust of knee, accentuating the compactness and solidity of the larger work. Many stones have veins, much as wood has a grain, and sometimes by following what these veins suggest you will get a finer effect than you had ever thought of when you were making your clay model."[21]

This quasi-creative fecundity in the very material itself, its ability to suggest novel formal and expressive aesthetic qualities, is a fact familiar to all sensitive and mature artists. For them the material of art is not a dead external physical matter but one alive with value possibilities, which long association has made increasingly rich and various. It is exhilarating, as well as adamant, material, and the artist watches it and follows it with the keenest attention. Of the very able Yugoslavian, Meštrović, Casson writes: "Unconsciously his hand is controlled by the stone; its planes and angles appeal to his eye; he is influenced by his material and by the natural cleavages of stone."[22]

Our account of the creative process so far may have seemed to suggest that inner vision invariably precedes the manipulation of physical materials in actual creation. But sometimes the very opposite is the case. The artist sometimes begins with the physical material itself and, so to speak, without an idea in his head. He fools around at the piano, he makes impulsive sketches on

[21] Putnam, *op. cit.*, p. 302; cf. also Eric Blom, *The Limitations of Music* (New York: Macmillan Co., 1928), p. 56.

[22] S. Casson, *Some Modern Sculptors* (London: Oxford University Press, 1928), p. 64.

paper following the suggestions of the lines and shapes, and slowly, as if from the material itself, an idea is born. The subjective vision is a relatively late arrival upon the scene. Where this is not the case, the material principle remains fertile in formal and expressive suggestions. It is usually far from a merely passive receptacle, as the Crocean account suggests. The material is a creative collaborator, provocative as well as docile, contributing as well as receiving; and the objective phase of creation is sometimes as much a process of discovery in regard to a work's formal and expressive aspects as it is the execution of antecedently formulated ideas.

Finally, the material principle is an important factor in the attainment by creation of many functional aims and gains. Thus the material principle is vitally instrumental in the attainment by the artist of certain private ends, e.g., the clarification to himself by objectification of his inner aesthetic vision and the deep satisfaction, the thrill of mastery, the maturity of personality, the growth of technique, and the catharsis and other medicinal results which may also attend successful objectification. Because all these are functions of physical objectification, they depend on physical objectification, which itself depends on a physical material. The material principle is also vitally instrumental in the attainment of certain public ends, e.g., the permanence and wide availability of the artist's novel aesthetic vision and its ability to serve not only aesthetic but multiple nonaesthetic purposes, from the economic to the religious.

The material contributes to these functions in varying degrees, besides providing the substance without which there could be no objective creation at all and consequently none of the functional gains attainable through it. Thus the material may be the chief factor in determining the quality of the private functional gains of an artist, e.g., a difficult material may make the clarification by objectification less complete, or it may make the satisfaction, the thrill of mastery, the maturity of personality, the growth of technique, and the catharsis and other medicinal results more profound. Similarly, the material may be the chief factor in determining the character of the public functional gains.

For example, a heavy, rigid material, such as stone, may contribute greater permanence but less wide availability to the novel aesthetic vision of the artist. It may also contribute greatly to a work of art's being more fit for certain nonaesthetic public purposes and less fit for others, e.g., more fit to be a permanent public memorial of some sort, less fit to be a widely circulated economic article.

This discussion of the fourfold role of the material principle in the creative activity puts us in a position to sketch tentatively the total process of artistic creation. This process swings between two extremes. At one extreme the process consists of a completely formed imaginative vision, transferred without emendation into physical materials. The creative aspect of the process here consists of the subjective phase and the addition by objectification of those literal material and functional properties inseparable from the embodiment of the subjective vision in physical material. This type of creation comes nearest of all to Croce's conception of the creative process as pure subjective formulation. In conception it differs from Croce's in recognizing as creative the addition of those novel material aesthetic properties and those novel functional aesthetic and nonaesthetic properties that appear in the objective phase and that are inseparable from objectification. It also differs in insisting upon a more "materialistic" interpretation of the subjective phase.

At the other extreme the total creative process consists of watchful experimentation with material under the guidance merely of some general functional aim, e.g., the aim to extricate from the material whatever interesting aesthetic effects can be extricated. There is no antecedent planning or inspiration. Piecemeal, the experimentation gives rise to ideas which come to the full flower of a complete subjective vision, if at all, only at the conclusion of the experimental operations and the completion of the objective work. This extreme is the very antithesis of the Crocean conception of creation as pure subjective formulation independent of physical materials.

Between these two extremes the great majority of creative processes in art are probably to be found. The typical intermediary process begins under the guidance of a general functional aim and with the projection of a specific imaginative idea. The artist is confronted by some problem, self-imposed or set by others—e.g., to decorate an area of a church or to compose a second and even finer piano concerto. His general aim is to solve this problem satisfactorily in terms of the materials of his art. His specific imaginative idea is an image that has occurred to him immediately or after long deliberation as a suitable suggestion for the solution of this problem.

Ordinarily, this imaginative idea as it emerges in the subjective phase is a general outline containing the chief essentials and many details of a possible work. And sometimes it is objectified in a preliminary way by a charcoal sketch, by a clay model, or by jottings in a notebook. The main objective phase, however, consists of an effort to work out the idea by constructing a material object that is a definitive solution of the problem. Sometimes this working-out consists of a swift and uninterrupted execution of the idea with only minor additions and alterations. Sometimes, however, it consists of the legendary 99 per cent perspiration, the process being slow, painful, laborious, and often embodying large additions, revisions, or alterations. In the end such a process may result in an object not greatly different in basic essentials from the object envisaged in the original imaginative vision. On the other hand, it may result in an object all of whose basic essentials are different from those of the object originally envisaged.[23] There is no fixed limit to the novelty that arises from overt material construction. The central constant factor in the objective phase of the process is simply the effort to shape an objective entity by technique so that it is a solution of the aesthetic and the nonaesthetic requirements constituting the artist's problem. The imaginative idea is only an intermediary or a means to this end, and its preservation in the final embodi-

[23] Cf. T. S. Eliot, *The Use of Poetry and the Use of Criticism* (Cambridge, Mass.: Harvard University Press, 1933), p. 138. The problem of the artist, as well as his imaginative vision as first conceived, may change radically during the creative process, especially if the problem has been self-imposed. Thus a musician whose original intention was to write a second piano concerto may decide, as inspiration unfolds, to cast the work into the form of a string quartet or a symphony, which would, of course, create a new problem.

ment, or even throughout the total creative process, occurs only to the extent that it proves itself to be useful in the achievement of this larger end.

V. THE ROLE OF ENVIRONMENT

Our account of the creative process up to this point has contained only scant explicit reference to what is regarded by some as one of the great factors in artistic creation, viz., the physicosocial milieu or environment. We must now try to repair this neglect by describing what seems to us to be the role played in artistic creation by this milieu or environment.

At a minimum, environment is the frame of the total creative process, the condition permitting its start, and the locale retaining its product. But environment is much more. Indeed, it enters creation at every point. First of all, environment furnishes the artist with the vast diversity of things by which his sensitivity is awakened and stimulated, and from which all his symbols are drawn.[24] It also supplies the artist with the occasions, joyous and tragic, in terms of which his personality is shaped and his sense of values formed.[25] Environment provides the artist with traditions, technical and social, that are the premises of his creation[26] and with the training that has developed his skill. It also provides the artist with a contemporary climate of opinion that indefinitely modifies the quantity and quality of his imaginative thinking as it moves into creative channels. Furthermore, environment furnishes the artist with catalytic agents of inspira-

[24] Cf. J. Wassermann, *My Life as German and as Jew*, trans. S. N. Brainin (New York: Coward-McCann, Inc., 1933).

[25] Cf. Edmund Wilson on Dickens, in *The Wound and the Bow* (Boston: Houghton Mifflin Co., 1941).

[26] Ribot (*op. cit.*, p. 128) writes: "Suppose, as Weismann says, that in the islands of Samoa a child were born having the unique and extraordinary genius of a Mozart. What could he achieve? He could at most extend the scale of three or four tones to seven, and invent a number of more complex melodies. But he would be as incapable of composing symphonies as Archimedes would have been of inventing an electric dynamo. . . . . So much is said about the free soaring of imagination and of the all-powerfulness of the creator, that we forget the social conditions (not to mention others) on which they depend at every moment."

tion;[27] and it supplies the physical materials of his art and the commissions, patronage, and social uses and occasions envisioned in the functional goals of his art. Finally, environment contains the conditions which determine the physical and cultural survival of the artistic product. Thus not only is environment the springboard and terminus of artistic creation, but it enters and deeply influences every aspect of the creative act and product.

Is environment, then, after all, the key explanatory principle of artistic creation? Some believe it to be. Romantic thinkers once sought to explain creation in terms of individual genius—a profound inner voice emanating from the depths of the soul. This subjective type of theory persists today in several different forms, the most fashionable being the psychoanalytic explanation of creation in terms of the tensions and disequilibriums of the unconscious, derived from childhood. The older romantic theory had its counterpart in the older naturalistic theory that explained creation in terms of the artist's milieu. The name in the philosophy of art most inveterately associated with the older naturalistic theory is Taine. This type of theory also persists today in several forms, the most fashionable at the moment being the Marxist explanation of creation in terms of economic forces.

Such theories, the subjective romantic no less than the "objective" environmental, have been valuable bases for investigation of special phases of the creative activity and have produced details of the greatest importance for understanding the creative process. But as philosophies, as comprehensive analyses rather than as limited hypotheses assumed for special inquiries, both types of theory leave much to be desired.

Even on subjective grounds, the usual romantic type of theory is inadequate. Functional ends and conscious critical intelligence,

---

[27] Lowes (*op. cit.*, p. 148) quotes Goethe's remark about hearing of the suicide of his friend Jerusalem: "At that instant the plan of *Werther* was found; *the whole shot together from all directions, and became a solid mass, as the water in a vase, which is just at freezing point, is changed by the slightest concussion into ice*" (italics in text). Whiskey, from Poe to Saroyan, has had its uses as a catalytic agent of artistic inspiration. Analogies discovered in reading and conversation or otherwise drawn from the social milieu are not the least important type of environmental catalyzer. Examples of a still different type are given in the references to Whitman, Rodin, Cézanne, and others in the last paragraphs of chap. ii.

as we have already seen, are as precious and influential in creation as are genius and the unconscious. Genius and a fertile spontaneous imagination are fundamental to the greatest art. But no less important are a keen sense of direction, standards, and a consciousness of where genius and spontaneity are succeeding and failing. There are the monstrosities of genius, as well as the inanities of cerebral art. There is no evidence in any case that a sense of direction and critical brain power of some sort do not generally operate in artistic creation, whatever one may think of the result. On the contrary, the sophisticated and professional art of the West invariably has availed itself of them, and they are not lacking in primitive art.[28] Instinct or the unconscious is a glamorous thread from which to weave the story of artistic creation, but it is much too thin to depict the whole story of this complex and highly differentiated process.

A similar stricture applies to the environmental type of theory. The constant and indispensable role of environment in creation cannot be denied. But environment would produce nothing artistic at all without a psychological agent with a creative gift and a discriminating intelligence. An analogy from the plant world might be helpful. Here climate and soil are extraordinarily important. They release certain genetic factors and inhibit others, so that you can grow fir trees in areas where you cannot grow corn or roses. But the fact remains that you need a certain kind of seed as well as a certain kind of climate and soil to grow fir trees or corn or roses. Similarly with fine art, the physicosocial environment is unquestionably important. But a certain kind of agent is equally required. The physicosocial environment is the total system of conditions and stimulations to which the artist reacts throughout his creative venture, from its dimmest preparation in the past to its final termination in a novel material product. The reactions of the artist are to this system of conditions and stimulations and consequently are in terms of it. Hence environment enters into and affects artistic creation at every point. But the reactions of the artist are not merely reactions to his environment but also reactions of his nature and spring from

[28] Linton, *op. cit.*

the peculiarities of his nature. They spring from his peculiar
seed, although they are in terms of his culture. And, just as fir
seed cannot produce corn or seed corn produce roses, so an artist
in reacting creatively to his world cannot produce work not
within the range of his endowment. The result is an emergent
from the inborn seed and the environmental nurture; and only
in terms of such a complex of factors, inner and outer, individual
and social, does a satisfactory theory of artistic creation seem
possible of construction.

This view is not intended to detract from the crucial creative
role of environment but to see this creative role in perspective.
The natural reaction to romanticism is to contend that all novelty in art is derived from without and to trace everything new in
art to physical and social sources. This is a healthy reaction,
based on an important and basic truth, viz., that fine art is not
self-contained but has an inveterate and fundamental connectivity with environment, before, during, and after creation. In
particular, fine art usually receives the first impetus to its great
new developments from the physicosocial milieu, as climate and
soil give the first favoring impetus to the release of the fir or the
rose. Thus relation to the environment is fundamental in understanding not only the existence but also the historical career
of the arts. Still it would not be in the interest of truth to let this
stand as a complete account. Fine art has an inner and distinctive
nature that differentiates it within its social context, and the
creator of art has an inner and distinctive seed that absorbs and
builds from the nutriment of the environment. The environment
is the great supplying and sustaining agent, hence its enormous
importance. But the alchemy of specific transformation is needed
for this sustenance to be fruitful in a particular specific way, viz.,
as diverse and individualized works of art.

We might express this rather differently by saying that the environment is a complex of forces that conditions the artist absolutely in certain very broad respects and inclines the artist relatively in certain specific directions. In consequence, the environment may be said to explain absolutely certain very broad facts
and relatively many specific features of works of art. Literacy is

absolutely necessary for literature. Had Russia been completely illiterate throughout history, there would never have been a Russian novel. Again, the censorship of Nicholas I inclined Russian novelists from Pushkin onward to make the "moral" of a novel implicit. "If it [the moral] were stated, the censor would suppress the book."[29] Thus one might say that environment furnishes not only a set of conditions absolutely necessary for the arts but also a system of possibilities of the greatest influence on art. Particularly important on this last point are the needs that the society wishes fulfilled by artists. Nevertheless, works of art are not systems of conditions or needs or possibilities. They are specific individualized actualities made for needs from the diverse available possibilities. They are selected personal reintegrations. The environment provides the broad conditions necessary for any such reintegrations and gives the artist "encouragement" in certain specific directions. But, beyond that, art is up to the artist, who must be able to make an individual actualization of possibilities within the broad conditions and contrive, in conformity to, or in defiance of, the specific environmental trends, the peculiar synthesis that is the work of art.

In summing up this analysis of artistic creation, we might say that the total creative process embraces a subjective phase and an objective phase, both environmentally nurtured. Each phase has its own central axis. The axis of the subjective phase is an imaginative reintegration of symbols, governed by functional ends and by the value system and critical intelligence of the artist. The central axis of the objective phase is the management of a public material by technique, so that it possesses the detailed plan and purpose envisaged in the final and complete subjective formulation. Thus the total creative process might be described as a twofold ideality seeking realization through a twofold actuality within the conditions and possibilities of a physicosocial environment. The idealities are the personally expressive dream and the ends for which it is dreamed, both environ-

[29] Edmund Wilson, "Historical Interpretation of Literature," in D. A. Stauffer (ed.), *The Intent of the Critic* (Princeton, N.J.: Princeton University Press, 1941), p. 51.

mentally conditioned. The actualities are the reintegration of symbols through which the idealities are realized, so far as they can be subjectively, and the environmental material technically handled, through which the idealities in their final subjective realization are embodied, so far as they can be objectively. There results from this complex collaboration a unitary public object with four major aspects: a material aspect derived from the physical material technically handled, a formal aspect derived from the reintegration as finally embodied, an expressive aspect derived basically from the value system underlying the reintegration, and a functional aspect derived from the purposes and ends which the material system is successfully shaped to serve.

We turn now to a detailed study of this four-dimensional public object whose nature has been indicated up to this point only in summary fashion. Our plan is to describe the properties and values of each of its dimensions—the material, the formal, the expressive, and the functional dimensions—and the relations between these dimensions. Since the public object enshrines probably the most important properties and the most widely influential values of art for society, the purpose of this book requires that we should carry out this plan on a comparatively large scale. Four chapters will be devoted to the task, and considerable illustration will be used in order to give our discussion sufficiently elaborate and diversified documentation. As a consequence, our pace in Part II will be slower. But, in addition to allowing us to exhibit more amply the properties and values of art of widest interest, our procedure will put us in the best possible position to describe in Part III the main public implications of the arts and will permit us to introduce considerations germane to Part I that could not be conveniently fitted into it. Part II will also complete, incidentally, our relational account of art's distinctive nature or triadic pattern, since the main analyses of the creative process and aesthetic experience—the two terms of the pattern additional to the public object—have now been given.

PART II
THE PUBLIC OBJECT

IV

THE MATERIALS OF THE
WORK OF ART

I. SOME PERCEPTUAL CHARACTERISTICS OF THE MATERIAL

IN PHILOSOPHICAL discussions of art, the term "materials" is often ambiguous. It may mean the physicosocial conditions, objects, or events which the artist has experienced and to which his work makes extensive reference; the mass of memory symbols from which the artist has drawn the contents of his subjective formulation, including psychological equivalents of his special physical medium; or the physical medium itself. In the present discussion the term will mean only the physical medium. The reason is that our present topic is the work of art as a public object, and this object is literally made of marble, tone, pigment, or physical media of some type. On the other hand, the antecedent physicosocial conditions, objects, or events referred to by a work of art and the memory symbols from which are drawn the contents of the artist's subjective formulation are not themselves constituents of the public object. If they appear in it at all, it is only as something suggested by the public object, part of what it indicates or expresses. The most proper and convenient procedure, therefore, seems to be to deal with them in connection with the dimension of expression and, not to include them with the physical media in the dimension of materials.

The physical media—pigments, tones, marble, and so on—are sometimes described as merely means for embodying the artist's subjective vision. This property is, of course, their most obvious characteristic. But in the public object these materials are not only the means of embodiment but the body itself. In general, the materials of art possess a number of important characteristics in addition to their medial properties.

They possess, for one thing, numerous sensory characteristics. Pigments have hue, "value," intensity; tones have pitch, timbre, volume; marble has grain, color, texture, sheen. The physical materials sensualize the public work of art and confer on it an abundant immediacy. The chief senses excited directly by the materials of art are sight and hearing. Nor is this surprising when it is remembered that the differential aim of art is to construct objects for aesthetic perception. Sight and hearing are superior to the other senses as avenues for aesthetic perception. This superiority rests upon several grounds.

First, sight and hearing are distance senses. Visual and auditory qualities can be discerned with a distance between the organism and the object. On the other hand, taste and touch are contact senses, while smell, although it is a distance sense and has been directly appealed to by some works of art such as oriental theater pieces, is an inferior distance sense, usually requiring longer time and more complex environmental conditions for satisfactory results. The aesthetic superiority of the distance over the contact senses lies in the fact that physical distance is more favorable to psychical distance, a negative condition of the aesthetic response. Physical distance between subject and object ordinarily makes it more possible for the subject to detach attention from action and to let attention explore the object for its intrinsic appeal with less practical danger and more perceptual latitude. A habit of aesthetic response, therefore, can be more easily built up. On the other hand, contact brings an object right to the biological danger-point, where its possible immediate threat to the welfare of the organism is at a maximum. As a consequence, contact arouses powerful impulses to subordinate attention to action and the aesthetic attitude is more difficult, more "unnatural," and more risky to try under ordinary circumstances.

Another reason for the superiority of sight and hearing as avenues of aesthetic appeal is that the sensory contents which sight and hearing discriminate are capable of superior perceptual organization and systematization. In the visual field, for example, a great number of hues, values, intensities, lines, and shapes can be easily distinguished and, more important, can be related for vision into complex and stable patterns without blurring their perspicuous individuality. A parallel situation exists in the case of words and musical tones, the chief auditory materials of art. On the other hand, tastes, smells, and touches have far less markedly the property of complex perspicuous perceptual organization. Most people, it is true, can distinguish a great number of tastes, not merely the four true tastes but the taste of rhubarb, the taste of chalk, and the like. But, in simultaneous combination, tastes tend to blur and lose their individuality; and, in succession, only the most elementary patterns remain clear in outline for most persons. This lack of perceptual clarity and stability in organization is also true for smells and touches, so that little of the lucid complexity and determinate subtlety of organization that can be achieved with colors or tones can be achieved with scents or tactile qualities.

Besides these two "natural" reasons for the aesthetic superiority of sight and hearing, there is the "artificial" reason that sight and hearing are the customary everyday sensory channels of expression and communication. A particular scent or the touch of a loved one may "mean" more to a particular person at a particular time than all the sights and sounds in the world. But smell and touch, and taste, too, are not the most usual sensory channels of public expression and communication in human life. Sight and hearing are. We express and communicate publicly by writing, pointing, speaking, gesticulating—by visual and auditory signs—and other signs are usually ancillary to these. Possibly major fine arts can be developed which appeal primarily to taste, touch, or smell. These senses have considerable potentialities as avenues of aesthetic perception. But at present they are aesthetically inferior to sight and hearing in at least the three ways just mentioned; and under existing circumstances the appeal of the materials of art primarily to sight and hearing is therefore inevitable in view of the differential character of fine art.[1]

The materials of art possess not only sensory qualities but

[1] Cf. DeWitt Parker, *The Principles of Aesthetics* (New York: F. S. Crofts & Co., 1946), chap. iv.

spatiotemporal form. They are fields for intuition as well as fields for sensation. Some materials, such as marble and pigment, are more obviously spatial than temporal. Others, such as tones and spoken words, are more obviously temporal than spatial. But spatiotemporality is actually present in all materials. Tones occupy space and can be discriminated as in space, as here or there. Marble exists in time and can be discriminated as in time, as now or then. And, just as a spatial property of a tone, e.g., whether it is sounded on the same platform as another tone or miles away, may be one important factor in its current terminal or instrumental aesthetic character, so a temporal property of a marble, e.g., whether its exposure to atmosphere and sunlight is age-old or recent, may be one important factor in its current terminal or instrumental aesthetic character. Thus both space and time may figure importantly in the total perceptual nature of each material. The spatiotemporal form of the materials of a work of art may harbor interior forms. A spoken word with one or more accent marks will set up a wave of rhythm in time. A color spread over a surface, with variation from light to dark will set up a gradation in space. These interior forms—rhythm, gradation, and so on—will receive more attention when we discuss the nature of artistic form. Here we shall merely observe that the spatiotemporality of the materials of art is foundational to the spatiotemporality of the work of art, and the spatiotemporality of the work of art is one of the chief bounding conditions within which arises the total form of the art work.

Besides engaging sensation and intuition, the materials of art stir feelings. Tones and pigments, white marble and dark granite, not only can be sensed and intuited but can stimulate moods vague or definite. Part of the explanation of this may be found in the physiology of perception. In perceiving tones and colors, for example, there is an impact on the receptor organ and the nervous system to which the organism reacts. Different types of impact entail different reactions. Thus, in experiencing musical tones, air vibrations strike the ear at a uniform rate per second, while, in experiencing noises, air vibrations strike the ear at a nonuniform rate per second. These different impacts modify differently the tonus of the organism, probably explaining in part the different affective reactions of the organism to musical tones and noises.

In addition to a physiological factor, a psychological factor based on association influences the feelings which the materials of art arouse. The organism congenitally experiences objects in terms of the ill or the good that they bode it. The organism is value-orientated. Green is the color of vegetation, red is the color of fire and blood. Our endless value experiences of vegetation, fire, and blood build up feelings about these and feelings about green and red. Mass, light, and space, which enter into all the graphic arts—into drawing, painting, sculpture, and architecture—are deeply connected with the essential conditions of our biological survival, and these connections build up a wealth of affective associations with these elements. All the visual and auditory materials of the arts are suffused with myriad affective overtones as a residue of innumerable life and death experiences and of the vast traditions in which these experiences are steeped. Even musical tones, the most esoteric of the materials of art, are experienced in endless contexts—military, sportive, religious, commemorative, recreative, commercial, festive, and funereal— and associations with these contexts, especially with those having stirring traditions, often subtly color the feelings which musical tones evoke. The materials of art are not pale stuffs withdrawn from the blood and fire of life. Owing to a web of almost unfathomable associations with the central circumstances of existence, they are moving and evocative materials. This is especially true for the artist, who combines with ordinary bases of feeling an intimate technical experience of his medium, which often develops in material extraordinary additional affective qualities. To him materials frequently seem possessed of an independent life—the stone quivering, the tones opening like flowers; and a whole special range of feeling is evoked by this autonomous "imaginary" life.

The materials of art appeal to imagination and in other ways besides the one just cited. What Berenson has called "tactile" values—the appeals to touch of the volume, bulk, substance, and texture of visual objects—are really appeals to imagination. We do not literally touch these visual elements as we watch them. We "touch" them in imagination. Often the motor responses to musical tones are imaginative. We may partly describe the movement suggested by music with overt gestures, but we may complete this movement in imagination or perform the total movement in this way. Similarly, the contemplative caress conferred upon the smooth, curving surface of a stone is an act of imagination. "His [Rembrandt's] opaque colors give the effect of floating in the varnish glazes."[2] This is an imaginative effect. So, too, is it when a patch of colors on a canvas appears as a pool of water or as a living head or a slab of marble appears as a writhing giant. All graphic representation consists of suggestions of the material which are completed in imagination.

The materials of art also engage intellect. They call out interpretations in terms of concepts. The simplest interpretations are immediate recognitions, the immediate recognition of a stone as diorite or of a tone as middle C. More complex interpretations of materials are the abstract conceptual descriptions of the scientist—descriptions of stones by the chemist and geologist, of tones by the physicist, of words by the philologist, of colors by the psychologist. Between these two extremes are the careful and concrete analyses of materials made by artists in discussing the elements of their craft. For the purposes of a philosophy of art the analyses of the artist are usually much more important than the descriptions of the scientist. The artist is customarily more concerned with the perceptual characteristics of his particular material and provides a wealth of particular detail about them. As a result, his analyses can serve as excellent factual bases for the more generalized description of these perceptual characteristics which it is part of the business of a philosophy of art to make, in dealing with the material dimension. For the purposes of aesthetic experience, also, the analyses of the artist are of superior importance, enriching one's background of knowledge of materials and, consequently, one's wealth of recognitions. Un-

[2] Max Doerner, *The Materials of the Artist* (New York: Harcourt, Brace & Co., 1934), p. 370.

fortunately, these analyses are scattered through a wide variety of contexts—letters, notebooks, reported conversations—which makes them less available than they should be, although some have appeared in formal publications of artists, as in the case of Berlioz, Coleridge, Hogarth, and Louis Sullivan, for example.

II. AESTHETIC STATURE OF THE MATERIAL

It should be clear from the general description of the materials of art up to this point that they can evoke all the powers of mind that go into a full-fledged aesthetic experience: sensation, intuition, feeling, imagination, intellect.

Consider the phrase "a perfumed night." As written or printed, the phrase is a visual mark with a size, shape, and color that vary with the way the phrase is written or printed, properties not negligible to a lover of fine writing or printing. As spoken, the phrase has other sensory properties—pitch, volume, intensity, and timbre—which vary with the way it is spoken, properties also not negligible to a person sensitive to fine speech or to differences of speech, e.g., the difference between the speech of an Englishman and an American southerner. The phrase written, printed, or spoken occupies a space-time, or has an intuitive aspect. And, even independent of a larger verbal context, the phrase can stir feeling, a balmy feeling, a feeling of disgust, any number of different feelings depending on the associations it arouses, as well as on the way it is uttered or written or printed. The phrase can also excite imagination. Reading it simply for its full intrinsic effect, one may hear its sound and rhythm in imagination or may imaginatively visualize pale clouds, shrouded trees, a night scene at a bazaar. The phrase also can excite intellect to a recognition of its reference, to a recognition of its rhythmic or metaphorical structure, etc. Thus a bit of the material of an art can bring into operation all the powers evoked in an aesthetic experience of even a complete work of art.

This point is not without its incidental importance for a philosophical understanding of the basic nature of creation. It suggests that artistic creation is not the invention and imposition upon an alien and irrelevant material of a supernatural or "spiritual" vision but that it is rather the articulation and development of potentialities already in the material into objects more completely satisfying to powers already satisfied in reduced fashion by the material itself. The artist is an agent capable of a larger vision of material potentialities; and creation in art is the overt elevation of the material to these larger potentialities by the skill and insight of such an agent. It is not the formulation and projection upon an alien surface of a completely independent "vision" or "thought."

The exact aesthetic stature of the material of art is realized more fully for the first time, however, only when one recalls that this material is not any old material but material of a special type. The great poet's words, as we have said, are not the flat stereotypes of a business letter. The sculptor's stone is not the lustreless shale of a river bed. The dancer's body is not the ungainly and ill-co-ordinated organism of the ordinary ten-year-old schoolgirl. The musician's tones are not the screeching noises of a city street. In other words, the material actually used in the arts is a perceptually select and vivid material as well as one possessed of the capacity for complex aesthetic apprehension. Moreover, its aesthetic stature is further enhanced in the best of art when this material becomes an actual dimension of the work of art, as we shall see in a moment.

Can one distinguish grades of superiority among artistic materials? Is any material the best? Some have argued that, of all the materials of art, words are the best. Words possess perceptual characteristics that interest human beings much more fully than any other material. Words can appeal to the senses, intuition, feeling, and imagination at least as much as any other material. In addition, words convey much more explicit and complex meanings. They "say" more. Against this, however, it has often been pointed out that words are much more frequently used than are other artistic materials for purely nonaesthetic, and especially for practical, purposes. As a result, their intrinsic sensory, intuitive, affective, and imaginative appeals, usually treated in roughshod fashion in these contexts, are much more blunted and deadened than those of other artistic materials. As materials of art, words lack sharpness, freshness, and purity in their sensory, intuitive, affective, and imaginative aspects; and in the appreciation of literature people usually read through these aspects of words to their mere meaning. This is not the case with many other materials of art, e.g., musical tones, whose sensory, intuitive, affective, and imaginative appeals remain comparatively fresh and unimpaired by usage in nonaesthetic contexts.

Such disputes about the aesthetic superiority of the different materials of art seem futile when formulated in a general or absolute manner. The fact seems to be that in certain respects and for certain purposes certain materials are definitely superior but that in certain other respects and for certain other purposes other materials are definitely superior. Were this not so, there would be no diverse arts. If words, for example, could be in every important way all that tones can be and more, music would be superfluous, and there would be no musical art. And this holds generally. Each material is unquestionably superior only in certain limited respects. The important question is not which material is best universally and absolutely but which material is superior in this specific way and better for this specific purpose? This question is constantly being asked by artists who are scrupulous about their medium and anxious to obtain a maximum of excellence in it without putting their work in jeopardy by attempting to do what can be done so much better in a different type of art. The more abstract question as to which material of art is best universally and absolutely is given scant consideration in practice, and in theory it appears to rest upon an assumption that would enable one major art to render some other superfluous, which seems to be mistaken.

III. PLASTICITY OF ARTISTIC MATERIALS

The purely relative character of the superiority of artistic materials is particularly evident when one considers these materials not in respect to the perceptual characteristics so far discussed but in respect to their plasticity and their utility as a means. Each material has a certain nature that makes possible a certain

range of effects; and, differing in range as they differ in intrinsic
nature, materials differ also in the superiority and inferiority of
these effects. "Thus stone is ideally suited to the sculptural rendering of heavy, massive bodies, and of whatever aspects of man's
experience are characteristically associated with such bodies;
. . . . bronze is the ideal sculptural medium for the expression of
sinuous and tensile grace; . . . . terracotta and colored porcelain
are perfectly adapted to soft and delicate rococo subjects. . . . . A
modern steel bridge or skyscraper cannot be built merely out of
stone, wood, or brick, and polyphonic and harmonic music cannot be produced on a one-stringed instrument or by one voice."[3]
Musical tones might express pure joy, but words "cannot express
a joy that shall be full and pure; for to keep the purity nothing
would have to be named which carried the least suggestion of
sadness with it, and, in the world that human language refers
to, such a condition would exclude every situation possible."[4]

Some of the plastic limitations and inferiorities of the diverse
materials of art are so evident and final that it seems childish to
mention them. Stones cannot talk or words run, and only a fool
would try to make them. On the other hand, some limitations
of materials are not, like these, sheer impossibilities. Thus one
might render a huge massive human body in colored porcelain—
this is not impossible. Still, in solidity, force, and majestic
strength, the effect would be definitely inferior to a rendition of
this body in granite or diorite. Some limitations of materials
can be overcome up to a certain point. "Beethoven's deafness
made him almost ruthlessly indifferent to the limitations of instruments and cruelly so to those of the human voice. There is
no doubt that his music, regarded as sheer sound, is often displeasing; what makes it not only bearable but positively admirable even from this point of view is the feeling one has that its
awkwardness is due to a visionary's magnificent disregard of human shortcomings which in the sphere of his visions count for

[3] T. M. Greene, *The Arts and the Art of Criticism* (Princeton, N.J.: Princeton University Press, 1940), pp. 41, 163–64.

[4] George Santayana, *Reason in Art* (New York: Charles Scribner's Sons, 1905), p. 62.

nothing."[5] Thus a Beethoven may compensate in the dimension of expression for a loss in the dimension of sheer sound. But the loss is there, and in the less magnificent works of Beethoven, one might add, it is sometimes more evident than the admirable Beethovenesque spirit that elsewhere may seem to compensate for it.

Deliberate attempts to overcome the plastic limitations of a material usually do not fare much better. Limitations remain in one form or another. A sculptor who paints a plaster cast to look like bronze may attain an initial pictorial effect only minutely different from that of bronze. But differences persist, even pictorial differences. Moreover, the materials wear differently. The original respectable appearance of the bronzed plaster may remain with time. But the bronzed plaster itself never can attain the peculiarly venerable green of time-patinated bronze. In addition, one may feel that a sculptor who paints his plaster to look like bronze is practicing a fraud, and this feeling may mar considerably the initial favorable reaction produced by the imitation of bronze. Recent artists have strongly advocated a candid use of materials which exploits their superiorities without disguising their limitations, and this usually gives a more permanently satisfying result. In any case, such a use of materials, as well as an effort to hide limitations, is an admission that materials do have limitations and are inferior, as well as superior, in certain plastic respects, which is the main point.

IV. POSSIBLE INSTRUMENTAL VALUES

Our discussion so far of materials, first as perceptual terminals, then as plastic agents, has been in abstraction from their position in works of art. We must now consider materials as a dimension and ask what position they occupy in the public object.

The answer seems to be that the materials here have a duality similar to the duality that we have just been describing. They have certain terminal perceptual properties and certain implemental perceptual properties. They have aesthetic values and disvalues as a terminus and aesthetic values and disvalues as an

[5] Eric Blom, *The Limitations of Music* (New York: Macmillan Co., 1928), pp. 101–2.

instrument of the other dimensions. First, let us consider the materials in relation to the other dimensions—the over-all form, the expression, and the function of works of art—and indicate the aesthetic values which the materials can have, and in the best works of art do have, as instruments of these other dimensions.

Materials can support aesthetically the over-all form of a work. Materials support form when their separate aesthetic weights fit into and reinforce the larger over-all design of a creation.

For example, the ample curving lines, the rich subdued hues, the powerful massive shapes especially in the central oval of Titian's "Entombment" (Louvre, Paris) vividly implement the surging re-strained balance which is the basis of the over-all design of the painting. The thick nervous lines, the compartments of pure color, the flat simpli-fied shapes of Matisse's "Woman in the Red Caraco" (Paul Rosenberg Collection, Paris) vividly accentuate the sharp organic contrast be-tween the figure and its setting, which is the chief formal principle of this work. In sculpture, to speak in more general terms, the properties of certain stones can be eminently appropriate to the simplified forms of abstract and stylized work. "Formal or 'styled' sculpture . . . . de-rived an advantage from being cut in a material of neutral colour which bears a clear but soft creamy polish. The quietness of the material and the softness of the surface polish do not distract from the simplicity of the outlines. So, too, where no harsh outlines or deep shadowed folds are required, limestones, sandstones, and oölitic stones such as Hopton wood, or Istrian limestone, are the best. They are the media *par excel-lence* of formal and abstract sculpture."[6] The qualities of certain build-ing materials can be eminently appropriate to certain architectural forms. "A light material like wood permits overhanging stories that would be dangerous in stone."[7] A tensile material, such as structural steel, is eminently adapted to the soaring form of the skyscraper. Similarly, the odd sprawling words that Whitman occasionally uses frequently fit felicitously into the sprawling form of his free verse, just as the heavy chords and complex orchestration very frequent in Wagner lend themselves to the massive, flowing forms of his musical composi-tions.

[6] S. Casson, *XXth Century Sculptors* (London: Oxford University Press, 1930), pp. 18–19.

[7] A. R. Chandler, *Beauty and Human Nature* (New York: D. Appleton–Century Co., 1934), p. 120.

In general, the greater artists are sensitive to the manifold aesthetic properties of their material and strive to weave out of them as rich and complex a unity as possible. This is, however, an extraordinarily difficult undertaking. It is easy to overlook or to be insensitive to some of these aesthetic properties and to weaken design aesthetically with materials inappropriate in various degrees. A painting of delicate linear structure with dull, inactive colors would be an elementary example of this. A poem of considerable formal elegance but with key words that were commonplace, trite, or faintly vulgar; a musical composition whose heavy instrumentation submerged its light, rococo themes would be other elementary illustrations. Artists who are very able in certain respects are sometimes flagrantly deficient in organizing all the salient qualities of their material so that they fit into and reinforce a unified form. The tangled cascading lines, the dispersed reds, the weightless shapes of Raphael's "Entombment" (Borghese Gallery, Rome) disintegrate rather than support form, scattering rather than strengthening the dramatic centrality which gives this painting whatever pictorial unity it possesses. To install in the material dimension of a work of art instrumental values to form of a very high order is a difficult achievement and not always found in otherwise fine works of very able craftsmen.

Besides the dimension of form, the materials of art can support effectively the dimension of expression. Roughly speaking, the sensory and intuitive properties of materials play the leading role in supporting form; and the affective, imaginative, and intellectual properties play the leading role in supporting expression. But in both cases all the aesthetic properties of the material are important. Materials support expression when their separate aesthetic weights fit into and reinforce the larger suggestions of a work.

The languorous lines, the balmy color, the soft full shapes of Giorgione's "Sleeping Venus" (Zwinger Gallery, Dresden) fit into and reinforce the expression of sumptuous repose in the figure of the Venus. The sinuous lines, the phosphorescent colors, the tiny needle-point shapes of El Greco's "View of Toledo" (Metropolitan Museum, New

York) vividly instrument the electric vision of the city expressed in the canvas. The heaviness and largeness, the multitude of swells and hollows and twists and lights and darks, of the stone of the Medici tomb figures (Medici Chapel, Church of San Lorenzo, Florence) lend themselves to the expression of massive languor and weary discontent which Michelangelo has embodied variously in these symbolic statues. The smooth surfaces and light colors of the glazes of Luca della Robbia implement the saccharine expression of his Madonnas and *bambini*. The heavy, soaring stone and colored glass of medieval cathedrals, such as Amiens or Chartres, contribute powerfully to the expression of solemnity, awe, and mystical intent of their interiors, just as the white sweeping surfaces, the clean lines, and the geometric shapes of twentieth-century architectural structures, such as Oud's workers' houses at the Hook of Holland, contribute powerfully to the expression of efficiency and communal intent of their exteriors. Examples of materials supporting expression are as abundant in music and literature as in painting, sculpture, and architecture. Musical tones of certain timbres and harmonies may contribute as much as rhythm or design to the evocation of expressive effects—funereal effects, as in the second movement of Beethoven's *Third Symphony;* delicate and dreamy effects, as in a piece by Debussy; exotic effects, as in a work of Rimsky-Korsakoff. The hardboiled clipped jargon of a contemporary work of fiction may contribute immensely to the evocation of a certain type of American scene and character, just as a less restricted language equally free of the clichés of tradition—fresh, supple, and germinal to a culture—may at any time implement vividly in prose or in poetry the expression of a great new vision of nature or of human life, as it has periodically from Homer to the present.

Here again the successful use of materials by the artist to instrument expression is not an easy task. Success, indeed, is usually a matter of degrees, and often materials have instrumental disvalues for expression. A painting of a highly dramatic subject, such as David's "Oath of the Horatii" (Louvre, Paris), may use dry and dull colors, which disfigure the expression. A musical composition, such as certain works of Richard Strauss, may use timbres and orchestrations which inject a note of bombast or vulgarity into an expression intended to be solemn or playfully gay. Motion pictures frequently "star" actresses of great physical beauty but of little flexibility of expressive range. Role after role in successive pictures receives the same stereotyped interpretation, which, undisturbing as it is to the admirers of great physical beauty, does not usually make for variety, poignancy, or depth of expressive effects. Popular story-writers, in dealing with great historical subjects capable of magnificent expression, will use not only commonplace plots but commonplace language and weaken at its very root the expressive promise of their themes. To demand of the average literary artist a supreme gift for vivid language, such as a Shakespeare had, is doubtless absurd. But some sensitivity to the nuances and niceties of language and to the possibilities of language in relation to theme seems not too much to ask, although often too much to expect.

Besides the dimensions of expression and form, the materials of art can support effectively the dimension of function. Materials support function when they contribute to the realization of the larger ends which the work of art itself serves. Materials support the nonaesthetic as well as the aesthetic functions of works of art, the religious, commemorative, commercial, and similar functions.

Thus the terse lines, the solid areas of blue and pure gold, the firm incisive shapes of Giotto's frescoes in the Arena Chapel at Padua not only help to make these paintings aesthetically delightful, independent of ulterior ends, but also help to make the paintings succinctly instructive religious and narrative pieces of great appropriateness to a medieval Christian house of worship. The great blocks of rusticated stone of which certain early Renaissance Florentine palaces were constructed implemented the utility of these buildings as protected seats of power, as fortresses and secure domiciles. Similarly, the metal of an equestrian statue intended to be a permanent public memorial to a military hero, such as Donatello's "Gattamelata" at Padua, helps in a marked degree to make this statue, in its climate and milieu, suitable for its intended function. Soft wood or soft stone, being more perishable and more easily disfigured, would have been far less useful for the purpose. The materials of music and literature also can support function, nonaesthetic as well as aesthetic. To accomplish this, of course, a judicious selection of materials is required. Music to be played at an American Fourth of July celebration might conceivably be written in quarter tones, just as a drama intended to be a commercial success in twentieth-century New York might conceivably be written in ancient Greek or Chinese. But tones from scales more traditional and familiar in America than the quarter-tone scale would appear to be better materials for Fourth of July music, just as the American English in which the usual Broadway commercial success is written is better than ancient Greek or Chinese for making a drama suited to commercial ends in twentieth-century New York.

As in the case of form and expression, materials may support function in varying degrees, sometimes grandly, sometimes badly. A material may support a nonaesthetic function well but the aesthetic function poorly. A very sturdy material may help a bridge to carry astonishing loads, yet be very ugly in appearance and to that extent undermine the total aesthetic effect of the work. Conversely, a material may support an aesthetic function well but a nonaesthetic poorly. A cheap architectural material may have a glamorous appearance but wear out easily and leave a leaky wall or roof in a building. To select materials suited to all the manifold functions which a work of art is sometimes called upon to serve is again a far from easy task. The problem is especially acute in architecture, where many of the parts of a work, such as the rooms of a house, may have very different nonaesthetic functions. Materials must be chosen not only in relation to the general requirements of the building but also in relation to each of these different functions as modified by the peculiar needs of the client. In addition, the architect must consider the relation of materials to climate and site, to his client's pocketbook and the commercial proprieties of the neighborhood, and to the form and expression and general aesthetic ends of the work. Few architects do all these things with great care or with distinguished success. But the considerable development of new architectural materials in recent times has been in part a response to the increasing practice of architects to seek materials suited in as many ways as possible to all the functions of their creations.

V. POSSIBLE TERMINAL VALUES

Besides having instrumental relations to the dimensions of form, expression, and function, the materials of art are themselves a dimension of the work of art, one of its final aspects. The media of art are rather unusual means. Usually means are like the scaffolding of a building or an airplane used for travel, things set aside when the end which they are used to gain has been reached. But the media of art are also part of the terminal being of the work of art and have terminal, as well as instrumental, values and disvalues.

By "terminal values" here are meant the values of the materials when taken as end-points of intrinsic perception within the work of art. We have already seen that artistic materials in the abstract, and even apart from the public object, appeal to sensation, intuition, feeling, imagination, intellect—all the powers of intrinsic perception. This appeal is intensified and greatly particularized when materials are taken as terminals within the public object.

It should be clear, first of all, that materials here do have their own terminal aesthetic values (and disvalues). The colors of a painting—the gorgeous purples of a Tintoretto, the iridescent blues and greens of a Monet, the powerful ribs of yellow of a Van Gogh, the juicy yellows, oranges, and blues of a Renoir— have an arresting and definite effect upon sensitive perception, just as do the graceful lines of a Leonardo or the rugged lines of a Cézanne. The materials of a building—the solid marble of an Acropolis temple, the bright white wood of a freshly painted Virginian Colonial house, the band concrete of a twentieth-century armory or recreation center—make an unmistakable impression on the alert observer. So also do the materials of sculpture taken within the frame of a particular work—the creamy surface of a marble delicately mottled with almost invisible veins and delicately suggestive of weight; or the brilliant high lights and warm shadows, the patina, or the light tensile strength of bronze.[8] The materials of music offer a feast of aesthetic qualities to sensitive perception. The tones from an instrument or an orchestra, with their multiplicity of pitches and timbres, may be hard, spacious, shrill, ragged, singing, blaring, rough, clear, mellow, brilliant, sharp, dull. Recent music is noted for its arresting material textures—the perfumed harmonies of Debussy, the iridescent frothy colors of Rimsky-Korsakoff. But even the less chromatic music of a Mozart or a Haydn has its material brilliance and simple charm. Nor do the materials of literature lack

[8] *Ibid.*, pp. 140 ff.

terminal values of their own. The language of poetry, for example, has intrinsic terminal properties as diverse as the poets. It may be the thick, sensuous language of a Keats; the homely language of a Wordsworth; the gusty, carefree language of a Whitman; or the artificial, clanging language of a Poe.

In some works of art the terminal material properties may, for various reasons, be the chief aesthetic asset. A poem recited expertly in an unintelligible foreign language may yet hold attention by the vivacious qualities of its sound. A complex orchestral piece may seem amorphous in form and vague in intentions upon first hearing; but its harmonies and timbres, the bounty of its material loveliness, may within limits be highly gratifying. The material of a statue, such as the japanned mahogany of Zadkine's "Mother and Child" (private collection), may be sturdy and brilliant and may far outshine in appeal the form or expression of the work. No doubt, a work of art whose major excellence, in the most adequate aesthetic perception, consisted chiefly of superb terminal material values is not properly describable as a "major" work of art. At least, it is not so describable if we agree, as we well might, that a major work of art is one with major excellences, both terminal and instrumental, in several or in all four of the aesthetic dimensions. Still sometimes, for "subjective" as well as for "objective" reasons, only the terminal qualities of the material dimension of a work do make a major aesthetic appeal. And if we decide, in those cases in which the reason for this is objective or in the work of art itself and not in the limitation of the percipient, that this work is only a minor artistic achievement, we must realize that, as with fine jewelry whose major aesthetic appeal often is only on the material level, the aesthetic values offered even by such works are not necessarily negligible and may even be of considerable magnitude and intensity.

Why do the materials of art have exactly the terminal aesthetic values that they do have in the public object? The answer seems to be twofold. First, there is the reason suggested in the earlier part of this chapter: The material of every art in itself is usually choice material with a superior appeal to sensation, intuition, feeling, imagination, and intellect. But very important in any complete account is a second reason. This is the aesthetic instrumentation that materials receive from the other three dimensions in the public object.

The instrumentation of materials in the work of art by the other dimensions will be illustrated serially and in detail in the discussions of form, expression, and function that follow. But perhaps a general preliminary illustration or two may not be inappropriate. A color in abstraction from a painting, for example, a bit of orange on a palette, may be mildly agreeable aesthetically but without startling power. Yet in a painting, amid the blues and yellows of a bathing scene, placed as a Renoir might place it, the color may have a vibrant aesthetic significance and a gleaming life. Why? Part of the reason, clearly, is the new arrangement in which the color now exists, the structure of contrast and balance and repetition which sets the color off and brings out more exquisitely and fully its distinctive sensory and intuitive qualities. Part of the reason also is the lively scene of which the color is now a part and the emphasis upon warm sensuous loveliness throughout the scene, which is expressive of the artist. Part also may be the fitness of the painting to decorate the area of the room in which it is, since this may allow the vigor and strength and flash of the orange to flourish at full aesthetic height. Thus form, expression, and function may equally help to vivify a material which, for all its a priori agreeableness, had only a mild aesthetic power outside the work of art.

A similar instrumentation could be illustrated from any of the other arts. A group of words outside a poem, arranged alphabetically and examined individually, may exhibit the most diverse and miscellaneous set of aesthetic properties, from which no clearly dominant over-all quality emerges. But in a poem where they are arranged in short, clipped sentences with certain ones emphasized, repeated, contrasted, and connected with certain others, where all of them are used to depict brutal actions and coarse attitudes with the intention of giving pleasure to a certain type of audience, the words may emerge with a definite quality, and the language of the poem be felt to be unmistakably pungent, earthy, ribald, and strong. What was nondescript and miscellaneous outside the work of art becomes defined and unified in terminal quality within the work, owing to the form, expression, and functional aim of the public object.

It should be emphasized that the properties which the form, expression, and function bring out in the material dimension—the flame of the orange, the strongness of the language—are intrinsic terminal properties of the material in the public object. They are instrumented by the other dimensions, but they are features of the material dimension. They are intrinsic features resting upon a relational structure. This notion of intrinsic material features resting upon a relational structure illustrates in a specific case the general relational interpretation of the dimensions of the public object. The contention of relationalism here is not that properties of dimensions are never intrinsic but that the full intrinsic properties of a dimension in a work of art rest upon the relations of the dimension to the other dimensions. As we proceed, we shall document this contention in regard to the other three dimensions of the work of art, and the result will be very significant for the relational standpoint. The result will be that the work of art as a whole will stand revealed as a complex relational pattern of four diverse dimensions, and relation or pattern will become the basic clue for seeing this work as a whole or as a system of diverse dimensions.

Apart from this general point, the preceding discussion illustrates two other fundamental points closely allied to it. First, it exhibits in a specific manner the intimate connection among the four dimensions. In the public object these dimensions are not external to one another but enter reciprocally into the nature of one another. For good or ill, each instruments the others and is instrumented by the others, so that, although the four dimensions can be distinguished for analysis, they cannot be separated in existence. Second, the preceding discussion also illustrates the fact that the terminal apprehension of any dimension in its concreteness is, in a sense, an apprehension of the total work of art. The total work of art comes to a focus in each dimension, since each dimension is fully what it is in a work of art only by virtue of its relations to the other dimensions. The terminal apprehension of any dimension, to be sure, is not the full terminal appreciation of the total work. This can be achieved only by using every dimension as a base of operations. But it is *an* appreciation of the total work of art, not an appreciation of one aspect of it in abstraction from the other three aspects.

V

FORM

I. ART AND FORM

FINE art at its best, we might say, is a selection, refinement, and vivification for intrinsic attention of perceptible material aspects of nature and the social world. It selects and refines these material aspects so that we are given a purified revelation of their perceptual properties, possibilities, and values on the aesthetic level. But we might equally say that fine art at its best is a selection, refinement, and vivification for intrinsic attention of perceptible unities or forms. In ordinary experience we usually perceive only confused and fragmented unities. Rarely do things or scenes, people or deeds, stand forth in highly organized and seemingly self-complete connections. In works of art, however, all this is shown abundantly. The unities of the world are reconstructed in miniature, so that we apprehend in ideal simplicity formal properties and values usually evident only obscurely, if at all, in ordinary experience. So much is this the case that fine art is often described as pre-eminently concerned with unity or form. Fine art is a process of introducing a certain novel fineness of form into the welter of incoherent fragments that enter our experience. Such a view is, of course, oversimple as a complete theory of fine art. But it does point to one of the salient achievements of art and to one of the basic aspects of the public object.

Works of art are highly unified entities. To begin with, they are space-time systems. Works of art exhibit togetherness in space and successiveness in time. In the so-called "static" arts of painting, sculpture, and architecture, the space is most highly organized. But the works of these arts also exist in time, sometimes briefly but often for long historical epochs. In the so-called "dynamic" arts of music, the dance, and literature the time is most intricately organized. But the works of these arts also exist in space, and sometimes, as in group dancing and in the acted drama, the space is extensively organized. Besides space and time, causality and teleology are present in works of art. The most obvious illustrations of cause-effect and telic structure are in the representational arts, especially opera, the dance, the drama, the novel, and the short story, where represented actions are depicted as in causal and telic patterns. But we shall find numerous other instances of causality and teleology in artistic creations.

Space and time, causality and teleology, however, are universal forms. They are the structure of all existence, not merely of works of art. Space and time are the bounding forms of the entire world of events and things; causality is as ubiquitous as events; and teleology, at least in the sense of self-determinacy, is as world-wide as continuants or things.[1] In its uniqueness, artistic form is clearly more than mere spatiotemporal, causo-telic structure. Artistic form employs these universal cosmic forms, and, separately or together, they constitute the general framework of works of art as they do of all other entities. But in its specific character artistic form at its best is rather a purification and vivification on a small scale of these cosmic forms in the direction of added intrinsic perceptual interest. It is enhanced spatiotemporal, causo-telic structure, the form of the world reconstructed and heightened in a certain area for multiple aesthetic effects.

II. PRINCIPLES OF ARTISTIC FORM

By what principles does the artist transcend "nature" and enhance existential structure in the direction of greater intrinsic perceptual interest? There are a number of these principles. Harmony is one of them. Two items together in space, for example, which also harmonize with each other are much more closely and complexly united for perception than are two such items which are merely spatially coexistent. And this is also true of two items successive in time, or of items connected causally or teleologically. As a principle of enhancing existential unity,

[1] D. W. Gotshalk, *Structure and Reality* (New York: Dial Press, 1937), chaps. iv, v, vi.

harmony may be secured by two methods. The first is repetition or recurrence of so-called "complete similars," e.g., separated areas of green of the same value and intensity in a painting, successive tonic chords in a musical figure, a pointed-arch form repeated in a building, the repetition at a later stage of an earlier action in a drama. The second method of securing harmony is partial similarity, e.g., vigorous colors and vigorous lines in a painting, a tonic succeeded by its fifth in a musical figure, a smaller triforium arcade surmounting the lower larger arcade, an action in a later part of a drama similar in motivation but otherwise very different from an earlier action. Gradation, a green surface, for example, with ever so slight differences in "value" or intensity between adjacent areas of the green; modulation, changing to a new musical key through a passage retaining something of the old key; theme and variation, restating a color, shape, line, or musical figure in various guises, are three well-known methods of linking diverse items by partial similarity and thereby attaining a harmony.

Balance is a second principle for building enhanced existential unity. Like harmony, balance can be secured by two methods. The first is by symmetry, the balance of so-called "similars," e.g., two equal and similar groups of figures converging toward the central figures in a late medieval Madonna and child or two similarly dressed dancers of equal stature approaching each other from opposite sides of the stage and executing the same pattern of movement. The second type of balance is secured by asymmetry, the balance of so-called "dissimilars," e.g., good and evil forces in a drama, theme and countertheme in a musical composition, a small compact group of figures on one side of a painting and a larger, looser group on the other side converging toward an area off center, as in Giotto's "Bewailing of Christ" (Arena Chapel, Padua).

Harmony achieves unity by recurrence, by items echoing each other partly or wholly, sometimes again and again, throughout a work. Balance achieves unity by contrast, by items opposing and equilibrizing each other. The opposing items form a system of complementary and neutralizing tensions, resulting in a complete and stable unity. Abstractly, balance and harmony are the reverse of each other. Balance emphasizes diversity in unity, and harmony emphasizes unity in diversity. Nevertheless, harmony and balance are effective collaborators and are often found together in works of art. A musical composition may exhibit numerous balances and harmonies—a balance of melody and countermelody or of theme and theme or of section and section, a harmony of tones within a melody or theme, a recurrence of a melody or theme or section. In combination, however, either harmony or balance tends to dominate over the other. In general, harmony tends to dominate in the so-called "temporal" arts, and balance in the so-called "spatial" arts. The temporal arts are by nature dynamic; and the tranquilizing principle of harmony tends to give them a stability and firmness of form which both amplifies and steadies for perception their intrinsically dynamic nature. On the other hand, the spatial arts are by nature static; and balance, by throwing opposites against one another, tends to give these arts a dynamic power which adds vitality to their form and enlivens their intrinsically static nature. Music and poetry are par excellence the arts of harmony, while painting, sculpture, and architecture are par excellence the arts of balance.

A very important principle of artistic form arising from a collaboration of balance and harmony or recurrence is rhythm. A rhythm is an organization of materials so that they possess or suggest patterned movement. It may be achieved in numerous ways, e.g., by quantities (long-short, large-small) distributed over the material in space or time, or by accents (beats, emphases) similarly distributed, or by both. The material may be colors, lines, shapes, tones, dance-movements, word-syllables. In any case the quantities or accents or whatever are so distributed that the material falls into measures either in the conventional sense, such as the ONE-two of a march rhythm, or in the sense of "figures," such as the up-and-down thrust of a horizontal, zigzag line. Regular rhythm is the occurrence in sequence of measures that are alike or only slightly different. It is achieved by repetition or by recurrence of the "same" measure pattern.

Irregular rhythm is the occurrence in sequence of measures of greater diversity—e.g., a small zigzag, followed by a long curved line, followed by a large zigzag, etc. It is achieved by the occurrence of measure patterns that are very diverse. But occurrence in sequence of measures of some sort, or recurrence of measure, is a basic trait of all rhythms organizing artistic creations, since a single measure is never extensive enough to constitute any but a fragmentary or negligible work of art.

Balance, however, is as fundamental in rhythm as is harmony or recurrence of measure. Balance exists primarily within the measure, as recurrence exists between measures. In most ordinary measures the balance is asymmetrical. Thus in accentual rhythm the ordinary measure is usually a combination of accent and balancing unaccent or unaccents: ONE-two, ONE-two-three, one-TWO, one-two-THREE, and so on. The accented item receives more stress than the unaccented item or items. But this greater stress is offset by the greater relaxation of the nonstressed or unaccented item or items. There is a balance within the measure of stress-relaxation or relaxation-stress. A similar analysis would apply to rhythm based on quantity, where the balance within the measure would be a balance of speed and delay, short and long. Incidentally, the peculiar balancing of items within the measure accounts for the characteristic phrasing and pulsation of a rhythmic unit. Thus rhythm is a combination of balance and recurrence. Balance is primarily the internal principle of the measure. Recurrence of measure is the principle of the larger measured movement.

A third major principle of artistic organization is the principle of centrality. This principle is employed when an ensemble of items is so connected that one item or group is given aesthetic dominance over the others which remain important but subordinate to it, e.g., Giotto's "Madonna Enthroned" (Uffizi Gallery, Florence) with its dominant mother and child; the statuary in the east pediment of the Temple of Zeus (Olympia) with its dominant figure of Zeus. This principle may govern the form of details as well as the form of an entire work. In a musical figure a certain tone or chord may dominate over the others, e.g.,

the chord for oboes in the third measure of the four-measure
figure that opens Wagner's *Tristan* Prelude. As a principle of part
or whole, however, centrality is not to be confused with mere
spatial or temporal centrality. In the Giotto and the Greek work
cited above, it is true, the Madonna and the Zeus are at the spatial mid-point of the ensemble. But centrality even in the spatial
arts can be attained without this. For example, in Giotto's "Bewailing of Christ," the center of the composition, toward which
everything else in the picture converges, is the head of the re-
clining Christ, which is located to the left of the spatial mid-
point of the fresco. Centrality means aesthetic centrality, con-
fluence of perceptual interest to, or dominance of perceptual interest at, a point. Spatial or temporal centrality may promote
this but is not necessarily identical with it. Other ways of pro-
moting it are to endow an item with greater size or fuller embel-
lishment or intenser color or superior expressive power and dramatic significance, or to make it the focus of subordinate harmonies, balances, and rhythms.

In some works of art centrality seems to be totally absent.
These works have no high spot, no focal point. Such works may
be constructed solely of certain harmonies or balances or rhythms
as a stylized relief in which reiteration or rhythmic recurrence of
the "same" figure is the chief formal principle. Compositions
lacking centrality, however, may differ from such stylized works
by unfolding not a series of similar figures but a single unstylized
idea, pattern, or figure. A short story may have neither a dominant high point nor a balance or recurrence of similars. It may
merely reveal progressively and without points of emphasis a
character, a dilemma, a mood, or a situation. Bit by bit the composition may evolve a pattern or expression in which everything
used is needed but nothing is merely repeated or balanced or
markedly outstanding. Such compositions seem to require the
recognition of a principle of organization different not only from
centrality but also from harmony and balance. This new principle might be called the "principle of development," and its
most striking illustrations are in the temporal arts, where the

elements of a work are set in a pattern of directional change and unified as successive steps in a progression.

This principle may be combined with harmony, balance, and centrality in varying degrees, e.g., in a drama. But it is distinct from them. Thus it is distinct from harmony. Harmony is based on repetition, on partial or complete reiteration of the similar. It is a harking backward, not a growth—a staying within the bounds of the past and the previous. Development is based on novelty, on partial or complete advance to the nonsimilar. It is a going forward, a growth, a leaving behind of the past and the previous. Development is also different from balance. Balance is based on equilibrium, on the meeting and neutralizing of opposites, on deadlock and stabilization. Development is based on disequilibrium, on the transforming of opposites into directional movement, on progression and the conversion of the primarily static into the primarily progressive. Finally, development is unlike centrality. Centrality is based on hierarchical order, on a superordination and subordination of items, on dominance. But the basis of development is an arrangement of items as prior and posterior, not as superior and inferior. It is based on sequence, not on rank, and may be carried forward solely by equals, as in the example cited, without the aid of items markedly superior or inferior in rank.

III. TWO LEVELS OF FORM

The four principles of harmony, balance, centrality, and development, with their associates and derivatives—recurrence, similarity, gradation, variation, modulation, symmetry, contrast, opposition, equilibrium, rhythm, measure, dominance, climax, hierarchy, and progression—are probably the chief formal principles used by the imagination of artists for the purification and enhancement of existential structure in works of art.[2]

---

[2] *Cf.* DeWitt Parker, *The Analysis of Art* (New Haven: Yale University Press, 1926), chap. ii; D. W. Prall, *Aesthetic Analysis* (New York: Thomas Y. Crowell Co., 1936), chaps. ii, iii, iv; T. M. Greene, *The Arts and the Art of Criticism* (Princeton, N.J.: Princeton University Press, 1940), chap. vii ff.; S. C. Pepper, *Aesthetic Quality* (New York: Charles Scribner's Sons, 1937, 1938), chaps. v–viii; Leo Stein, *A B C of Aesthetics* (New York: Boni & Liveright, 1927), chaps. xii, xiii. The preceding section is greatly in debt to all these works but particularly to the excellent chapter in Parker's *Analysis of Art*.

Employing these principles, artists build up perceptually vivid spatial, temporal, causal, and telic unities in the details and the over-all designs of their works.

Before considering this achievement, it should be noted that artists may use the four major principles of design and their associates and derivatives on two levels: the presentational and the representational. In a painting there may be a harmony or balance between colors or shapes or lines. But there may also be a harmony or balance between suggested actions or attitudes or between represented personages within a scene or between the glint in the eye and the gesture of an arm of a single represented personage. The representational side of the painting may be as composed, as harmonized, as balanced, as are the lines or shapes or colors. Centrality and development may be similarly employed on the two levels. In a statue there may be a dominance of a certain shape over others, but there may also be a dominance of a certain represented attitude. In Rodin's "La Pensée" (Musée Rodin, Paris), the head shape is not only dominant over the block, but the reflective attitude represented in the face is dominant in the head and central to the statue. As to development, it may appear merely on the presentational level as in the progressive unfolding of an abstract dance pattern or a pattern of musical sounds. But it may equally appear on the representational level in the progressive unfolding of a character, a course of action, or an idea in a drama, an opera, or a novel.

This fact—the operation on two levels of the principles of design—is important not merely for understanding the nature of artistic form but also for the light it throws on the problem of representation in fine art. Writers who have contended that the sole business of art is the creation of form have sometimes maintained that representation is irrelevant to art. But if representation itself is a field for the operation of the principles of form, it would seem contradictory to call representation irrelevant to art, at least on a theory that described the business of art as the creation of form. If the operation of formal principles on the representational level necessarily conflicted with their use on the presentational level, the case might be different. But this is not true. In a painting, such as Renoir's "Three Bathers" (Cleveland Museum of Art), a balanced organization of expressive subject matter may amplify, prolong, and enrich the balanced organization of colors, lines, and planes; and the balanced organization of colors, lines, and planes may give sensuous depth, complexity, and enlargement to the balanced organization of expressive subject matter. It is, indeed, a question as to whether the operation of formal principles on the representational level is not absolutely necessary to enable such arts as painting and sculpture to compete in formal power with such an art as music, as formalists wish them to do. After describing the marvelous complexity of musical form, Abell writes: "To attain a similar richness, painting and sculpture must definitely avoid abstraction. Only when they employ their innate resources of spontaneously evoked meanings do they present a sufficient variety of elements, a sufficient range and complexity of relations, to make possible the achievement of forms worthy to compare with symphonic music in exalted beauty."[3]

The chief merits of the polemics of formalists such as Clive Bell and Roger Fry have been to call greater attention to "abstract" or presentational form and to deprecate nonaesthetic sentimental "life"-attitudes toward subject matter, especially in painting. But to restrict art to abstract form and to dismiss representation as irrelevant to art because it may be used to indulge sentimental nonaesthetic life-attitudes, as Bell does,[4] is, to put it mildly, a paradoxical procedure. Bell admits, it is true, that the representation of the third dimension or of deep space in painting gives opportunity for greater formal realizations and is therefore permissible. Here would seem to be the principle to hold to. In the end the basic artistic consideration regarding representation in art is certainly this: Does the introduction of representation into art permit the creation of works which provide richer aesthetic experiences? And even if we accept the formalist restriction of aesthetic experience to the experience of form, the answer would seem to be affirmative. Representation

[3] W. Abell, *Representation and Form* (New York: Charles Scribner's Sons, 1936), p. 168.
[4] Clive Bell, *Art* (London: Chatto & Windus, 1914), p. 225.

opens a vast field for the operation of formal principles, and this operation can be synchronized with the operation of these principles on the merely abstract or presentational level, so that there is not merely an extension but also an enrichment all around of the form of the work of art.

IV. OVER-ALL DESIGN

What is to be understood by "artistic form" taken as a dimension of the public object? Artistic form in this sense might be described as the system of relations uniting the materials of the public object into a perceptual whole or the system of patterns pervading and organizing the presentational and representational levels of the materials of a work of art. This will be its primary descriptive meaning in our account. We have, however, described artistic form at its best in different language, viz., as enhanced existential form. It is the form of all material existence—space, time, causality, teleology, one or all—transformed in a certain area by the application of such principles as harmony, balance, centrality, development, and their associates and derivatives. More precisely, artistic form at its best is such a unification of materials that all the conflicting ramifications and loose ends of ordinary existential patterns are eliminated and a certain systematic self-completeness is installed in the work of art. Every material item is connected so subtly and amply with [other material items that the work of art becomes for perception a tiny island universe. Such a complex, thoroughgoing, and self-complete unity of the materials is, of course, an ideal not necessarily exemplified by every work of art, and even flagrantly violated by some works of art which are of very great merit in other respects.

The descriptive meaning of artistic form as the total system of relations in the materials of the work of art is not to be confused with two other meanings. The first is pattern—the pattern of colors or lines in a painting, the pattern of shapes or masses in a statue or a building, the pattern of words or actions in a novel, poem, drama, or opera. Such patterns are true forms, but they are only fragments of artistic form in our sense. Artistic form is rather the system of such patterns found in any given creation. The second meaning defines artistic form as the total body of relations in a work of art. Artistic form includes not only the total system of relations of the materials but also the relation of this system to expression, function, and materials, and the relation of these dimensions to each other and to the system of material relations. Artistic form is the interdimensional system of relations as well as a dimension of the public object.

In our sense, artistic form is a dimension only and is exactly coextensive with the other dimensions, e.g., the dimension of material. Artistic materials, as we have seen, have a sensory-intuitive and an imaginative-intellectual side as well as an affective side, which is evident upon sensory intuition (non-"associational" reaction) and fully disclosed upon imaginative intellection ("associational" reaction). When artistic materials are placed in a composition and the sensory-intuitive-affective side of them is composed by rhythm, harmony, development, and so on, the work of art presents certain relations or relational patterns, and these are what we have called "artistic form on the presentational level." When the imaginative-intellectual-affective or associational side of the material is similarly composed and its suggestions or connotations are organized into a coherent and meaningful system, the work of art represents, as well as presents, certain relations or relational patterns, namely, relations or patterns in the "subject" represented; and these are what we have called "artistic form on the representational level." Thus artistic form as the system of relations pervading the presentational and representational levels of a work of art has a point-for-point correspondence to the multiple sides of artistic materials. It is simply the organization installed in the major perceptual aspects of these materials, and it extends only so far as and in the degree that, these aspects are composed into definite features of the artistic creation.

As the system of patterns pervading the presentational and representational levels of a work of art, artistic form might be called over-all form or over-all design. The magnitude of this design will vary with the artistic creation. In a simple work devoid of definite representational form or content, such as an abstract two-dimensional painting, the basic over-all design will be merely the pattern of lines, shapes, and colors as integrating into a unitary scheme. In a simple work with definite representational form and content, such as a short story by Bret Harte or Poe, the basic over-all design will be the pattern of incidents, characters, and moods, together with such presentational patterns as have been contrived by placing words in relations governed by rhythm, balance, recurrence, and similar formal principles. In a complex work of art the detailed wealth of relations constituting the over-all design may stagger comprehension. In the first movement of a great symphony the themes and the relation of the other sections as expositions, extensions, variations, developments, and repetitions of these themes may become clear upon careful study and hearing. But the detailed relationships within the components of the movement, even the total rhythmic, melodic, harmonic, coloristic, and dynamic relations between the tones and chords of the themes, may be grasped only in the most summary and incomplete fashion by all except the most expert and tenacious musical analyst.

One of the delightful paradoxes of great art, however, is that, with all the dense and infinite complexity of design it frequently has, it tends, upon familiarity, to create an impression of singular formal simplicity. The reason for this is that the highly complex detailed orders in great works, although they are the basis of the works' extraordinary formal strength, are usually organized by the imagination of the artist as incidental strands within large sections. They are like the threads in a tapestry, whose individual convolutions elude us, although the broad design of the tapestry itself seems perfectly clear. In each case microscopic details are fused into a few macroscopic unities, such as the musical themes and sections just mentioned; the fine complexity becomes absorbed in the larger simplicities and is grasped in terms of these simplicities instead of in terms of its own separate and perplexing diversity.

The study of the over-all design of particular works of art belongs to history and criticism, not to philosophical analysis. But a few additional general remarks about over-all design may not be out of place before we consider more specifically its characteristics and uses as a dimension of the public object.

V. TYPE DESIGNS

Every over-all design, simple or complex, is as individual and unique as the work of art possessing it. To reproduce the design of a picture by Tintoretto, one would have to copy the shapes and lines and colors in the various patterns given them by the painter and the personages represented in their dramatic relationships, since these also enter into the total structure put there by the artist. Change a shape, substitute in Tintoretto's "Miracle of the Slave" or "Miracle of St. Mark" (Academy, Venice) a tiny rigid body for the great St. Mark, and the pattern of the shapes is perceptibly altered. Change a personage, substitute Christ for the executioner, and the structure of the drama is perceptibly altered. To reproduce the over-all design of a work with absolute completeness, one must reproduce the work itself with absolute completeness. To alter any feature is immediately to alter the presentational or representational relations radiating from that feature and so to alter the precise over-all design that the artist has given to his work.

Nevertheless, designs can be considered at a certain level of abstraction as mere schemata, or, more exactly, patterns within designs can be so regarded. In this sense the "same" design may occur again and again in the works of an artist. The swirl pattern in the "Miracle of St. Mark" recurs in one form or another in innumerable Tintoretto compositions. Artists generally tend to reuse similar patterns. As an artist matures, he develops a characteristic manner of organizing the aspects of his materials. "Each artist creates his own type of co-ordination, it is special to himself, it is his own personal language."[5] The artist uses this personal method of co-ordination again and again, usually suitably varied, in diverse works. The terse, monumentally simple linear patterns of Giotto; the vertically elongated shape patterns

[5] Vernon Blake, *The Art and Craft of Drawing* (London: Oxford University Press, 1927), p. 65.

of El Greco; the dense, weighty, color rhythms of the later Titian, are repeated by these artists in different pictures with endless modifications. Similar type patterns are used by creators in the other arts. A person may recognize an excerpt from a poem as a quotation from Whitman or Dante by the rhythm of the language or by other formal features of the verse. A person may equally recognize a piece of music as by Bach or Beethoven or Wagner by its rhythmic, melodic, or harmonic structure. The characteristic form traits that artists impart to their diverse individual designs, it is true, often change considerably over time. Historians speak of the early, middle, and late manner of a Titian, a Beethoven, or a Wagner. An artist's manner of construction, like any habit, may be discarded for a new one or for a very different one. Still it is usually possible to abstract a set of recurrent formal traits from some group of any great artist's individual designs. Manners may change, but a manner is a manner and results in a type of form.[6]

Type patterns, however, include much more than type forms peculiar to individual artists. Indeed, the most familiar of all type patterns are traditional forms, often obscure in origin, that are employed equally in the work of numerous artists. Illustrations are the sonnet and ballad, the minuet and mazurka, the sonata and fugue and *passacaglia* and rondo, the orders of Greek architecture, the canons of Greek sculpture, the formal conventions of Byzantine or Japanese painting.

Type designs, individual and traditional, are important to all concerned with the arts. To the ordinary perceptive person they can be the starting-point of an apprehension of the total individual design of a creation. The swirl of a Tintoretto, the *terza rima* of a Dante, the sonata form of the first movement of a Haydn symphony, can be tools for entering more fully into the over-all design and apprehending it in great detail. They supply a spacious frame which can be clothed in the flesh and blood of the individual form. To be sure, type patterns can be used by per-

[6] Ernest Newman, *The Unconscious Beethoven* (New York: Alfred A. Knopf, 1927), is a good example of an interesting detailed study of a creative artist's peculiar habits and unconscious traits of construction.

cipients as mere tags of identification and can become the dead ends of devitalized perception instead of tools to implement detailed appreciation. Often they are no more than this in so-called "appreciation courses" in colleges. But, if type patterns are used as instrumentalities instead of as finalities and as methods for starting on the quest of an over-all design, they can open up the general outlay of an individual structure and become the dim beginnings of aesthetic wisdom regarding form.

The critic and the historian of art can also make good use of type designs. Not only can these designs serve as starting-points for that full appreciation of form which should precede the distinctive critical and historical tasks, they can also be used in the critical and historical tasks themselves.

The critic, for example, can use type patterns as a basis for judging the originality of an artist. Has this artist merely borrowed a stencil from tradition and filled it with timely commonplaces or inconsequential novelties? Has he given new and glowing life to a traditional form that seemed played out and dead before he revived it? Has he invented a powerful type form peculiarly his own? Often the difference between a genius and a hack is revealed more clearly in the difference of the handling of a traditional type pattern or in the difference of strength of their individual type patterns than in any other formal difference or in any differences in the material, expressive, or functional features of their works.

As to the historian of art, he can use type patterns as tools of clarification and correlation of individual designs. A type pattern, such as a sonata or an epic, is a schema of recurrent formal traits. In his analysis of form, the main business of the historian, I believe, is the analysis of concrete forms, not of schemata. But type patterns, as schemata of recurrent formal traits, can highlight generic formal features of concrete forms and formal similarities between different concrete forms. The general pattern of the sonata can help to point up certain general properties of a Beethoven or a Mozart sonata and supply a language in terms of which to compare the individual design of this Beethoven sonata with that, or this Mozart sonata with this Beethoven sonata.

Thus, while the analysis of type patterns is not the main concern of the historian, these patterns can supply bases for the clarification and correlation of individual designs, which is his main business, and so make a substantial contribution to his analysis of form.

Type patterns, finally, can be of considerable service to the creative artist. To the apprentice in an art, traditional type patterns can provide good discipline. They can require him to hew to a line while allowing him a certain freedom of |invention of details. They can teach him general conceptions of artistic ordering and can help to inculcate precision and a certain amount of elementary technical facility. To the alert apprentice they can even be means to the discovery of new forms by stirring his imagination to conceive alternatives and variants of traditional forms.

To the mature artist, traditional type patterns can equally be an asset. Such types as the ode and ballad and prose epic in literature or the sonata and theme and variations and fugue in music can serve as fruitful bases of original productions. A certain superior richness of inventive imagination and a certain temperament are probably required to create works in such traditional forms that are outstanding and permanently valuable. But when artists with these qualities do take over these forms, they can usually make something very fine out of them. In literature there have been myriad examples of artists of this sort from the Greek poets to Fielding and Coleridge and Keats. In music, Bach is an obvious example. "Bach was one of the most conventional composers who ever existed. He accepted forms and formulas ready-made from his predecessors, chiefly German and Italian, but French and English also, and he was none the worse for it, because he succeeded, in spite of these self-imposed blinkers to his fancy, in making something greater out of precedent than it had ever been before."[7] An artist less virile than Bach, or a slavish copyist who took traditional type patterns as rigid schemata and traditional examples as absolute models, would be unlikely to turn traditional forms to very significant account. But an artist who extracted their principles, adapted them to his own needs, and

[7] Eric Blom, *The Limitations of Music* (New York: Macmillan Co., 1928), p. 114.

filled them with rich new matter from his own abundant fancy would be perennially able to find them profitable.

Besides traditional forms, individual type patterns or the characteristic formal twists that artists employ in designing their works have an obvious creative usefulness. Ordinarily, these patterns are developed as a consequence of the artist's personality maturing and gaining stability. Their usefulness to the artist is similar to the usefulness of a habit in everyday life. Our habits of walking and running facilitate our everyday responses to stimuli. The individual type patterns of artists, at least as technical "manners" or traits, can facilitate artistic responses to stimuli. They can constitute mechanisms of action ready to cope with creative impulses, and they can enable the artist to ride the crest of his inspiration by supplying devices adequate to his personality that automatically shape the energy going into his work.

It should certainly be added that type patterns, traditional and individual, can be a disadvantage and even a danger to the creative artist. An ambitious apprentice may be handcuffed and ill at ease writing drama in neoclassic patterns or music in seventeenth-century forms and may produce only undistinguished work in these molds. A change to designs of his own invention, adapted to some compelling contemporary purpose, may release unsuspected creative powers, and the young artist may eventually become the founder of a new type of drama or musical form. In the work of a mature artist who lacks fertility of invention, the use of traditional type patterns may not curb his creativity, but it may underline his mediocrity. His Greek-temple banks and memorials, his statues of grand antique design, his facile heroic couplets, or his carefully classical sonatas and fugues may have the slickness of high-grade studio pieces. Flavored by a cool or dulcet personality, they may even have a mild gracious charm. But in the end they will bespeak a feebleness of imagination, and their charm will be clouded by recognition of the hackneyed, derivative, out-of-date, otiose, and irrelevant.

One of the most frequent uses of traditional type forms is as easy short cuts. A veneer of novelty spread upon a tried and true artistic pattern usually produces a very salable product. The mon-

etarily successful hackworks of the great often follow this
formula. So do many of the popular songs of the commercial
theater, which sell immensely, then vanish immediately. Motion
pictures frequently use for plots stereotyped dramatic forms
which have been spruced up by novelties of setting and dialogue,
by popular actors, and the like. Such works are entertaining
when their additions are lively or clever, but they usually do not
stand up under close or repeated scrutiny. To the gifted professional artist, traditional type patterns can be a means to quick
commercial success but also to quick artistic death or to low-
grade creative performance.

Nor are individual type patterns free of disadvantages and
perils for the creative artist. A painter such as Corot may hit upon a type of composition warmly approved by the public and,
deserting his earlier and more solid work, spend his days repeating
his new formula. For any number of reasons the manner of any
artist may degenerate into a conscious mannerism or, remaining
unconscious, be used too profusely or mechanically. People there
are who would gladly do without some of the more synthetic
of Haydn's compositions or some of the more pretentious of
Liszt's forms. Others would gladly forego some of the patterns
of sweet *bambini* of the Della Robbias or some of the clouds of
corpulent nudes garnishing the more lush works of Rubens or
pupils of Rubens. Every artist—a Bach as well as a Haydn or a
Liszt, a Michelangelo as well as a Rubens or a Della Robbia—has
a limited set of gestures manifesting his personality and modifying his forms; and no artist has a personality so profoundly complex that these gestures are without danger, upon occasion, of
protruding too insistently and, by so doing, marring the aesthetic effectiveness of his forms.

With these remarks about type patterns, their importance to
the ordinary perceptive person, the critic, and the historian, and
their uses and perils to the creative artist, we must return to the
discussion of over-all designs or concrete individual form. Type
patterns are partial forms, abstractions from concrete forms. In
the public object, it is the concrete form, the total individual
system of relations pervading the materials of the work of art,

that is artistic form in the fullest sense. What roles does this concrete form have in the public object? What are the chief aesthetic properties and values to be found in it? The correct answers to these questions are similar, I believe, to the answers already given to similar questions regarding materials. In the public object artistic form has instrumental properties and terminal properties. It is related to the other dimensions as means to an end and can have—and in the best works does have—considerable value as instrumental to the other dimensions; and it is itself an aesthetic end and can have—and in the best works does have—considerable terminal value as an end to which the other dimensions are subordinate.

VI. POSSIBLE INSTRUMENTAL VALUES

First, artistic form has instrumental relations to materials and can help to bring out qualities of materials.

A primary color which in itself is charming but not distinguished may take on a striking brilliance in an arrangement of colors constructed to support and accentuate it. Two complementary colors by proper placement on a canvas often acquire a surprising and glowing intensity. A series of musical tones sounded discontinuously may seem pleasing but unremarkable. Joined in a certain melodic and rhythmic progression, enriched by gradations of volume, the tones may exhibit a material loveliness of the most unexpected type. "The aesthetic character of the primary medium as such [i.e., of the materials in our sense] is intensified by skilful formal organization. The artist makes clear to us his appreciation of this immediate aesthetic quality and helps us to realize it as we never did before. Thus, the successful composer exploits the aesthetic character of timbre, tonality, and dynamic variation, and the musical significance of rests. In good architecture, the aesthetic character of evident tensile strength, weight, color, and surface-texture of the materials employed, and of the geometrical proportions of space and light, are all artistically realized. . . . . Good sculpture exhibits the lithic character of stone, the distinctive qualities of wood, and the like."[8] Poetry might be described generically as heightened speech, the formal structure of meter, rhyme, and the like being a means of heightening the speech.

[8] T. M. Greene, *The Arts and the Art of Criticism* (Princeton, N.J.: Princeton University Press, 1940), p. 408.

The skilful instrumentation of materials by form, however, is not axiomatic in the arts. With consummate technicians—a Debussy or a Ravel, for instance—the use of forms that show off brilliantly qualities of the material medium (e.g., orchestral sound) is familiar enough. But in some works—a symphony by Schumann, for example—the harmonic and coloristic forms may be more suited to piano than to full orchestra, and, as a consequence, the material texture of the music may lack the density and opulent variety attained in the texture of expertly contrived orchestral works. Similarly, in a building the steel skeleton may be loaded with a heavy neo-Romanesque body, and the light tensile qualities of the steel may be obliterated for perception by the ponderous form of the work. To achieve distinguished enhancement of materials by form, an artist not only must have the intention of using his material honestly but must know his material medium intimately and be able to judge the potentialities of forms for materials with great accuracy. In the absence of such superior knowledge or judgment, the best of intentions will usually result only in mediocre attainment of this instrumental value of form.

Artistic form has instrumental relations to expression as well as to materials and can help to bring out qualities in the dimension of expression of the public object. Form supports expression when it lends its unity and its aesthetic weight to accentuating the perceptual qualities of the expression.

In Giotto's "Death of St. Francis" (Santa Croce, Florence), the organization of the figures surrounding the horizontal body so that they lead in slow, intense rhythms toward the haloed head of the saint serves to space and bring out more effectively the quietly intense sorrow that is variously expressed by each attendant figure and group. In Rubens' "Rape of the Daughters of Leucippus" (Old Pinakothek, Munich), the great pyramidal design, with its interior system of sweeping intersecting swirls, bulwarks energetically the powerful drama and pagan exuberance expressed in the picture. In Michelangelo's "Bound Slaves" (Louvre, Paris), the *contrapposto* composition of the figures—the torso and head turned in one direction, the thigh and leg turned in the opposite direction—underlines the struggle and heaving exhaustion which the figures express. The vertical form of a medieval Gothic cathedral instruments the expression of romantic aspiration everywhere embodied in the building. It instruments especially the expressive quality of the ornamental details. "Removed from their setting the ornamental animal forms, like the cathedral statues, are dead, senseless, and expressionless." They acquire, however, a lively expressiveness when they are absorbed into the outlines of the building and become fitted into the over-all design.[9] In Tschaikowsky's *Fifth Symphony*, the recurrence of the signet theme in the various movements impresses the emotional qualities of this figure upon the expressive substance of the whole work and, as a consequence, helps markedly to color the expressive dimension of the work.

Contrasting the current novel and drama, Joseph Wood Krutch incidentally indicates how the form of the successful drama generally helps to sharpen its expressive effects. "The novel as currently written is so often nearly without form as to permit its author a casualness . . . . fatal to any genuinely artistic effect. . . . . No play is, on the other hand, even producible unless the author is master at least of a certain minimum skill in the more mechanical aspects of craftsmanship, and for that reason it is very rare to see a play which is, in this elementary sense, as badly written as a good half of published novels. . . . . Nor do I see any evidence that the author who can rise above the merely mechanical elements of craftsmanship usually finds in the relatively rigid requirements of the dramatic form any difficulties the mastering of which does not contribute to, rather than detract from, the final artistic effectiveness of his work. The limitation of length necessitates careful selection and condensations; the necessity for climaxes necessitates the bringing of his conceptions to a focus; and there comes a moment when the intended effect must be produced without the fumbling of which the majority of novelists, obviously themselves often uncertain in which scene, if any, their prime intention is fully realized, are very commonly guilty."[10]

It should be clear from the references to the novel in this quotation that the relation of form to expression is not invariably a happy one. The form of a novel, indeed, may be so confused or indeterminate that what the work is trying to say or express may become equally dim, baffling, and uncertain. A form may be an aggregate of discrete units like the two or more distinct plots of a cumbersome historical drama, and, as a consequence, the expressive content of the work may fall apart into separate and dis-

[9] W. Worringer, *Form Problems of the Gothic* (authorized Amer. ed.; New York: Stechert-Hafner, Inc., 1920), p. 61.

[10] "How I Stand It," *Nation*, CL (February 10, 1940), 223–24.

jointed segments. Above all, the form of a work of art may be inappropriate to its expressive content. A decentralized or static color pattern may weaken the dramatic force of an incident depicted in a painting, just as a slackening of the tempo and a de-accenting of the rhythm of a lively song may take out of it much of its mirth and zest and laughter. Orchestral conductors sometimes exaggerate fortes and pianos or alter tempos and rhythmic accents in symphonic works, thereby painfully distorting the expressive substance of the pieces. Similarly, a writer adapting to the stage a novel containing subtle gossamer characterizations may employ a melodramatic plot to give "punch" to the dramatic presentation. But by such a plot he may disfigure or destroy many of the essential qualities of the original characterizations.

In general, artistic form can be a means of introducing a wholeness into the materials of the public object that focuses and reinforces the qualities of the dimension of expression. But, if this form lacks complete appropriateness or clear-cut wholeness, it will usually weaken, confuse, divide, or distort the expression.

Over-all form, finally, has instrumental relations to function and can facilitate the attainment of both the aesthetic and the nonaesthetic functions. As a terminus of intrinsic perception, successful form can be of great aesthetic interest and value and can thus contribute to the total aesthetic wealth of a work and enhance its utility as an aesthetic object. Of this we shall say more in a moment. As instrumental to the other dimensions, artistic form can also add to the aesthetic wealth of a work and so again to its utility as an aesthetic object.

Form may equally be of use in the attainment of nonaesthetic goals. The rhythmic and melodic form of a piece of music may help to make it highly appropriate to dancing or to a church service. The rhyme and rhythm of a poem may help to make it highly fitting to a commemorative occasion. The design of a painting, as congruent with rugs and furniture, may help to make an otherwise rather unimportant picture a commercially valuable part of a set of interior furnishings. The design of a statue may help to fit it to be an icon or an integral part of a fountain. Of all the fine arts, architecture is most profuse with illustrations of form aiding in the attainment of nonaesthetic goals. Buildings constructed to house office corps, families, or great public assemblies may, simply by the arrangement and organization of their interior space, take a long step toward becoming efficient instruments of the functions that they are intended to serve. This instrumentation of nonaesthetic functions by form is very evident in the better products of the industrial arts, where the parts of successful utilities—e.g., the trigger, the barrel, etc., of a first-class gun—are so arranged as to permit the maximum of efficient practical use. Here form follows function completely and is pre-eminently the willing servant of nonaesthetic purpose.[11]

Clearly, however, form may fail, as well as succeed, in varying degrees to facilitate function. The squat heavy form of a building may make it aesthetically unpleasing and pragmatically unsuitable as the commodious library of a large city. The principle here is the same as in the cases of materials and expression. Superior facilitation of function by form is not an axiom but an achievement of art and usually requires the same sort of detailed attention and knowledge and high-grade skill and felicity of conception as are required for the superior facilitation of expression and materials by form.

VII. POSSIBLE TERMINAL VALUES

The form of a work of art is more than merely an instrument of the dimensions of function, expression, and materials. It is itself a dimension and offers itself as a terminus to be appreciated for its intrinsic properties, for its adroitness, subtlety, laxness, vigor, spareness, ease, austerity, coherence, artificiality, wholeness, or the like. In uncritical aesthetic experience the focus of attention is usually elsewhere, on the brilliance of the materials or on the represented personages and actions and other expressive content. But form, or at least good form, can weave its spell and exert a fascination; and in great art, where every major aspect of a work has merit, this is invariably what, given a chance, form does do.

[11] Cf. Thomas Munro, "Form in the Arts," *Journal of Aesthetics and Art Criticism*, II, No. 8 (1943), 5 ff., especially on functional form.

Ordinarily, the apprehension and appreciation of a total concrete form is a far from simple process. In some works, certain
unities are immediately evident: e.g., the rhythm of dance music
or the arrangement of figures in simple representational paintings. But the total unity of which these more obvious unities are
fragments is rarely disclosed at first glance. Perhaps the best approach to it is to seize upon a pervasive and fairly basic pattern
in a work and to appreciate the other formal elements in relation
to it. Illustrations of patterns useful for this purpose, besides the
two just mentioned, are the plot of a short story or a novel, the
posture of a statue, the general ground or elevation plan of a
building, the type forms of fugue, sonata, or rondo in music. In
art that is successful in its form, the total design is constituted by an integration of all the formal elements or patterns into
a single complex whole. Accordingly, if any pervasive pattern is
selected and used as a clue to the whole, the character of the total
concrete design should be clear from such integration of the other
patterns with the selected pattern as is found in the work examined.

In Jan van Eyck's "Jean Arnolfini and His Wife" (National
Gallery, London), for example, the representational pattern—
the arrangement of the two personages, the dog, the mirror, the
bed, the window, and so on—might be taken as a pervasive pattern, useful as a clue to the total design. Then the light and dark
and the linear and the color organizations might be studied and
seen in relation to the larger representational ensemble. When
this is done, it will be found, I think, that the various presentational patterns fuse with the representational pattern and constitute with it a complex, balanced design of extraordinary variety, richness, and delicacy. The quiet asymmetrical balance of
the representational ensemble is amplified and diversified by the
presentational ensembles, especially by the light and dark, which
are arranged in an asymmetrically balanced pattern of great subtlety and complexity. In works formally inferior to such masterpieces as the Van Eyck, some of the patterns composing the total
design will usually be found to be either in conflict with, or in
disrelation to, one another, e.g., the color scheme of a painting

will conflict with the linear scheme or be irrelevant to the representational organization on the canvas. But the principle of appreciation will be the same—the perception of all the patterns in their interrelevance. This tracing-out of the patterns and seeing the complete system of relations that the artist has installed in his materials, as I have said, is not a simple task, and to do it in even an approximate fashion usually requires prolonged study and analysis. At the same time, the process is not a merely intellectual activity. Analysis and cognition are a part, but the aim is rather to attain an imaginative intuition of the wholeness of the material organization, together with a vivid sense of the terminal perceptual qualities of this wholeness: its quietude, vigor, lightness, thinness, animal robustness, dryness, richness, animation, etc. This requires sensation, intuition, imagination, and feeling, as well as intellectual analysis.

As a terminus, artistic form at its best can give a lively satisfaction and possess great intrinsic aesthetic value. Numerous reasons have been given for this besides the obvious one that something instrumentally useful and also well done is usually itself a pleasure to perceive.

Good artistic form harmonizes in a very marked degree with man's basic biophysical organization. Man's muscular, vascular, and neural systems are governed in a very fundamental way by the principles of balance, rhythm, and dynamic equilibrium, and the larger processes of man's biophysical being are connected in an organic unity. Good artistic form embodies all these principles for perception. It invariably employs balance and rhythm in a major or minor role; its apprehension involves an excursion over a diversity that ends in an equilibrium or unity; and, to the degree in which it is imaginatively successful, artistic form possesses organic wholeness. Good artistic form embodies principles which are at the very foundation of man's biophysical mechanism. Hence in alert intrinsic perception, which brings this mechanism into action, good artistic form easily fits the pattern of the mechanism and is able to lead from it a response which is natural, agreeable, and capable of very great intensification.

Good artistic form also gives agreeable scope to the psychological powers that are released in intrinsic perception. As Kant has said of form in nature, artistic form sets these powers into harmonious free play,[12] or, to use other terms, it allows our impulses of response "free play . . . . with entire avoidance of frustration."[13] More specifically, in the aesthetic perception of good artistic form the powers of intuition and imagination are given a field for ample and unimpeded exercise in agreeable harmony with sensation and intellect. Neither the sensory diversity is so great or so meager nor the intellectual difficulties so insuperable or so few that imaginative intuition in its quest for perceptual unity is not able to achieve a full and free use of its powers. There have been many descriptions of successful design. Hopkins' is regularity within irregularity; Bell's, absolute necessity; Tovey's, integrity.[14] But, whether described in these ways or, as we prefer, merely in terms of unity in variety, a successful design does open the way for the full use of imaginative intuition (the power to grasp perceptual *unity*) unhampered by sensory extremes or intellectual tedium or bewilderment (defective or excessive *variety*). It makes possible the agreeable play of the "form" powers of intrinsic perception in harmony with the "content" powers and so is as satisfactory psychologically as it is biophysically.

Just as basic as these two reasons are two other reasons that are frequently cited. First, good artistic form is harmonious with the general pattern of human aspiration. This pattern has been described in numerous ways, e.g., in terms of complexity and simplicity, of richness and economy. Certainly, a very basic way to describe it is in terms of novelty and stability. The human being constantly aspires to novelty, yet equally he desires to retain stability. This is illustrated by all ordinary purposive activity, which is an effort to attain something-not-yet and so something

[12] Immanuel Kant, *Critique of Judgement*, trans. Bernard (London: Macmillan & Co., Ltd., 1914), e.g., pp. 159 ff.

[13] C. K. Ogden, I. A. Richards, J. Wood, *Foundations of Aesthetics* (London: George Allen & Unwin, Ltd., 1922), p. 75.

[14] G. M. Hopkins, *Notebooks and Papers* (London and New York: Oxford University Press, 1937), pp. 54–91; Bell, *op. cit.*, p. 230; D. F. Tovey, *Integrity of Music* (London and New York: Oxford University Press, 1941), p. 42.

new, and yet to attain it according to forethought, a plan, i.e., a principle of stability. Sheer novelty is madness, sheer stability is deadness, and the human being generally aspires to a life which is more than death, yet less than madness. Now, in good artistic form the combination of novelty with stability is given exemplary illustration. As it unfolds, a good artistic form constantly reveals something different, often something surprising and utterly unexpected. The able musician and dramatist contrives ever new changes and turns in their sequences. The able painter and sculptor and architect contrive ever fresh novelties for the main areas of their spaces. The aim is variety, with entire avoidance of monotony. Yet, for all its variety, good artistic form exhibits an over-all system and order. Its novelties are arranged according to a unity which embraces them completely and gives them an underlying stability. Good artistic form combines an ample novelty with perfect stability and is thus an ideal image of the general pattern of human aspiration stated in terms of novelty and stability.[15]

Second, good artistic form is connected with the basic form of man's past, as well as with the basic pattern of his aspiration toward the future. Plato has described the pleasure taken in ideal Forms as due to reminiscence, or the recollection of a prior existence among such Forms. This might be stated less mythically by saying that an ideal form, or at least a good artistic form, taps a vast subterranean mass of associations. Human life is passed within a spatiotemporal framework everywhere diversified by causal and telic relations. This complex structure is as basic to human life as breath and movement and clings to all its memories as these memories cling to it. In the perception of an artistic form no specific structural associations may be aroused. In viewing the form of a painting, one may not recollect any specific vista of space which in the past had seemed extraordinary; in listening to form in music, one may not recall any specific temporal sequence which had charmed one in prior experience. But, if the spatial

---

[15] Cf. Eliseo Vivas, "A Natural History of the Aesthetic Transaction," in Y. H. Krikorian (ed.), *Naturalism and the Human Spirit* (New York: Columbia University Press, 1944), pp. 107–8.

and temporal forms of the painting and music have been expertly contrived, the pleasure in their perception doubtless derives part of its force "from arousing some very deep, very vague, and immensely generalized reminiscences,"[16] such as a generalized memory of space and time when they were most pleasing in antecedent everyday life. The same would be true in viewing in a drama, for instance, a magnificent rendition of causo-telic structure. This underground association of the structure of art with the structure of existence at its best seems, indeed, natural and inevitable, if the structure of art is simply a perfected version of the structure of existence, bringing out the perceptual felicities as well as the novel possibilities of perceptual value in it, as we have contended.

These reasons—the biophysical, the psychological, the teleological, and the associational—together with others, such as the joy of perceiving something instrumentally useful that is also well done or the joy of rediscovery of a fine artistic form previously known, certainly go a long way toward explaining the terminal satisfaction and value found in a good artistic form. But a further factor, I believe, requires recognition. This is the instrumental relations of the other dimensions to form. The reasons cited above may explain the satisfaction that percipients take in good form in general; but the form of a given work of art is not merely a good form in general. It is the light, sturdy, extremely lively form of a Mozart symphonic movement or the large, muscular, extremely dynamic form of a Michelangelo fresco. Qualitative individuality is perceived in the form and affects the satisfaction and value we find in the form; and, to explain this, the other dimensions of a work of art must be taken into account, since they help to bring out the individual qualities of the form dimension.

In Michelangelo's ceiling fresco, "The Creation of Man" (Sistine Chapel, Vatican City), the ample masses and flowing lines and the colors that are used help to make the design large, muscular, and extremely dynamic. So do the great dramatic fig-

---

[16] Roger Fry, "The Artist and Psycho-analysis," in *The Hogarth Essays* (New York: Doubleday Co., 1928), p. 302.

ures of God and Adam, as represented in the ceiling space, and the function of decorating the large ceiling area that the work serves. Similarly, in a piece by Mozart: its light material texture, its darting terse expression, and its charming aesthetic viability help to make its form light, sturdy, and extremely lively, as in the Finale of the *Haffner Symphony*. Since these diverse individual qualities greatly affect the peculiar satisfaction and value that we find in a particular good form and since these qualities are there to be enjoyed, owing in good part to the instrumental relations of the other dimensions to the form dimension, the relations of these dimensions to the form clearly should be given a place in the explanation of the terminal satisfaction and value that are actually found in a specific good artistic design.

It is of considerable importance for a proper understanding of the view of form set forth in this chapter to realize that the form of a work of art, the possessor of the terminal formal values, is not an abstract Platonic form-in-general but a specific and qualitatively unique design, rooted in the total being of the public object.

In the preceding chapter we saw how materials instrument form, how they can enhance it, and how they may debase it. In succeeding chapters we shall see how expression and function also instrument it. The result is an "emergent" of a distinct type with individual qualities that mark it off and give it a particular nature within its generic station. It becomes a particular Mozartian or Michelangelesque form, and, far from a mere abstraction, might be said to sum up the individual artistic creation. Its full appreciation is actually an appreciation of the total work, the form being in relation to all the other dimensions and its specific qualities reflecting dimensional qualities of the whole artistic creation. Thus the theory of the formalist is to this extent correct, that form is a principle opening up a view of the total work of art. Of course, form is only one such principle, and to this extent the formalist theory remains as limited and incomplete a philosophy of art as was suggested in previous discussions.

VI

EXPRESSION

FINE art, then, can select, refine, and vivify for intrinsic attention the structural features as well as the physical qualities of our world. As its treatment of materials can show us in new and enhanced light the material variety of perceptible things, so its treatment of form can show us in similar light the formal principles of the universe in which we dwell. But fine art can do more. It can select, refine, and vivify for intrinsic attention a great wealth of content—feelings, ideas, character, and personality—lying behind the material surface and within the structural frame of our world. It can express much that it cannot literally present, a whole region of imagination transcending the presentational immediacy of the materials and form.

What is meant by "expression" as a dimension of the work of art? Most simply, it is that organized wealth of over-all suggestions that emerges as an element of the public object. The form of a work is the organization of its materials. The materials themselves, as we have seen, harbor certain suggestions. A color or tone suggests a feeling, a line or shape suggests a thing, a few words suggest a person or action. By selecting and organizing these suggestive materials into a functional whole, emphasizing and suppressing as the case requires, fine art can build an object suggesting a unified complex of feelings, a complete scene filled with a variety of things, a developed human character or personality. This larger system of suggestions emerging within the materials as organized by form into a functional whole is the dimension of expression in the work of art.

A painting, for example, may suggest a complex mood, a scene in the country, an artist's technique and personality. These features are not literally present in the work, as are its colors or its pattern of lines. The painting itself does not literally feel ardent and vehement; nor is it a wheat field or Van Gogh's technique and personality. These items are merely "said" in terms of the colors and patterns. They are indicated or suggested as there. At the same time, their suggestion is not a free addition of our fancy. It is the painting itself that suggests ardor and vehemence, a wheat field, Van Gogh's technique and personality. Our imagination does not arbitrarily invent these contents, although for apprehension they require us to use our imagination. The suggestions are planted in the work, often unconsciously, by the artist himself. Such is the dimension of expression. It is the body of suggested content present in a work as a result of the materials being organized by form into a functional whole, and it is experienced as an intrinsic part of what the work is in the fullest aesthetic perception of its content.

How a work of art can suggest as present in it a multitude of things not literally present is a problem for the genetic psychologist. Apart from imitation, authority, and convention, perhaps the chief reasons are two: direct reaction and association. For example, a person may assert that a certain nonrepresentational painting expresses calmness and gentleness. Now he may assert this because it is conventionally believed or because the title of the work suggests it or because someone has said it.

But, apart from such reasons, he may assert it for one or both of two other reasons. When he perceives the painting, the visual, conative, and other psychophysical reactions stimulated by its colors, lines, and patterns may themselves be calm and gentle in feeling quality. Or the colors and lines and patterns, being similar to those already associated in his past experience with calmness and gentleness, may automatically evoke by generalized association these general emotional qualities. In either case, since the painting is the clear causal source of the feeling qualities evoked, these qualities are immediately taken as suggested by the painting, and their suggestion is taken as an integral feature of the painting's being. But, whatever the explanation, works of fine art do arouse us to find in them a wealth of suggestions over and above their literal sensory properties and presentational forms. They awaken imagination—the power to perceive, in the present, the absent or the merely suggested; and imagination, aided by the resources of feeling, memory, and intellect, apprehends as internal to the work of art a unified multiplicity of content beyond what is merely sensed or intuited.

II. RANGE OF EXPRESSION

At first glance the expressiveness of works of fine art may seem almost infinite in variety; but, upon analysis, it appears to consist of a few broad types, of which the following are probably the most important.

The first is universal abstract expressiveness, by which is meant the suggestion of general properties and attributes ranging from sensory qualities and feelings to philosophical thoughts. "The pure dance can . . . . express with great eloquence the primary sensations of weight and lightness, thrust, rising and falling, floating, soaring and sinking, opening and closing, and the like."[1] Music can express sparkle, gaiety, lightheartedness, swiftness, melancholy, yearning, resolution, uncertainty, or, like "hot" jazz, a rowdy animal gusto. A painting may express tenderness, terror, bleak loveliness; a statue, animation, coldness, grace, twisted vigor; a building, power, dignity, poise, squat heaviness, soaring aspiration. Included in this first type of expressiveness is the general view of life or so-called "philosophy" that works of art are said to express. This philosophy may be expressed very explicitly, as when a literary artist gives us a voluminous outline of his views of love, honor, ambition, death, the church, communism, God, man, and the universe. Or the philosophy may be expressed only implicitly. "It is the province of the plastic arts to compress within the nature of a line, of an arrangement of shapes, of a harmony of tint, an entire outlook upon life and thought."[2] Whether this is the province of

[1] T. M. Greene, *The Arts and the Art of Criticism* (Princeton, N.J.: Princeton University Press, 1940), p. 67.

[2] Vernon Blake, *The Art and Craft of Drawing* (London: Oxford University Press, 1927), p. 26.

the plastic arts or not, these and the other arts can put in the presentational content of their works suggestions of a general attitude toward life that can be elicited by an imaginative reading of this content.

The second type of artistic expressiveness is representation, the suggestion of concrete persons, places, things, incidents, situations, or events. Not all the arts, of course, are representational. Abstract poetry and two-dimensional nonfigure painting, architecture and absolute music, for all their wealth of suggestion, are not. Narrative dance, dramatic literature, three-dimensional painting, and sculpture, however, are full of representation. The works of these arts suggest, definitely and unequivocally in many cases, particular persons, circumstances, and actions not literally present in fact. They give us Petrouschka or Hamlet, the surrender of Bréda or David after slaying Goliath, not literally but in terms of perceptual marks that suggest the outer and inner nature of these particular personages or events.

Ordinarily, representation of even everyday particulars in the arts is based not so much on an imitation as on an interpretation of them. Representation is concrete interpretation. It is based on a selection and marshaling of suggestive details according to an idea, and it expresses a particular according to an artist's idea. This is true no less of historical than of fictitious subjects—e.g., of David or Hamlet, if there was a Hamlet. The representation consists of a body of details marshaled according to an idea. Comparing the Davids of Donatello, Verocchio, and Michelangelo, one is aware at once of differences not only of detail but also of underlying idea.

While universal abstract expressiveness may occur in a work possessing only a presentational level, representation can occur, of course, only in a work of art possessing a representational, as well as a presentational, level. The two other major types of artistic expressiveness deserving special mention, however, can occur both in representational and in merely presentational artistic creations.

The first is the expression of the personality of the artist or, more precisely, of his character as a technician and as a man. In nonrepresentational works this can be suggested by the sort of materials that the artist selects and emphasizes, by the way his presentational designs are built, by the abstract expressive content that he reiterates or underlines, and by the aims or goals or functions of his works. In representational art, it can be suggested by the interpretation of the subject embodied in the representation, as well as by the factors just mentioned. From all these clues an imaginative percipient can often obtain very vivid suggestions of the characteristic manner or technique of the artist and the individual scale of values and telic inclinations of the man. Literally, of course, neither technique nor scale of values and telic inclinations are in the public object. The technique is a feature of the antecedent creative process, the cause from which the public object springs as effect. The scale of values and the telic inclinations are literally possessions of the artist, who controlled the creative process of which the public object is the effect. Nevertheless, suggestions of, or clues to, these causo-telic factors become deeply imprinted upon the public object just because the artist by his technique, inclinations, and scale of values has shaped this object as his effect. And, with imagination, a percipient can apprehend these clues as properties of the public object suggestive of the artist as technician and as man.

A certain caution, however, should be sounded in this matter. The clues in a work of art by no means always point unmistakably to the individual technician behind it, nor do they always sum up to a complete picture of the artist's character as a man. In creating a given work, an artist may employ technical manners and methods used by others, and, as a result, his work may be technically very similar to the work of others. There is much of Haydn and Mozart in Beethoven's *First Symphony* as well as something of Beethoven, and the music by itself is far from unequivocal in its indications of the individual technician who created it. The greater artists, such as Beethoven, do develop strikingly characteristic manners which are unmistakable in many works. But this cannot be said about all artists or about all the works of all the greater artists, including Beethoven. Works of art may also be incomplete pictures of the character of an artist as man. It is fairly clear from the mature music of Wagner—*The Ring* and *Tristan*, for example—that its author is no meek and piddling traditionalist, that here is a man of large and original mold, of great ardor and mammoth imagination, of a certain brutal coarseness and delirious tenderness. And such properties, as well as others in the music, may add up to a fairly differentiating picture of the character of Wagner as a man. Yet that they will add up to Wagner's total character or form a system of traits from which one might deduce the exact nature of all the particular life-actions of Wagner can hardly be maintained. The fact is that the total character of anyone is manifested only in relation to all the stimuli to which the individual might respond, and the field of any art, however broad, will usually supply to a given creator only a certain set of these stimuli and therefore will draw out only a segment of his total character.

Within these limitations, however, works of art do express the character of artists not only as technicians but especially as human beings. "He [Brahms] was a forceful character, who expressed his strength through gruffness and ponderosity, and his profound feelings through a lyricism that could occasionally grow maudlin. He is nearly always admirable and seldom wholly lovable." "She [Edith Wharton] based her values not upon a free and rich feeling for life but on a feeling for decorum and pre–Wall Street merchant respectability." Such summaries of the human character of a major musician and a minor novelist based on critical observation of their works[3] could be repeated indefinitely regarding major and minor artists in all the arts. Nor is this surprising. Despite the limitations mentioned above, the world of art is one in which the artist usually can command, far more successfully than in almost any other region of his experience, the type of effect that satisfies his nature. In this world he is ordinarily more at home, and more free, as well as more able, to achieve a realization of deeply cherished aspirations. That his creations should therefore record and suggest to a considerable

---

[3] Eric Blom, *The Limitations of Music* (New York: Macmillan Co., 1928), p. 161; Louise Bogan, "The Decoration of Novels," *Nation*, CXLVII (October 22, 1938), 419. The complete accuracy of these particular summaries is, of course, not under discussion.

extent the slant of his being and the value inclinations of his nature seems logical and inevitable, since usually these are given fullest expression where one can attain in a superior degree a fulfilment of one's deeply cherished aspirations.

The final major type of artistic expressiveness is social expression—the expression of the nature of a people, an age, a milieu. The music of a German by its spontaneous accents may vividly suggest the aggressiveness, pompousness, and solid thoroughness widely characteristic of the German, just as the music of a Frenchman may equally suggest the lightness and sparkle, the horror of ponderosity and dulness, that have been widely characteristic of more literate Frenchmen.[4] A fifth-century Greek statue or temple may express the restrained, opulent vigor and worldly ideality widely venerated by leading figures of the Periclean age, just as an Elizabethan play may suggest the abundant vitality, love of variety, and lack of great intellectual rigor widely characteristic of leading figures, as well as of the masses, in the Renaissance. Social expressiveness clearly need not be the suggestion merely of the more admirable or original traits of a people, age, or milieu. A derivative architectural work—an American government building that is a copy of a copy of a Renaissance work that is itself a copy of an ancient Roman building—may express a feebleness of creative power and an admiration of elegance divorced from functional excellence that are very typical of a whole circle of the society of its day. Nor need social expressiveness be effected merely by accents in the abstract expression of general traits. It may be achieved by representation. A painter may achieve it by depicting typical or striking personages and scenes from contemporary London or Moscow, from the American Southwest or the Maine coast. A novelist may achieve it by depicting, as did Dreiser in *The Financier* or Sinclair Lewis in *Babbitt*, the American businessman and the American business life of the late nineteenth or early twentieth century.

As in the case of the expression of personality, certain limitations must be recognized regarding the social expressiveness of works of art. A people, an age, a milieu, are very complex and

[4] Blom, *op. cit.*, pp. 146 ff.

possess a multitude of traits. No work of art can suggest more than a fraction of these traits, and even works of vivid social expressiveness usually suggest no more than some of the more prominent or valuable or peculiar. Moreover, in one work the social characteristics expressed may be mass traits or characteristics widely prevalent, while in another the social characteristics expressed may be leader traits or characteristics highly restricted. Thus, even works vividly expressive in the social sense may be limited not only in the number of social traits suggested but also in the social area of which the traits that they suggest are expressive.

It remains true, however, that works of art do express traits that are overindividual or social in character and in some instances traits that penetrate deeply all levels of a society. This last is frequently true of works belonging to what are generally regarded as the greater historical epochs of artistic production. For example, during the sixty-seven years of its existence, the Elizabethan theater "does seem to have been the expression of all that was most vital, most genuine and most joyous in the lives of the people, and to have received from them the most spontaneous and intelligent response. It was an audience of all classes, aristocrat and bourgeois, riff-raff and intelligentsia; and it was a drama of all sorts, of sensationalism and buffoonery, of crude horror and romantic love, of satire and patriotism, of bawdry and moral passion, of rubbish and of riches. But, like Greek drama, it drew its strength from the close co-operation between playwrights and populace. The people and the theatre understood one another, they stimulated one another, they drew vitality from one another. And, except in very specialized and local instances, they have never done so since."[5]

The four types of expressiveness just outlined—the abstract and the concrete, the personal and the social—constitute, I believe, the main content of the dimension of expression. We must now ask: What position does this dimension occupy in the public object? What are its chief aesthetic properties and values there?

[5] Elizabeth Drew, *Discovering Drama* (New York: W. W. Norton & Co., Inc., 1937), pp. 88–89.

Here again, as in the case of materials and form, I believe the correct answer is twofold. Expression has instrumental and terminal aesthetic properties and values in the public object. It is related to the other dimensions as means to end and can have—and in the best works does have—considerable instrumental value for these dimensions. And it is itself an aesthetic terminus or end to which the other dimensions are means, and can have—and in the best works does have—considerable aesthetic value as a terminus or end.

III. POSSIBLE INSTRUMENTAL VALUES

First of all, expression has instrumental relations to materials and can help to bring out vividly for perception qualities in materials. The expressive lightness and soaring suggested by a figure in bronze may forcefully underscore the sturdy tensile qualities of the bronze. The dramatic expression that an actor gives a line or passage may make words that seemed ordinary and undistinguished upon casual reading seem vibrant and choice. Tones of a melody expressing liveliness or melancholy may seem more lively or melancholy in the light of the total feeling quality of the melody. Purple in a painting, by being the purple of velvet cloth, may seem more rich and luminous and soft, just as yellow, by being the yellow of the light of an interior, may seem more subtly subdued and radiant and golden. Of course, expression may fail as well as succeed in supporting materials, as a heavy unarticulated figure represented in bronze may fail to bring out any of the more peculiar and characteristic qualities of the bronze.

Expression has also instrumental relations to the form and can help superbly to bring out for perception qualities in designs. The swagger and cocky air expressed in Verocchio's "David" accentuate the vigor of its graceful form, just as the delicate flesh and relaxed dreamy attitude represented in Praxiteles' "Hermes" accentuate the rhythmic softness of its graceful form. The terse lively representations in the Giotto fresco, "Death of St. Francis" (Church of Santa Croce, Florence), invigorate its simple monumental design. The expression of massive desire in a passage of Wagnerian love music may make more intelligible and more endurable its lengthy labyrinthine form. To be sure, expression may fail to support form as conspicuously as it may fail to support materials. An overabundance of characters in a short story or novel may augment the expressive range of the work, but it may also overload the plot and help to split it apart. Conversely, the sentiment expressed by a piece of music may be insufficient to fill out the lengthy form given the music, as happens sometimes in the adaptation of folk tunes to symphonic designs.

Finally, expression has instrumental relations to function and can effectively help a work to carry out its function. The stirring expression of romantic militarism in Rude's "Hymn of Departure for War" helps to make the relief an eminently appropriate adornment of that architectual monument to romantic militarism, the Arc de Triomphe in Paris. The expression of delicate serenity in an Ionic temple, of massive dignity in a Doric temple, of energetic exuberance in a Gothic cathedral, help to make each type of building a fitting shrine for diverse types of worship. The expression of a timely sentiment in a drama, story, painting, novel, or motion picture may be a leading factor in its great success as a commercial article. Moreover, all expression that is aesthetically effective when considered terminally is, by that fact, an effective aid in the total aesthetic functioning of the public object. Expression may be instrumentally unhelpful, as well as helpful, to function. The expression of an unstriking or untypical attitude in the statue of a great historical personage may diminish or even destroy the value of the statue as a memorial of that personage, just as the expression of unseemly hatred or violence in a Christian church fresco, may impair the usefulness of the fresco as a fitting ornament of a church dedicated to the religion of mercy and love.

IV. POSSIBLE TERMINAL VALUES

In the eyes of most people, far more important than the instrumental role of expression is its role as a terminus. Indeed, to most people expression is, par excellence, the end of art and the aspect of works of art to be apprehended above all others. That

expression is at least one of the most powerful and voluminous
terminal aspects of works of art should be obvious from the description of its types already given. In this realm one "meets"
the most diverse and fascinating personalities: the crafty Titian,
the dreamy Shelley, the sensational Cellini, the darting Mozart.
In this dimension images of whole peoples, ages, and milieus appear: the ancient Greeks, the Elizabethan era, the *grand siècle*, the
landscape of Provence. One finds trenchant interpretations of innumerable historical figures—Philip IV and Innocent X by Velasquez; Moses by Michelangelo; Napoleon by Tolstoy—and
equally trenchant interpretations of innumerable fictional individuals—the Falstaffs and the Shylocks. One also catches
glimpses of innumerable historical and fictional events and of the
endless miscellaneous circumstances and details of these events:
the glory of a brilliant sky, the sheen of armor, the titanic
strength of lightning, the creamy softness of delicate skin. Finally, there is the endless array of abstract contents, of suggested
sensations, feelings, and ideas—roughness, brilliance, sweetness,
calm, restlessness, longing, hope, torture, and the infinite flashes
of truth and insight of poets and others.

Although the dimension of expression is vast and various, not
all its contents have been enthusiastically praised or even accepted. Two types in particular have been recently attacked, representation and truth. Representation has been declared irrelevant to art, and art as a source of truth has been rather vigorously disparaged.

The main argument against representation has come from the
formalists. Fine art, they say, should give us something that
"life" does not give. Otherwise, fine art has no particular excuse
for being. But life gives us Philips and Shylocks and the creamy
softness of delicate skin. Representation merely repeats life and
takes us back to the sorts of interests that operate in life. It gives
us neither a new subjective thrill nor a new objective factor capable of being experienced only in art, such as significant form, for
example.

At this stage of our discussion, an answer to this argument is
not difficult to formulate. We have already seen that representa-

tion opens up vast opportunities for the creation of novel forms so that, even on a theory that conceived the essence of art to be the construction of form, representation would have sound reasons for being retained. But the argument here can be met more directly. The fact is that life does not give us Philips and Shylocks and the creamy softness of delicate skin *as art gives them*. Instead of clearly rendered and coherently interpreted suggestions, life gives us such persons and properties, if at all, in their actual shifting existence. Accordingly, they usually appear with obscuring details or lacking in essentials vitally necessary to making them of maximum perceptual import. Moreover, they are not detached for perception. They are given within a whirl of cross-claims and dynamic relations that makes steady and detached perception of them often difficult and frequently impossible. Life outside art ordinarily gives us neither the perceptually accentuated vision nor the thrill of perceiving in full detachment such a vision that representation at its best supplies. Thus, representation can easily be defended if it needs for justification merely the ability to provide an objective factor and a subjective thrill not ordinarily provided in everyday life.

This point is strengthened and properly qualified by observing for a moment what a formalist who attacks representation is led to say about the objective factor which he claims works of arts should, and alone do, provide, viz., significant form. Thus Clive Bell is forced to admit that significant form is sometimes found outside art. "Who has not, once at least in his life, had a sudden vision of landscape as pure form? For once, instead of seeing it as fields and cottages, he has felt it as lines and colours. In that moment has he not won from material beauty a thrill indistinguishable from that which art gives?"[6] The obvious answer is that he has. The person has found in ordinary objects outside art the same property that the formalist claims is the exclusive possession and justification of works of art. The truth seems to be that there is no general type of objective factor in works of art, a form or an expressive content, that does not occur *in some degree* and *in some shape* in life outside art and that art differs from

[6] Clive Bell *Art* (London: Chatto & Windus, 1914), p. 53.

life outside art not in the presence of an objective generic factor altogether absent from life, but in the presence of generic and other factors that are aesthetically detached, accentuated, and perfected as they usually are not in ordinary life. These are the novelties of art. And in the arts this sort of aesthetically detached, accentuated, and perfected factor is found as profusely on the level of representation, with its endless historical and fictional images trenchantly rendered, as on the level of form. If the rationale of any level of art must be its difference in objective nature and subjective effect from life outside art, as formalists say, representation is as different from life in these respects as form and is certainly found no more in its full artistic stature in ordinary life than is significant form.

The disparagement of art as a source of truth has come from many quarters, most recently from the logical positivists. The general theme is as old as Socrates and amounts to this: that art gives us piquant nonsense or emotive falsehood, not sober and solid knowledge, and that, far from communicating genuine truth, art is mostly intriguing (and Socrates would add dangerous) lies.

There is a certain downright prosaic sense in which this view is correct. The particular representations in art, as just suggested, are rarely, if ever, literal transcripts of empirical facts; and, taken in a certain straightforward, rigorous, and simple-minded way, they are inaccurate and false, even nonsense in the positivist sense. The ancient tale used by Goethe in his ballad "The Sorcerer's Apprentice" is clearly open to criticism of this sort. To begin with, a sorcerer is a myth, not an empirically discoverable being; and that his apprentice by a magic spell could induce a broom to carry water or that a broom chopped into two parts could arise and carry double the original amount of water seems utterly fantastic. The tale is a lie, or, certainly, not a scientific statement of empirical facts. To this extent the position of Socrates and the positivists is clearly correct.

There is more to such a tale, however, than this surface content, and, read imaginatively, the tale can be seen to contain an overtone of insight. Often enough, like the apprentice, human beings out of curiosity or mischief start a chain of events whose consequences they do not fully foresee; and, often enough, their efforts to circumvent these consequences, once the consequences have begun to appear, only lead to greater involvements and worse consequences. Events get out of hand and move straight toward disaster, which only the intervention of an older or wiser person, like the sorcerer in the tale, prevents at the last moment. This is the overtone of insight embodied in the tale—a general truth about human character, action, and consequences. And this sort of truth, together with lesser and larger philosophical truths, is provided by endless works of art that on the surface seem, like "The Sorcerer's Apprentice," false or even nonsensical in the positivist sense.

Nor is insight into human life the only type of truth in works of art of this sort. Insight into physical nature can be found as well. There may not be and may never have been an empirical scene to which Cézanne's "Landscape" (Louvre, Paris) or his similar "Landscape, Mt. St. Victoire" (Phillips Memorial Gallery, Washington) exactly corresponds. The paintings are too simplified and structurally too well ordered to be likely to have a complete one-one correspondence with any empirical fact. Yet such paintings hold up to us vivid images of the linear contour and bony structure of physical nature, such as keen perception often does discern to a certain extent in innumerable scenes. They give us an idealized and simplified version of natural aspects on the perceptual level, just as the mathematical laws of theoretical mechanics incidentally give us an idealized and simplified version of natural aspects on the conceptual level. Thus, correct in one sense, the positivist is wrong in another sense about truth in works of art. Works of art do not give us truth of one type, but they do give truth; and the positivist's dismissal of art as emotive nonsense is a hasty generalization based on an arbitrary restriction of truth to one type of truth—that type most precisely realized by factual statements in the empirical sciences.

Often, however, those who recognize the error of positivism fall into an opposite error. They identify truth with the essence of art: Truth is Beauty, Beauty is Truth, and all that sort of thing.

Or, they say, the central aim of art is to give insight into Reality. Now there is certainly more to such claims than is indicated by our examples from Cézanne and Goethe. The scope of truth in art is very wide. Music can give us amazing insights into the qualities of innumerable nameless emotions, as well as into the qualities of innumerable nameable ones: rage, eagerness, love, tenderness, fervor, and the like. Painting and sculpture can image for us the most subtle and fleeting, as well as the more central and characteristic, of outer appearances and reveal to us trenchantly the basic inner bent of a personality or group. Architecture can give us knowledge ranging from insight into the possibilities of certain materials to an understanding of the aspirations and needs of a society. Literature, even more fully than the other arts, can give us literal, as well as metaphorical, truths about nature and human life.

But diverse and important as are truth and insight in the arts, it seems incorrect to say that they are its central aim. We have already considered this view in discussing cognitive theories of aesthetic experience. Let me add one comment here. If truth and insight were their central aim, the arts in their long professional career would certainly have gone into the business of truth and insight as professionals do, systematically and thoroughly. They would have isolated and analyzed their truths and insights and have developed them with the greatest detail and care, not left them merely suggested and sketched, to be read off in passing by the imaginative intellect. And, once having started down this path, they would have turned quickly into science or philosophy, whose main business would then be identical with theirs. An occupation so professional and so intensely and persistently pursued as the arts have been would not have escaped this fate. Yet the arts have escaped it, and the reason must surely be this: that truth and insight have not been their main or central aim but only incidental to a larger aim. This, of course, has been our theme, that the aim of art is the construction of full-orbed perceptual systems in which truth exists merely to engage one element of intrinsic perception and to fill out the content of the perceptual field by supplying it with one more factor of intrinsic interest. Such a view explains quite precisely, I believe, the suggestiveness, incompleteness, and half-and-half condition that truth usually has in art.

V. BASES OF TERMINAL VALUES

What are the bases of the terminal values found by perceptive human beings in the dimension of expression? We have already noted that imagination may be awakened to the suggestions constituting this dimension by direct reaction or association. This would seem to mean that the dimension of expression is interesting to perceptive people because the direct reactions or associations involved are interesting. As to the direct reactions, we can say at once that where they are interesting it must be because they satisfy immediately the telic factors brought into play in them. These factors are immediately gratified, and so their object has immediate value and interest.

Associations seem to present a more complex problem. Part of the interest of associations in the experience of art—but only part, I think—arises from the fact that these associations touch life-interests that thrive outside art. Formalists, as we have noted, assert that the operation of life-interests in our experience of art destroys the distinctive character of the experience. Art should appeal to different interests, or it has no excuse for being. Stated in the unqualified way that formalists sometimes phrase it, however, such a view really cuts the ground from under the formalists' own position, since an interest in form itself is a life-interest, i.e., it operates in life outside art. And it operates there prior to its operation in the experience of art. In all the daily experiences in which a child is curious to discover how things go together—how one building block fits another, how one room connects with another room or one street with another street, how a key fits a lock—the interest is in relationships, connections, form. An interest in form, in the "hang" of things, is one of the most elementary of life-interests; and, if life-interests were barred in an unqualified sense from operating in our experience of art, the type of interest described by the formalists as alone appropriate, viz., an interest in form, would not be permissible in the experience of art.

The formalist is correct in one sense. Used in a certain way, a life-interest may destroy the aesthetic character of the experience of art. If a person acted toward a playful dog in a sculptured relief or toward a dramatic heroine in distress as he would act toward similar beings in daily life, his experience would not be aesthetic. Nor would it be aesthetic if he used the suggestions of art as he might opium or a strong drug, as an opportunity for day dreams, as an aphrodisiac, or, in general, as a means of self-indulgence. Life-interests in the experience of art, including the interest in form, must be controlled and subordinated to a new end, the aesthetic end; and only in that condition are they admissible as a factor in the explanation of the interest in expression in art.

But only part of the interest in artistic expression here can lie in the life-interests touched through association. After all, the contents of life itself can be taken aesthetically and can be viewed as an array of expressive aesthetic events and objects which stimulate associative processes. If the dimension of expression of art did not offer something more than this, perceptive people would not turn away from life and become so keenly interested, as they often are, in the expressive content of art. The dimension of expression must exhibit an excellence that the ordinary run of life as a perceptual spectacle does not possess. And at its best, I believe, the dimension of expression does exhibit such an excellence. It excels ordinary life quantitatively and qualitatively. It brings before a human being innumerable personages, incidents, feelings, and facts from the remotest regions of space and time and from the boundless world of fancy, which quantitatively far exceed the restricted contents of his everyday world. And at its best it does this with an aesthetic detachment, grace, subtlety, clarity, and force that are rarely, if ever, matched by the incidents and figments of his everyday life.

This aesthetic superiority of the dimension of expression, which incidentally extends to factors arousing direct reactions as well as to those arousing associations, is by no means independent of the other dimensions of the public object; for what a person experiences in the dimension of expression is not a disembodied, formless, purposeless expressiveness but an expression that is materialized, formed, and embodied in a functional unit. Materials, form, and function enter profoundly into what the expression of a work of art is as an aesthetic terminus, and they contribute greatly to its aesthetic superiority, particularly its qualitative superiority.

The materials of a work of art, for example, give the expressive contents a sensuous, concrete, bodily presence that anchors them immediately to the realm of direct experience. They also present this expressive content so that it is not mistaken for pragmatic content and acted upon pragmatically. The pears and bananas of a painting are so clearly paint and canvas that one is immediately inhibited from taking them as "real" pears and bananas. Moreover, when the materials of a work of art are terminally choice, they give the expressive content not only a direct and sensuous presence but also a charming and intrinsically pleasing presence; and when these materials are instrumentally well chosen, they support and reinforce the expressive content. The colors of a painting, the well-chosen word-sounds of a poem, fit in with and reinforce by their qualities what the painting or poem is trying to express.

The form of a work of art may equally contribute to the aesthetic superiority of the dimension of expression. Good form supplies coherence, clarification, elimination of nonessentials, and unification to expressive contents, so that these contents are able to make an intense, intelligible, and total impression on intrinsic perception that is very rare with comparable objects of everyday life. A human career dramatized in a well-made play becomes a unified, clarified, and vividly organized field for perception, unlike a human career happening before our eyes in everyday life, which is usually broken in its unity, teeming with uncertain starts and stops, and encumbered with endless miscellaneous details. The qualities of a good form can also be fused with the contents expressed and can invigorate as well as elucidate them. The sharpness and climactic power of a good dramatic form can be fused with the substance dramatized so that this substance takes on for perception the appearance of sharpness and climactic power, as a human career in an excellent dramatization.

Finally, function can make a contribution to the aesthetic superiority of the dimension of expression. The primacy of the aesthetic function of a work of art gives its expressive contents a superior opportunity to show their intrinsic perceptual strength and force. The objects of everyday experience are usually of such immediate pragmatic concern, if they are of concern at all, that to look at them merely to perceive their intrinsic perceptual character usually seems idle, irrelevant, or perverse. Not so works of art. Their distinctive function is to be taken in that way. This function releases to the full a perceptual interest in their expressive contents and saves this interest from being deterred by the habits, or smothered by the inhibitions, built up around the objects of everyday experience. Other functions of a work of art may also contribute to the aesthetic superiority of its expressive content. A suitable place for hanging a picture may help to highlight its expressive content, just as a suitable place for the rendition of music may give its expressive content a chance to be more effective than sounds buried in the obscuring mazes of everyday circumstances.

Materials, form, and function, then, can help and, properly used, do help immensely to make the dimension of expression in art aesthetically superior in quality to the expressive contents of everyday life. And this dimension has quantitative as well as qualitative superiority, for works of art—novels, poetry, music, drama, and the like—spread before the ordinary percipient an expanse of items far exceeding in diversity and extent the limited run of expressive content of his everyday life. Thus the bases of the terminal values of the dimension of expression are at least three: direct reaction, the incidental play of life-interests, and the general aesthetic superiority of the contents of the dimension over the expressive contents of everyday experience, quantitative and qualitative.

VII

THE FUNCTIONS OF THE
WORK OF ART

I. ART AND FUNCTION

IN A sense the functional aspect of works of art is the most fundamental of all. The other major aspects are what they are because the work of art has an end or function. Materials, form, and expression react on function, modifying it to some extent, as we shall see. But initially they are selected, refined, and projected into a work of art to fulfil some telic propulsion of the artist, to bring forth an object that can function in a certain way. First and foremost, works of art are implements for achieving ends, and the functional aspect of a work of art is simply its uses in the achievement of ends.

The uses of works of art in this respect are extremely various. Works of art, of course, serve the ends of intrinsic perception. But as vivifications of the physical, the formal, and the human and social features of our world, works of art project vistas and ideals that go far beyond the moment of intrinsic perception. Works of art also have economic, religious, sportive, and medical uses. They are public ornaments and historical documents. Indeed, works of art reach into all the major extra-artistic channels of social living; and a detailed discussion of the functional dimension would carry us far into a discussion of the implications of the arts for the various phases of human living. This is the topic of later chapters, while in this chapter, as a necessary preliminary of it, I should like merely to indicate the broad scope of the functional dimension and the main roles of the dimension in the public object.

II. NONAESTHETIC FUNCTIONS

Various as are the functions of works of art, they can be divided into two basic types—aesthetic and nonaesthetic—and the chief nonaesthetic functions can themselves be divided into two types—individual and group functions.

For the artist or creator, works of art may be means of making money and winning fame, prestige, and social power, as they may also be to some extent for individuals who obtain these works from their original creators. For the appreciator and to some extent for the creator, works of art may also be occasions for the playful expenditure of unused energies, for pastime, escape, entertainment, and excitement or for knowledge and insight. Of the manifold nonaesthetic uses of a work of art to the individual creator or appreciator, two deserve special mention above all the others.

The first is the satisfaction of the will or of the drive for mastery and achievement that the public object may embody for the creative artist. A work of art for him may be, not the thin wish-fulfilment of a reverie indulged in, but the solid wish-fulfilment of a reality achieved. It may stand in his eyes as a reassuring landmark in the development of his talent, as a symbol of his power to accomplish, and as a victory of his self as a creative force over enormous obstacles and difficulties. The second outstanding non-aesthetic function for the individual is the modification of the scale of values that a work of art may effect, especially in the appreciator. "Yesterday," writes Nietzsche, "I heard for the twentieth time—will you believe it?—Bizet's masterpiece. . . . . How such a work perfects a person! He becomes a masterpiece himself."[1] In general, a work of art to which one fully submits may affect all the more vital aspirations and value inclinations of one's being and modify in all sorts of ways the powers and vision that guide subsequent reflection and action. The complex implications of this function—indeed, of all the functions to be mentioned here, aesthetic and nonaesthetic—will be considered in later chapters, as I have said, our aim now being merely to indi-

---

[1] Friedrich Nietzsche, *Der Fall Wagner* (Leipzig: C. G. Naumann, 1899), p. 7.

cate briefly, first of all, the major types of functions that works of art possess.

Besides the manifold nonaesthetic uses of works of art to individuals, works of art have manifold nonaesthetic uses to groups. A building may shelter an industry, an educational institution, a congregation, or a family. A sculptored figure may serve as a religious icon or as a memorial to the fallen soldiers of a nation. Poetry, music, the dance, may bolster the morale of a group or play a vital part in a great festive occasion. Painting may record the deeds of a celebrated citizen, a king, or a prize-fighter. In so-called "primitive" societies the art impulse is invariably combined with nonaesthetic group purposes. What are called works of "primitive art"—statuary, music, dances—have usually been created primarily to propitiate the gods of war, marriage, earth, or sea or to whip up communal spirit for a group activity. These works usually possess a powerful simple form and a lively expressiveness, which much more sophisticated or "civilized" works, divorced from nonaesthetic group ends, rarely equal. In these primitive creations, of late greatly admired by Western artists, there is illustrated the enormous fruitfulness of social needs as a basis of artistic production, a lesson that is probably of inestimably greater importance for the Western artist today, as we shall see, than the instruction in abstract design, which is the chief benefit that so far he has gained from them.

Of all the nonaesthetic group functions of works of art, two seem of greatest importance. The first is the function of satisfying certain so-called "physical" group needs, e.g., shelter, transportation. The second is the function of satisfying certain so-called "mental" group needs, e.g., the communication of feelings and experiences, the welding of the individuals of a group into a purposively active, unified society.

III. AESTHETIC FUNCTION

The aesthetic function of the public object is, of course, its service as a terminus of aesthetic experience. We have already discussed aesthetic experience in general. It remains to say something in particular about the aesthetic experience of works of art in order to indicate the range that the aesthetic function may have here. I will do this by contrasting two opposite and extreme types of aesthetic experience of art—naïve and disciplined experience.

Naïve aesthetic experience perceives a work of art as if it were an everyday object elevated momentarily to the purely perceptual level. In so far as it is aesthetic, it is an appreciation of obvious perceptual features of the object taken in this way. The naïve percipient admires the cozy setting given a house in a painting. He relishes the sweetness of the melody played by an orchestra. He delights in the graceful posture of a sculptured figure or the lively gestures of the comedian upon a stage. In general, he catches the intrinsic perceptual quality of evident aspects of the artistic object before him, and to that extent his experience is genuinely aesthetic. But his experience is naïve in a number of ways.

First, it is highly limited. It is usually confined to the apprehension of a few of the more evident expressive features of a work and misses most of its material and formal, as well as all its more subtle expressive, and functional features. Moreover, naïve aesthetic experience tends to treat the expressive features which it does apprehend as if they were properties of a "real" object. The landscape of a painting is contemplated as if it were a real landscape perceptually apprehended. It is viewed as a "natural" object and appreciated for its natural qualities, in ignorance of the relevant conventions, limitations, and aims of the artistic enterprise.

Furthermore, the object is usually judged very subjectively and dogmatically. The naïve percipient tends to insist that the object immediately satisfy his acquired preferences in perceptual matters, and he is usually very quick and sweeping in condemnation of a work that fails to meet these a priori prerequisites. If a landscape looks "unnatural" or "cockeyed" to him, he says so without hesitation and with considerable finality. Cockeyed art—e.g., "modernist" art—he ascribes to incompetence. It is the sort of thing any child could do. The naïve percipient usually is blissfully unaware that there might be other and perhaps even better standards in terms of which many of the things which seem incompetent to him possess competence in a very high degree. Finally, his experience is usually unsustained and impure, constantly slipping from the aesthetic to the nonaesthetic. If an object is markedly displeasing to him, the naïve percipient is usually quick to push it aside or to take himself from its presence. If the object is very pleasing, he usually lapses intermittently into sentimental reflections upon it or into reveries, nostalgic, sexual, or heroic, depending on the subject matter. A thin line of pure aesthetic response or intrinsic perceptual appreciation usually runs through his experience, but the line is not only thin but usually broken in many places.

Naïve as it is, the experience just described probably embraces a great majority of the usual experiences of works of art. Moreover, there is a large industry, not to be confused with serious art, that produces tons of books and songs and pictures yearly simply to supply persons with objects for this sort of experience. These works usually project suggestions that are more glamorous or sensational than the perceptual properties of everyday situations, and so have for the naïve an instant appeal. And they offer him a never-never land or substitute world in which he can indulge himself fully while taking in a minimum of the qualities of this world on the pure perceptual level. Having the appearance of works of art, such confections are more basically anti-art, vehicles for self-indulgent, rather than for object-centered, experience.

Disciplined aesthetic experience is in most fundamental respects the exact opposite of naïve aesthetic experience. Perhaps its most basic difference is in orientation. Disciplined aesthetic experience begins by taking a work of art not as a natural object momentarily viewed aesthetically, but as a work of art, a special type of creation. It is aware of the general character of art, its possibilities and limitations, and is not easily surprised or offended by a work simply because it differs from a natural object in perceptual appearances. In treating a work of art as an object of a special type, disciplined aesthetic experience might be described as narrower than naïve perception. But at the level on which it views the object—the aesthetic level—disciplined experience is immensely wider, exploring all aspects of the object and the interrelations of the aspects and attaining a vastly broader experience of the object as a created aesthetic entity.

Moreover, disciplined aesthetic experience is usually deeper as well as wider, since it is ordinarily much more analytical and brings to bear upon a work a much larger volume of relevant knowledge and training. Its appraisals also are usually far less dogmatic. It allows the work itself to speak out more fully, and its critical decisions customarily come as precipitates of a voluminous experience of apprehension rather than as consequences of an instantaneous interaction between the object and fixed preconceptions that often have little to do with art or art criticism. Finally, disciplined aesthetic experience is ordinarily much more pure, sustained, and active than naïve experience. At its best, it treats the work of art with the single-mindedness, seriousness, vigor, and respect that the creative artist presumably bestowed on it. The object is the center of the experience; to perceive its intrinsic character energetically and fully is the sole aim; and every thing tangential to or inhibitory of this—sentiment or reverie, pleasure or pain—is brushed aside as irrelevant and inconsequential in the persistent pursuit of this aim.

Of the differences between naïve and disciplined aesthetic experience, one deserving special emphasis, in view of the next chapter, is the difference in critical mentality of the percipients. A critical vein runs through both types of experience. All aesthetic experience is basically telic in character. It is therefore evaluative, at a minimum an implicit measuring of objects in relation to inclinations, demands, ends, or other telic factors. But this feature is different in the two types of experience. In naïve experience the critical evaluation is more extrinsically and subjectively based. The naïve percipient possesses a set of demands formulated primarily in terms of his everyday private preferences and desires, and he requires that the work of art meet these demands or be damned. On the other hand, the critical evaluation of disciplined aesthetic experience is much more intrinsically and objectively grounded. The experient possesses a set of demands formulated primarily in terms of the aesthetic possibilities of art itself, and he requires that the work of art meet these demands or reveal a better set of possibilities. The naïve aesthetic percipient says: "My will be done." The disciplined aesthetic percipient says: "Art's will be done." Thus the critical vein in the two types of experience is exactly opposite in basic character.

Disciplined, as well as naïve, aesthetic experience, we have said, is an extreme type. Disciplined experience is indeed the aesthetic response to art in its most elaborate form, as naïve experience is this response in its most attenuated form.

There is, however, a good deal of even casual aesthetic experience of art that approaches the disciplined type, e.g., when a well-equipped aesthetic percipient subjects a work to a single rapid examination. In reading a poem in this fashion, the percipient is likely to consider its aspects, not methodically and systematically but in a more cursory and incomplete manner. He may first be most attracted by the rhythm of the opening lines, then note certain verbal felicities or infelicities in sequent lines, then find himself dwelling most on certain abstract expressive qualities of the poem, and end by feeling that the poem as an aesthetic object is rather neat or tiresome or pretentious. That is, his single reading of the poem shifts focus, now making one dimension central, now another, and ultimately taking in all four to some extent; and from this incomplete multifocal perception of the work he comes to formulate his first estimate of the poem as a work of art. Perhaps the most inevitable examples of this sort of experience are one's first hearing of unfamiliar music at a concert or the opera. Now disciplined aesthetic experience at its best is merely a more complete and systematic execution of what is here done in a more cursory and incomplete fashion, an active perceiving and reperceiving of a work until perception has taken in fully its dimensions and their interrelations. But such hasty and incomplete experience as just described is akin to disciplined aesthetic experience at its best in at least these respects: it is complex and purely aesthetic, and there is usually lying behind it, certainly with well-equipped aesthetic percipients, a conception, perhaps vague and unformulated, of the full aesthetic possibilities of works of art.

Just what the full aesthetic possibilities of works of art and so the appropriate bases of disciplined evaluation are has been a central topic of the present part of this book. We must now complete our account of the matter by describing the possible values of the functional dimension. In the three preceding chapters we described the aesthetic possibilities of materials, form, and expression, respectively. What are the aesthetic possibilities of function? The answer, I think, is, in principle, the answer given in the discussions of the other dimensions. Function has a two-fold role as a dimension of the public object. It is related to the other dimensions as means to end and can have—and in the best works does have—considerable value as instrumental to the other dimensions. And it is itself an aesthetic end and can have—and in the best works does have—considerable terminal aesthetic value.

IV. POSSIBLE INSTRUMENTAL VALUES

Both the aesthetic and the nonaesthetic functions of works of art can possess considerable instrumental value for the other dimensions.

The aesthetic functionality of a work of art can bring out excellently the qualities of all the other dimensions as termini of intrinsic perception. Place a well-made utility, heretofore considered merely for its practical values, upon an aesthetic plane, and the intrinsic properties of its material, form, and expression, previously unnoticed or obscured, may become vividly apparent. Often a work of fine art that was disappointing upon hasty perception turns out to exhibit surprising merits when its function as an aesthetic object is permitted its full or proper operation. In general, the unobstructed aesthetic functioning of a work effectively brings out the full aesthetic qualities of all its dimensions. Even with inferior works of art, this is the case. With inferior works, this may seem a disservice, since it means the revelation of their aesthetic inferiorities. But this view overlooks the fact that such a revelation is a display of the aesthetic qualities of these works to their fullest extent and so is a service to whatever these qualities can be for adequate aesthetic perception.

Aesthetic functioning, however, can be a genuine instrumental disservice. A work of art functioning poorly—a painting exhibited in overdull light or a piece of fine music heard in a reverberant concert hall—illustrates this. Such aesthetic functioning may obscure, confuse, or disfigure the material, formal, or expressive qualities of a work and thus do harm to their nature as terminals. Even in such cases, however, the functional dimension clearly remains connected with the other dimensions, illustrating our general point that the dimension of function is everywhere related instrumentally to the other aspects of the public object.

The nonaesthetic functions of works of art also have instrumental relations to the other dimensions, and may also obscure or disfigure the aesthetic qualities of these dimensions, as the pragmatic functions of a well-made utility may obscure or disfigure the aesthetic merits of its material, form, or expression, to revert to the instance above cited. The nonaesthetic functions, however, can also implement in a high degree the other dimensions. Soldiers marching to a piece of music may stirringly underline its pulsing rhythm and gripping martial spirit, just as a great celebration may bring back the glow of fresh life into an old song, as a New Year's Eve celebration often does to "Auld Lang Syne." The reading of a memorial poem, not at first glance impressive, at a banquet in honor of a great and lovable person may set off poignantly its feeling and form, just as the revival of a celebrated drama in honor of an anniversary of its author may help to give a fresh perspective on all its aspects and qualities. The economy and convenience of a modernist house, its functional adroitness, may emphasize the light, precise, trim, clean-cut qualities of its materials and form. The quiet simplicity of the broad, pale colors, the flattened forms, and abstract symbolic expressiveness of a mural painting may derive a certain sturdiness from its function of decorating the wall of a room without hollowing it out and weakening it in fact or in illusion, just as the material and form and content of a mural or bas-relief may de-

rive an extra smartness and daring from its function of decorating
a night club or a bar.

V. POSSIBLE TERMINAL VALUES

Besides possessing instrumental values for the other dimensions, the dimension of function can itself serve as a terminus of
aesthetic attention and possess terminal aesthetic values.

Even the aesthetic functionality of a work of art may be an
end-point of intrinsic perceptual interest. This occurs when one
is concerned not so much with the intrinsic perceptual properties
of materials or form or expression separately as with the total
aesthetic functioning of a work. "The music played tonight was
marvelous in every way." "That painting is simply perfect in
every respect." Such statements, summing up the total aesthetic
functioning of works, are based upon taking this functional
dimension as the terminal point of interest. It is evident that here
the other three dimensions are instrumentally related to the functional dimension. They are means to it as end. Indeed, taking the
total aesthetic functionality of a work as a terminus is in large
part an integration of taking each of these other dimensions as a
subterminus. It is taking in all of them and the interrelation of
all of them and the nonaesthetic functioning of the work as well,
as subordinate parts of a larger perspective in which each is seen
as contributing to a larger aesthetic totality.

Less comprehensive than this perspective, yet fully appropriate, is the taking of an outstanding nonaesthetic function as a
terminus of perceptual interest. This has always been one of the
basic ways of viewing architectural works. A building is constructed to serve as a school. How adequate is it to this purpose?
Do its rooms and halls have the proper space and light, the efficient healthful heating and ventilation, the appurtenances and
décor most appropriate to a school of its type? Do its outer members—entrances and wings and elevation—fit in with, and at-
tractively point up, the characteristic functions of the building?
A practiced eye, surveying current American school buildings
from this functionalist standpoint, probably would not have a
very luxurious aesthetic repast. But the standpoint is pertinent,

and its standard of perceptible adequacy of a building to its central nonaesthetic function has always been superbly satisfied by the greater monuments of architecture: the Parthenon, Hagia Sophia, Amiens Cathedral, etc. Moreover, many current works often satisfy it vividly. A modern steel bridge, with its majestic sweep, clean-lined channels, and tensile stability, may offer in operation an impressive vision of an efficient mechanism of travel. Nor is this point of view applicable only to works of architecture and the industrial arts. It can be applied to music, literature, painting, and sculpture. Viewing a piece of music in relation to a ritualistic role, a poem in relation to a festive role, a painting or statue in relation to a commemorative role each is performing and apprehending such perceptible adequacy as each has to the role in question are instances of taking an outstanding nonaesthetic function of music, literature, painting, sculpture, as a terminus of aesthetic attention and considering the elements of each in relation to this nonaesthetic function, taken as the end-point of the intrinsic perception.

VI. FUNCTIONALISM AS A THEORY OF ART

This discussion of the adequacy of works of art to nonaesthetic functions brings up the doctrine of functionalism. As a theory of art, functionalism has usually been advocated in connection with arts that are inseparable from the "physical" needs and "practical" life of human beings, such as the industrial arts and architecture. Its theme has been that materials, form, and expression should follow function, meaning a practical, physical function. Make an object such as an automobile or a building into a material mechanism with a form as suitable as possible to its practical, physical function, and it will be "beautiful" or aesthetically satisfying.

This theory has been taken to mean that the useful is *ipso facto* beautiful. Then opponents have pointed out that a rattletrap automobile may be useful in getting a person from one place to another, but it is certainly not beautiful. This is not, however, the burden of the theory. Its chief thesis is rather that in the degree that a constructed object is well adapted to its practical, physical function—and a rattletrap automobile is by definition not so—it will give satisfaction on the aesthetic plane. And this doctrine seems correct so far as it goes. Indeed, in the later part of the preceding section we were illustrating such a view and were insisting upon the validity and fruitfulness of taking the practical, physical function of a modern steel bridge, for instance, as the terminus of aesthetic attention and using the perceptible suitability of the bridge to such a function as a standard of aesthetic judgment.

Functionalism in the above sense, as a general theory of art, has defects of a different type. Many works of art, including some of the finest music, painting, literature, and sculpture, have no ostensible practical, physical function. They do not directly surmount, or protect man against, physical obstacles, as do automobiles, bridges, or buildings. Functionalism in the narrower sense seems inapplicable to them. Moreover, works of art generally, including those having practical, physical functions, have numerous psychological functions—such as play, escape, compensation, consolation. Functionalism in the narrower sense seems very incomplete, even in regard to the nonaesthetic functional side of works to which it is applicable. Finally, two works of art that do have practical, physical functions may be equally efficient practically and physically, yet not be aesthetically equal. Two automobiles may be able to travel at the same speed and may handle with the same ease and last equally long. Yet one may look much more slick, trim, elegant, and inviting than the other. Of two equally efficient practical solutions, there are usually several possible material, formal, and expressive embodiments. You may make equally efficient buildings of marble and reinforced concrete with equally efficient forms. But aesthetically they will be very different materially and formally—and expressively also. A well-known contemporary American architect writes regarding function and form in a building: "In a great many cases function only *indicates* the form in a general way—it does not *dictate* the form. The artist (that necessary part of the architect) must choose from several forms, which are equally possible and which would function equally well, that one form which is to him most satisfactory aesthetically."[2]

In sum, many works of art do not have practical, physical functions at all; and, in those that do, the practical, physical function is often only one element of their complex functionality. Moreover, in these works the practical, physical function is usually only one explanation of their total aesthetic qualities. The selection of alternatively possible materials and form and expression permitted by the physical functionality is also required to explain the totality of these aesthetic qualities.

Accordingly, in order to become a satisfactory theory of art, functionalism in the above sense must be broadened considerably. The way to do this with best results, I believe, is to introduce the standpoint of relationalism. That is, the best way to emend functionalism is to view fine art not merely in its practical, physical functional relations but in its total relational pattern and to describe the needs it can serve within this larger relational pattern.

Viewed in this way, fine art is seen to be capable of serving a large number of nonaesthetic individual and group needs and to be distinguished among human enterprises by the comparative centrality in it of the relation to the aesthetic need. A transformed functionalism would therefore develop a theory of fine art along this dual line. It would recognize the relation of art to the multiple nonaesthetic needs and would emphasize the relation in art to the aesthetic need. And this is, of course, the theory of art that we have been developing in these pages. This theory embraces the conceptions of fine art as the creation of material surfaces (impressionism), the creation of forms (formalism, classicism), and the creation of expressions of various types, especially the emotional (expressionism, romanticism), in the conception of fine art as the construction of four-dimensional perceptual fields or systems for aesthetic attention; and it embraces the conception of art as an instrument of certain practical, physical needs (functionalism) and of play, escape, conscious self-de-

[2] William Lescaze, *On Being an Architect* (New York: G. P. Putnam's Sons, 1942), pp. 9–10; italics and parenthesis in text.

ception, and similar individual and group psychological needs (psychologism) in the comprehensive conception of fine art as the construction of functional units that have multiple values, in addition to their central aesthetic values, for the nonaesthetic interests of creator, percipient, and human beings generally.

With this summary, our answer to the first major question of our inquiry "What is art?" is as complete as we can make it without discussing in some detail the second major question: What of art? What is the importance of the arts to human life generally? Accordingly, we turn now to this second question, our particular intention being to describe the implications of art as interpreted in the preceding pages for critical and social attitudes toward the arts and for the enterprise of art itself at this moment in its history.

PART III

IMPLICATIONS

VIII

ART CRITICISM

I. THE PHASES OF ART CRITICISM

A PHILOSOPHY of art implies a general theory of art criticism. By stating what fine art is, a philosophy of art implies what criticism of art should be about, if it is to be art criticism. Nor are the implications of our philosophy along these lines difficult to see. The distinctive nature of fine art, we have said, is the creation of objects for aesthetic experience. It follows that criticism of art as art, or in its distinctive nature, should be an evaluation of the objects created by art as objects for aesthetic experience.

This general conception of art criticism conceives its major business as judgment or evaluation. But subordinate phases can be distinguished within the critical process. The chief of these are the genetic and the immanent.

The genetic phase of art criticism is a study of the factors that have shaped a work of art. In our chapter on the creative process we described these factors as subjective and objective. The subjective are psychological factors, such as sensitivity, imagination, personality, taste, aims, the value system, and the peculiar experiences of the artist. The objective are environmental factors, such as materials, physical milieu, traditional influences, social needs, and what is usually called the "cultural climate" of the creator. Accordingly, the genetic phase of art criticism would be the delineation of some or all of these factors with a view to an evaluation of the work of an individual creator or a period of art history.

Sometimes such psychological and environmental studies are made in abstraction from the aim of tying them in with a critical estimate of the works of an individual or period. This abstraction

173

may be motivated by modesty, i.e., by a feeling that the task of tracing out the subjective and objective factors that go into the works of an artist or a group of artists is of sufficient magnitude to be an independent project. Or the abstraction may be motivated by a zeal to be "scientific"—i.e., to be descriptive and not normative. In any case the resulting studies are not, strictly speaking, art criticism at all. They are biography or history. Only when these studies are tied in with some attempt to evaluate the aesthetic stature of the work of an individual or period do they move beyond biography and history into the province distinctive of art criticism.

The second, or immanent, phase of art criticism is a study of the major features within the work of art itself. We have described these features as four: materials, form, expression, and function. The immanent phase is, first of all, an effort at clarification and elucidation of these dimensions of the public object by description of some or all of their terminal or instrumental properties. In contrast to the genetic phase, the aim here is not so much to describe what has shaped a work—the background—as what is actually in the work—the foreground. The aim is sympathetic penetration and vivid adumbration of the actual intrinsic perceptual properties of the public object with a view to making an adequate critical judgment of the work under consideration. Some works are internally less intelligible than others; and often, when we come to learn what is actually in them, our critical opinions change radically. This is the great service to criticism of the immanent phase, providing, with the genetic, the documentary bases of the judgmental activity.

Sometimes, like the genetic phase, the immanent also is conducted in abstraction from evaluation. A book on opera tells us the stories of the operas. An article on a painter tells us the subjects of his paintings and the "manners" that he has employed in them. Such descriptions are not, strictly speaking, criticism at all but mere reporting. Only when they are tied in with, and are used to aid, an attempt to evaluate the work of an artist or of a group of artists are they more than reporting and properly a part of art criticism.

In a sense the judgmental activity of art criticism itself might be considered a phase—the third phase—of the critical process. In this sense the judgmental activity would be considered as the culmination and completion of the genetic and immanent phases. To know the genetic factors of a work of art or its immanent features, with a view to estimating their worth, is not yet to estimate this worth explicitly. An additional element is needed, viz., the application of a set of general standards. The genetic and immanent phases prepare the way for the judgmental. They characterize the background and foreground of a work in such a way that an informed estimate is possible and standards can be applied. But the standards must be applied and an estimate delivered. The judgmental phase of art criticism at its best is simply the systematic application of a set of relevant general standards to a work of art that is known genetically and immanently. The standards used, it should be emphasized, must be appropriate or relevant. They must enshrine value possibilities that works of art can actualize to some extent, since it is plainly futile to ask a work of art to do something impossible for it to do. But these standards are not genetic or immanent actualities. They are ideals, and the judgmental phase of art criticism is the explicit evaluation of the actualities of a work of art in the light of a canon or an appropriate set of relevant value possibilities or ideals.

Art criticism, then, might be described as embracing a genetic and immanent phase, but as aiming at an explicit appraisal of works of art for aesthetic perception, according to a canon or a set of relevant standards. The genetic and immanent phases of art criticism are subordinate and auxiliary to the judgmental phase, which is the essence of the process. In this sense art criticism is simply the fullest possible appraisal of works of art as aesthetic objects according to a set of appropriate standards. This, it is understood, is criticism of art-in-its-distinctive-nature, or art criticism as such, not criticism of art-in-its-total-nature or in all its ramifications and connections beyond the process of aesthetic perception.

II. PROPOSED CANON OF JUDGMENT

Since the essence of criticism is the evaluation of works of art as aesthetic objects according to an appropriate set of standards, the basic problem for a philosophical analysis of art criticism is to determine what the appropriate standards for art criticism are. What are the value possibilities that can be demanded of works of art because they are works of art? What is the total set of aesthetic values capable of realization by artistic creations?

In the four preceding chapters one of the main aims was to describe just such a set of value possibilities. We may summarize the results as follows: Each dimension of a work of art is capable of possessing terminal values, and, in relation to each of the other dimensions, it is capable of possessing instrumental values. Each dimension can itself be a focus of intrinsic perceptual interest, and each can be a means of implementing for intrinsic perception the quality of the other three dimensions. Accordingly, a work of art ideally is capable, at a minimum, of four terminal values and twelve instrumental values or of sixteen different aesthetic values, and any work of art is capable of being judged in at least sixteen different respects aesthetically.

Stated in this way, our proposed canon of art criticism may seem too complex and unwieldy for practical use or theoretical discussion. But the canon can be stated more simply. Primarily, the canon asks two major questions of a work of art: first, do the dimensions of the work of art, its materials, form, expression, and function, constitute intrinsically satisfying aesthetic foci? And, second, do these dimensions work together, augment and implement one another, co-operate to reveal and to reinforce the nature of one another? Do they harmonize, or are they discordant? These are the two leading questions for any comprehensive evaluation of a work of art, according to our theory.

Stated in this generalized way, these two questions involve certain subquestions integral to the judgmental process: e.g., the first question involves the subquestion as to what in particular might make the dimensions of works of art intrinsically satisfying aesthetic foci. Such subquestions will receive attention later,

as occasion permits. But the two leading questions, as such, outline the scope and the main demands of a comprehensive evaluation of a work of art as art; and the aim of art criticism is simply
to formulate the most precise possible answers to these questions,
according to our theory.

III. OBSTACLES TO THE APPLICATION OF THE PROPOSED CANON

Even when the proper questions of art criticism are understood,
there are certain obvious obstacles to formulating precise answers to them. At least three conditions must be fulfilled.

First, the critic must be able to encompass a work of art adequately, discerning all its major aspects and the relations between
these aspects. This is a very difficult feat. A distinguished critic
says regarding the form of a novel: "To grasp the shadowy and
fantasmal form of a book, to hold it fast, to turn it over and survey it at leisure—that is the effort of a critic of books, and it is
perpetually defeated. Nothing, no power, will keep a book
steady and motionless before us, so that we may have time to
examine its shape and design. As quickly as we read, it melts and
shifts in the memory. . . . . A cluster of impressions, some clear
points emerging from a mist of uncertainty, that is all we can
hope to possess, generally speaking, in the name of a book."[1]
Nor is the form of the works of the so-called "static" arts always
easy of apprehension or retention. Usually, this form is composed
of a dense variety of elements, e.g., in a painting, of color, line,
shape, mass, light, dark, texture; and, as a rule, the patterns of
these elements can be grasped only by lengthy sequential perception. In the case of larger works, such as great buildings, the
apprehension of form may take much more time and much more
memory, with their concomitant uncertainties. And what is
true of artistic form is often true of the other dimensions of the
public object, which are frequently complex, and of the relations
of form to these dimensions and of these dimensions to form and
to one another. Generally speaking, works of art spread before
attention a vast and often elusive array of offerings requiring

[1] Percy Lubbock, *The Craft of Fiction* (London: Jonathan Cape, Ltd., 1921), p. 1.

time, effort, patience, experience, knowledge, and capacity of a high order before one can even begin to encompass them adequately.

This objective complexity not only makes difficult the successful operation of such a canon of judgment as that proposed above but also helps to explain much of the apparent diversity and conflict in criticism. Usually, a few features of a work of art are ample to supply a theme for a critical discourse. And, as there is no important work of an artist without merits, so there is no important artist without defects. To revert to the novelists: "Fielding lacked at least one-half of all the 'finer feelings'; the structure of Goldsmith's one novel would shame a kindergarten; Jane Austen regarded the failure to possess an inherited income as placing a man outside the pale of humanity; Dickens had the sentimentality of a nursemaid; Theodore Dreiser cannot write the English language."[2] Accordingly, two able critics may give the most divergent judgments on the work of an artist without actually being inaccurate, irrelevant, unintelligible, or even biased beyond excusable limits. One critic may write at great length on the lively characterizations or skilful designs in the novels of Jane Austen. Another may write at equal length on the deficiencies of this novelist's social perspectives. Thanks to the complexity of works of art, each critic may be right and his criticism sound, although the critics may seem both to themselves and to others to be disagreeing about the artist completely.

Besides the objective complexity, there is a subjective complexity—the nature of the critic. This nature can also make the successful operation of the proposed canon difficult, since for its successful use the canon requires that a critic attain a very clear and comprehensive grasp of a work. Temporary conditions may interfere with this: inattention, ill-health, distractions, and pressures of various types. Equally interfering may be irrational sympathies or antipathies for the race, creed, nationality, or personality of the artist or biases induced by nonaesthetic factors, such as the commercial success, popularity, or partisan backing

[2] J. W. Krutch, "The Half-truth of the Whole Truth," *Nation*, CXLIV (January 2, 1937), 21.

of a work. Below such obvious impediments are deeper obstacles—defects of sensitivity, feeling, imagination, knowledge, education, intellectual penetration, germane experience. Freedom from these defects is needed in a high degree if the proposed canon is to be applied properly. With a simple canon the necessary equipment of a critic may be simple, sometimes no more than willingness to open his mouth in public. But with a highly complex canon applied to a highly complex object, method and diligence must be combined in the critic with an equally complex power to see clearly and fully, before he is in a position to operate with the canon at all adequately.

Incidentally, much of the conflict, confusion, and divergence in art criticism can probably be traced more directly to this second obstacle than to the first. Particularly is this true of criticism of new works of art. Often critics do not know enough, have not sensitivity or imagination enough, or are not sufficiently free from powerful preconceptions and preferences simply to see new works in their actual nature, as a study of the critical pronouncements made upon the works of innumerable great artists when they first appeared eloquently reveals. Nor is this true merely of new works. Even in the criticism of the "classics," critics often reveal surprising deficiencies in orientation or imaginative grasp, or they ride favorite hobbyhorses at a fast clip. All this makes for conflict and diversity in criticism, as well as for poor criticism. The requirements for a good critic, especially in subjective equipment, are of a very high order, as will become increasingly clear as our discussion proceeds. And, as long as these requirements are not fulfilled in a reasonable degree, criticism will not only fail in its proper aims but be mired in interminable conflict.

A third obstacle to the successful application of the proposed canon is the language with which art criticism traditionally operates. By and large, it is a language of concealed comparatives. For example, a critic may describe the posturings in an opera as "exaggerated." What he means is that, in comparison with some implied standard—say, attitudes prevalent in twentieth-century Western life—the posturings are exaggerated. But in comparison with some other standard—say, attitudes prevalent in the eighteenth-century court life depicted in the opera—the posturings may be "realistic." In general, the language of ordinary criticism, both descriptive and evaluative, moves against a background of standards that the critic often leaves so shadowy that his language conveys no more than an emotion of approval or disapproval. The cure, of course, is constant overt comparison and constant specification, as far as this is possible, of the sense in which a term is applied. "A perfectly honest review of a very ordinary novel in the critic's own opinion, may make use of adjectives that are equally applicable to novels that the critic himself would rank enormously higher in the very aspects indicated. Constant overt comparison is required to other works of the same author or of other authors to indicate any precise meaning for the terms applied. It is this inadequacy of language to the needs of criticism that makes valuable criticism one of the more difficult literary arts. . . . . The critic's standards . . . . will function to communicate the character of specific works of art to others, only if these others have the same basis to relate them to, unless the critic by various means indicates with some precision his own peculiar qualitative scale, the indifference points at which the degrees of any quality attributed by him positively begin to apply. Except in the very few cases where our adjectives—like those for color and pitch—are systematized pretty fully, the available descriptive terms are so extremely indeterminate that their application alone would hardly differentiate in degrees at all, without explicit comparison. Criticism, as we have it, is too vague in its terminology to be taken very seriously as more than roughly descriptive on the one hand, and on the other as expressive of the critic's personal feelings, and this only to the degree in which his literary powers are adequately creative."[3]

IV. POSSIBILITIES OF UNIVERSAL AGREEMENT

The common assumption regarding art criticism is that its aim is to produce statements about the aesthetic merits and demerits of works of art that are valid without exception for all informed

[3] D. W. Prall, *Aesthetic Analysis* (New York: Thomas Y. Crowell Co., 1936), pp. 201–2.

and intelligent people. Everyone is quick to observe that in practice art critics never come very close to doing this. But the explanation is usually that art critics are jealous or biased or overopinionated or constitutionally quarrelsome or in some other way limited people. The belief that there is only one right verdict about a work of art and that the art critic should deliver it is usually not questioned fundamentally or seriously.

In a moment we shall question this belief, but, in the meantime, let us suppose it to be valid. And let us ask: If the three obstacles mentioned above were overcome—if the objective complexity of the work of art were surmounted, the complex subjective equipment necessary for a critic to see clearly as well as comprehensively were provided, and the impediments of the language of criticism were eliminated—and our proposed canon of criticism were permitted to operate without obstacle, would the result be statements about the aesthetic merits and demerits of works of art valid without exception for all informed and intelligent people? What are the possibilities of universal agreement? Since our canon has two parts, one concerned with terminal values and one with instrumental values, let us answer this question by considering these types of value, beginning with the terminal.

Suppose two persons are judging the terminal worth of the materials of a work of art, say, the colors of a painting. One person approves their intrinsic perceptual qualities, describing the colors as robust and powerful. The second person disapproves of the qualities, describing the colors as harsh and garish. Theoretically, both persons have applied the same general standard —terminal aesthetic adequacy of materials. But the result is two diverse and conflicting judgments. The judgmental phase, however, need not end here. Let us suppose that the first person is relatively inexperienced regarding colors and works of art, the second relatively experienced. By further clarification of the nature of colors through comparisons and elucidations and by increased experience of works of art, the first person may come to agree with the more experienced person. He may agree, now that he has seen, for example, the color realizations in the greatest paintings, that the colors of the painting mentioned above are comparatively harsh and garish—the judgment of the second person. In this sense nothing is more profitable than disputes about tastes and nothing diminishes the differences between the critical judgments of persons intelligently concerned with the arts than a common understanding and experience and an education of sensitivity that can be fostered in the process of resolving disputes about tastes.

Nevertheless, disputes about terminal values may end not in complete agreement, as here, but in complete disagreement. Even with critics whose education, sensitivity, resources of language, and insight are very superior and roughly equal, this may be the case. Human beings are constructed differently as well as similarly, and there is a temperamental individuality in them that seems at present incapable of eradication. Some people are dominantly phlegmatic, some dominantly volatile; some are dominantly intense and quick, some dominantly slow and mild. And these bents of human nature, as well as the sheer power and resources to see and hear, will obviously affect terminal evaluations. Suppose that the two persons mentioned above had been of opposite temperaments, for example, hearty and fragile, and the painting in question a very brilliantly colored modern Mexican work. It is possible that, after the fullest examination of the color realizations of the greatest paintings, the first person might still hold that the colors of the painting are robust and powerful, while the second continued to hold that they are harsh and garish or to hold that they are robust and powerful and to be sickened by such robustness and power.

And what is true about the terminal values of materials may also be true about the terminal values of form, expression, and function. To one temperament the form of a work may be too sprawling and heavy, to another the same form may be of accommodating ease and grandeur. To one temperament the expressiveness of a work of art may be deep and profound, to another it may be too mystical or turgid. To one temperament a work of art may be a magnificent memorial, to another it may be overpretentious. Such disagreements in critical judgments seem

ultimate, assuming them to arise not from education, environment, capacity for discernment, or similar factors but from the
natural temperament that these factors release as well as modify.
On this basis, if on no other, some ultimate diversity of critical
judgments regarding terminal values of works of art seems theoretically inescapable in the application of our proposed sixteen-
value canon, even when the three obstacles described above have
been removed from the path of the critic.[4]

Besides the four terminal values, there are the twelve instrumental values. Do these entail an equally irreducible diversity of
critical judgments? Is universal agreement possible here? I think
that universal agreement is always theoretically possible here,
for such judgments are not, in the strictest sense, matters of temperament at all. They have to do simply with interdimensional
adequacy within the work of art. To be sure, art criticism here
lacks mathematical precision. It cannot demonstrate in Euclid-
ean fashion that the colors of a painting, for example, are appropriate to the expressiveness, that they fit and reinforce the expressiveness. Yet it can exclude from such judgments temperamental affinities either for the colors or for the expressiveness. A
person may not be charmed either by the reds or by the melodrama of a Delacroix. Yet he may be capable of agreeing with
another who is charmed by both that the reds are judicious and
effective in implementing and reinforcing the melodrama. The
chief basis for judging interdimensional competence as such is
not temperament but sensitivity to an artist's instrumental
achievement and knowledge of what other artists in the same
field have achieved. To be sure, two critics chosen at random
may disagree in their interdimensional evaluations of a given
work of art. But if both have sufficient sensitivity to discern accurately what is there and if both have wide and roughly equal
knowledge of interdimensional achievements in the art in question, the disagreement is likely to be small, and even to vanish.

[4] Of course, if biochemistry should ever be able in the future to produce human beings so
that all were in all psychophysical respects absolutely alike, this position would become
untenable. But, at present, this prospect seems improbable, not to mention slightly mon-
strous.

In this sense disagreements about interdimensional competence seem even more capable of resolution by discussion than do disagreements about terminal values. Mathematically precise agreement, as I have said, is not possible. Art criticism by its language is limited to rough comparatives which are capable only of very crude and approximate mathematical correlates. But, given wide knowledge in an art and equal sensitivity to and experience of interdimensional achievement, given more generally the removal of the three obstacles mentioned above, very great agreement on instrumental values seems possible, and ultimate agreement is not an irrelevant ideal.

In view of this, it may be thought that the only worth-while art criticism is interdimensional or "technical" criticism. This conclusion is correct under two conditions: first, that the proper aim of art criticism is merely to make statements capable of winning universal agreement and, second, that interdimensional criticism exhausts the possibilities of making such statements in art criticism.

As to the second point, it is important to observe that terminal criticism by no means produces only conflict and diversity and that it harbors possibilities of much judgmental agreement. Temperaments differ, and, at some point in a wide and searching criticism of works of art, two critics of diverse temperaments will disagree. But temperaments have neutral zones. There are areas of value into which the mild and intense, the phlegmatic and volatile, enter without sharp conflict. Moreover, there is much more in the termini of works of art than temperamental appeals. A good artistic form, for example, as we have seen, synchronizes with the basic biophysical and attention structure of the human being and with the basic pattern of human aspiration and remembrance. It has a larger than temperamental appeal. Having different individual qualities, a specific good form by Giotto, it is true, may appeal more to a given temperament than a specific good form by Rubens, or vice-versa. But, because each form is finely constructed simply as form, it may make a definite appeal to the most diversely tempered critics and bring a deep terminal satisfaction to all. If, because of temperament, a critic

who has felt the power of both still rates one form slightly higher than the other, his differences with a second critic on this
score may be almost completely neutralized by the deeply universal appeal of both forms.

Something of this sort is also true about the other dimensions.
The dimension of expression, for instance, frequently contains a
vision of some phase of human life and experience that reflects
the artist's value inclinations and realizations and personality
operating on a certain "subject." In creations of the greatest
artists, this vision may reveal very forcefully certain basic qualities of human feeling, character, and conduct—qualities that,
for all their sketchiness and incompleteness and temperamental
colorings, may yet convey stimulating insights into the actualities and possibilities of human life and the conditions of human
good. Owing to temperament, different critics may differ in the
exact degree of worth that they accord the insight of a Sopho-
cles or a Shakespeare, a Mozart or a Beethoven. But certain
works of these artists may seem to disclose so clearly the logic
of certain human actions or the nature of certain human feelings that the differences of critics due to temperament may be
minor and incidental notes in a largely unanimous approval.

In general, works of art at their best give us in their termini a
refined and clarified perceptual "vision" or revelation of material properties and aesthetic and nonaesthetic functions, as well
as of the existential structure of our world and the characteristics
of action, things, and human beings. And this vision or revelation can be measured by its comparative perceptual refinement
and clarity, i.e., by the comparative incisiveness, inclusiveness,
and coherence for perception that the peculiar terminal realizations of the artist possess. Here, incidentally, is a set of criteria
for the judgment of the termini of art, a set of substandards under
the more inclusive standard of terminal adequacy, which answers the subquestion mentioned at the end of Section II of this
chapter as to what in particular might make the dimensions of
works of art intrinsically satisfying aesthetic foci. These substandards cannot be wholly freed from temperamental entangle-
ments, since they involve measuring the degree of refinement and

clarification of the *personal* realizations of artists which naturally will be rated differently by different temperaments. But such differences can become quite minor features in the judgment of termini in terms of their comparative depth, width, and consistency for perception and can lead to judgments that are, on the whole, free from radical disagreements arising from merely temperamental preferences.[5]

Thus, given a reasonable neutralization of the three obstacles mentioned above; given, in particular, critics who have the knowledge and the receptor competence, the breadth of view and the verbal skill, to overcome the main objective and subjective complexities and the more elementary linguistic difficulties confronting criticism, much agreement regarding the terminal values of works of art is also ideally possible. It seems right, therefore, to conclude that art criticism should not exclude terminal criticism and be confined solely to interdimensional criticism, even assuming that the proper aim of art criticism is to make value statements about works of art capable of winning universal agreement.

V. THE AIM OF ART CRITICISM

But are value statements commanding universal agreement the proper aim of art criticism? I wish to suggest a different view which retains what is possible in this commonly assumed belief but does not involve the frustration of criticism by temperament in the region of terminal values that this belief does when taken as stating the proper aim of art criticism.

This new view conceives the business of art criticism as that of pointing out, with what clarity the language of criticism permits, the stature of a work of art in the eyes of the critic in such a way that others can find out better what in an adequate perception its stature would be for them. The business of criticism is not to formulate value statements, all universally true as they stand, but to make value statements that, if not universally true,

---

[5] Cf. S. C. Pepper, *Aesthetic Quality* (New York: Charles Scribner's Sons, 1937, 1938), chap. ix, and *The Basis of Criticism in the Arts* (Cambridge, Mass.: Harvard University Press, 1945), and Bertram Morris, *The Aesthetic Process* (Evanston: Northwestern University Press, 1943), pp. 180–81, on the substandards mentioned in this paragraph.

are translatable into the personal value language and understanding of others.

In this conception of art criticism the universal interdimensional and terminal value statements possible to criticism retain their position intact. But the status of temperament is different. The set of deep-seated and peculiar value attitudes constituting a critic's temperament becomes an instrument of suggestion instead of an instrument of decision regarding terminal values. Its business is not to determine the terminal values of works of art for others but to be a medium for the projection of judgments that will help others better to determine what these values are for themselves. Thus, under this conception not only can the universal truths that criticism can reach be preserved, but the universal service of criticism, curtailed under the other aim by temperament, can be extended. Nothing a critic says need be wasted private talk, provided he sets it off so that others can translate his peculiar terminal enunciations into their own private perspectives. On this view the good critic is not only the judicious critic, able to discern the universal values of works of art, but also the suggestive critic, able by his projections to lead us to find the peculiar and unique terminal values that exist for us in works of art. He contributes to an articulation of our own individual experience of art, as well as to an articulation of the common thread that can run through all experience of art by his peculiarly suggestive judgments of the public object.

This view of the aim of the art critic and art criticism is recommended by a number of circumstances. The first has already been mentioned. The view enables criticism to retain what is possible in the commonly assumed aim and to circumvent the frustrations of criticism entailed by this aim in the region of terminal values. A second circumstance is probably even more important. This is the belief that the individual values of works of art—the temperamental colorings, the purely personal slant of artists—are as basic and precious in certain respects as the universal values and that, since such values will be judged somewhat differently by different temperaments according to whether the artist and judging percipient are temperamentally akin or not, criticism should not try to do more here than facilitate the judgments of diverse percipients. To deny the temperamental colorings in works of art is not possible. To deny their authentic value to percipients temperamentally harmonious with the temperament of the artist would be callow. Under such circumstances the best plan for criticism would seem to be to illumine these temperamental colorings in such a way that their value to diverse percipients is immediately clear or can be discovered and known with greater clarity. And this should be the aim of art criticism according to the view we have been stating.

Two other arguments also favor the view here set forth. First, art criticism is not open to many of the usual criticisms made of it, for example, that it is exhibitionism, that it is setting up one's self as a world norm, that it is an effort to inflict a critic's predilections on others, all of which statements are to some extent true so long as it is assumed that the aim of criticism in all areas is the enunciation of judgments universally binding as they stand. Second, art criticism can be of very great and genuine usefulness to appreciation, creation, and other activities. This last point is so important for understanding both our general position and certain views expressed in later chapters that it deserves extensive attention.

VI. SOME USES OF ART CRITICISM

With the aim just described, the canon previously outlined, and a reasonable freedom from the three impediments already mentioned, art criticism, I believe, can, first of all, be of very great assistance to appreciation. By means of the standards of interdimensional competence and of universal terminal achievement, it can separate a vast quantity of inferior works from those more rich in universal values. So many so-called "works of art," from current escapist confections to the more sentimental and bombastic of traditional creations, possess merely a few piquant terminal features, usually in the dimension of expression. In interdimensional competence or solid workmanship they are usually weak, and in depth, width, and coherence of terminal achievement they are invariably deficient. Such works often provide agreeable illusions and pastime to persons who wear sufficiently heavy aesthetic blinkers. But just for that reason they can help to clog the paths of appreciation. In particular, they can overpower the popular mind and rear a high wall between the mass of men and man's superior artistic achievement. Good criticism can do an inestimable service here by ceaselessly reducing the size of this wall and by keeping alive in as many people as possible the sense of the superior.[6]

As to superior works of art, besides evaluating their interdimensional excellences, art criticism in the sense and spirit above suggested may have two other uses for appreciation. To persons who have not experienced the works in question, the terminal evaluations of such criticism may provide useful starting-points. The danger here is that the evaluations of the critic may become prepossessions, inhibiting the free personal reactions of the appreciator. But this danger can be avoided if these evaluations are taken as hypotheses, not as dogma—as value apprehensions to be tested and to be accepted only in terms of one's own vivid experience. To persons who have experienced the works in question, criticism in the present sense may be useful in a different way. It may bring out interdimensional, as well as terminal, values which were missed in prior experience. It may also help to make more explicit any judgments previously formed or, by the challenge of its analyses, stimulate the appreciator to re-experience the works and check and retest his perceptions in the light of the critic's experiences. Finally, criticism of superior works can be useful in suggesting general methods of appreciating works of art of all types, as when a stimulating critical analysis of a series of fine paintings suggests a general method of critical appreciation of all types of paintings—indeed, even of all types of works of art.[7]

[6] A simple example, and there are literally thousands, would be Margaret Marshall's critical review of John Steinbeck's *Cannery Row* (*Nation*, CLX [January, 1945], 75–76). The example is simple because the critic deals only with expressive features of the novel, but it is very effective in distinguishing for the reading audience a bit of chaff from the wheat of literature.

[7] A. C. Barnes, *The Art in Painting* (New York: Harcourt, Brace & Co., 1925, 1928, 1937), and Thomas Munro, *Great Pictures of Europe* (New York: Coward-McCann, Inc., 1930), contain critical analyses of this type.

Art criticism in the sense intended in this discussion can also be of considerable use to creation. Although creative activity in the arts is based on a number of unconscious factors, it is rarely, if at all, a merely automatic process. It also employs reflective guidance, and often artists can improve here immensely. An artist may choose subjects not well suited to his talents or be unaware of certain possibilities of his peculiar idiom. He may become careless and imperceptibly relax his standards or be puzzled by the general direction of his growth. By analyses of specific works, the good critic can illumine all these things, as well as encourage all the fine things. The labor of the creative artist is one long ceaseless process of self-discovery in his art, and the keen and able critic who also appreciates the nature and hardship of creation can assist and accelerate this process in many ways.

It is probably true that the majority of artists, particularly recent artists schooled in the romantic tradition, furiously resent critics, feeling that critics generally are envious, incompetent, and parasitic people who see art from the outside only. Critics are people incapable of understanding or coming to close grips with the problems of creation. Otherwise, they would not be critics, but artists themselves. This view ignores the fact that many of the best critics are and have been creative artists. But the view is certainly correct to this extent, that, artists or nonartists, good critics are very rare. The great scarcity of good critics, however, should not blind one to the considerable usefulness to creation that good criticism can have when it does occur. The chief business of good criticism is reflective, analytic object judgment, such as the artist himself must perform to some extent on his works if he is to profit markedly from his own creative experience. Moreover, the good critic usually possesses to a far greater extent than the majority of artists those powers of abstraction, comparison, and generalization that make possible superior reflective object judgment. If critics too frequently have used these powers ignorantly or offensively, the good critic can use them constructively and as a respectful mentor of the artist. Indeed, criticism has frequently championed artists vigorously and intelligently against immense obstinate and ignorant opposition, as the *Neue Zeitschrift für Musik* championed Schubert, Chopin, and Weber; Griepenkerl, Berlioz; Ruskin, Turner; or Gustave Jeffrey, Cézanne.

Good criticism can also contribute to creation in general, as well as in specific, ways. If artists refuse to learn from critical analyses of their own works, they frequently do learn from sage and penetrating analyses of the works of other artists, particularly the works of rival artists or of the greater artists of the past. By seeing wherein others have succeeded or failed, artists may renew in their own mind the aims of their undertakings and augment these aims by lessons drawn from the present and the past. Furthermore, good criticism can disseminate a body of ideas and foster an atmosphere favorable to the best creative work. By provocative and trenchant analyses of artistic problems and achievements, not only can good criticism influence artists directly or indirectly, but it can help to develop a wider and more discriminating audience for the arts, which demands and relishes the best that artists can create[8] and rejects the counterfeit works of spurious talents.

Finally, art criticism in the above sense can be of considerable use as a source of knowledge. This is particularly apparent when one remembers that the full range of art criticism in this sense would include the genetic and immanent phases. These phases clearly can contribute richly to our knowledge of the origins and properties of works of art, while the judgmental phase, although its sole aim is not the enunciation of propositions universally valid, can nevertheless formulate estimates of the interdimensional and certain dimensional values of works of art which have general validity. That the total body of propositions thus resulting sums up to a science, the science of criticism, as some might claim, is largely a matter of terminology. If a narrow meaning of science is preferred, e.g., a science is a body of statements based upon controlled experiment and capable of formulation in mathe-

---

[8] Cf. *Paul Cézanne, letters*, Eng. trans. by Marguerite Kay, ed. John Rewald (London: Bruno Cassirer, 1941), p. 248, on the value to the creative artist of a public of intelligent amateurs.

matical terms, this knowledge is clearly not a science. If a broader meaning of science is allowed, e.g., a science is a body of statements based on experience and capable of verification by competent observers, this knowledge at its best is a science. At its best it is based on analytic aesthetic experience and is verifiable by all persons competent to undertake criticism in the present sense of the term.

Art criticism can contribute to philosophy as well as be a science in the broader sense just mentioned. I have said that a philosophy of art implies a theory of art criticism. It is equally true that criticism of art implies a philosophy. All criticism proceeds in terms of certain broad assumptions about the nature and purport of fine art which constitute what the critic believes the arts should offer human beings. These assumptions underlie and control the critic's approach to works of art and generate the expectations governing his diverse particular procedures. Without such a philosophical substratum, indeed, art criticism would be helpless. It would lack intelligible direction or goal. It would be unaware of what art or works of art are and so of what criticism should seek to estimate in regard to them.

Critics, it is true, rarely state explicitly their general assumptions about art and are often unconscious of them. Nevertheless, as necessary to criticism, these assumptions can be found in their writings, and the philosopher can often learn much from detecting and formulating them. In a sense the business of the art critic and the philosopher of art is the same, the reflective analysis of fine art, and the philosopher should be something of a critic and the critic something of a philosopher. The difference between the two is that the critic is primarily concerned with the analysis of particular works of art, artists, schools, and periods, while the philosopher is primarily concerned with the general nature and importance of art. But, just as the philosopher's concern with the general involves some consideration of the particular, so the critic's concern with the particular involves at least some vague conceptions of the general. These general conceptions can be analytically separated from the particular and often contain general insights into art that the philosopher might never have reached except for the critic, since the philosopher does not have the detailed concern with the particular that first called forth these insights as premises or framing assumptions of the analyses of the critic.

VII. A HISTORICAL RETROSPECT

It may help to set our theory of art criticism in a proper light to take a brief glance at certain historical positions. Art criticism, we have said, has three phases—a genetic, an immanent, and a judgmental phase—and invariably, we might add, it involves all three phases to some extent as parts of one complex total activity.

During a given historical period, however, one phase or more tends to be dominant, and during the early "modern" era—the era of classicism, embracing the seventeenth century and the largest part of the eighteenth —the judgmental phase was dominant. Fine art, the classicist believed, should conform to certain fixed canons and universal laws, and the chief business of art criticism is to measure particular works of art by their conformity to these canons and laws. The classicist identified art with fine workmanship, and to this extent, of course, he was right. But he identified fine workmanship mainly with the achievement of a certain limited type of pattern or form. In consequence, when he propounded his canons and laws, they turned out to be such criteria as the three unities of the drama, the "classical" rules of musical harmony, the Greek orders à la Palladio, the revived canon of Polyclitus, the golden section, the serpentine line; and at once works of art were found or produced that ignored or broke these criteria and yet were marvelously effective aesthetic objects.

In this early modern era, opposition to the prevailing classicist creed was to be found in the writers belonging to the so-called "School of Taste"[9] and in Hutcheson, Hume, and Kant, all of whom denied that beauty was conformity to rational concepts and that artistic excellence was mere consistency with authorita-

[9] Cf. Joel E. Spingarn, *Critical Essays of the Seventeenth Century* (Oxford: Clarendon Press, 1908), I, lxxxviii–cvi; see also my article, "Taste and Its Education," in *Encyclopedia of the Arts* (New York: Philosophical Library, 1946), pp. 996 ff.

tive rules and laws. Art, Kant held, was founded on genius not on rules, beauty was a matter of "taste." And from these beginnings, which were especially vigorous in the late eighteenth century, the modern romantic conception of art sprang to full flower, and the juridical emphasis in criticism associated with classicism ceased to be the dominant factor in all except academic and ultra-conservative critical circles.

During the next one hundred and fifty years, the heyday of modern romanticism, the immanent and genetic phases of criticism received most emphasis. Romanticism itself directly favored an immanent type of criticism. The artist as genius was viewed by the romantic as the maker of the law, a free creative titan. To hold up rules for his guidance or to measure him à la Beckmesser was sheer pedantry and arrogance. The first business of the critic should be to follow sympathetically in the footsteps of genius and feel in his own soul the manifold nuances of the experience portrayed by the artist. Criticism should be a record of personal adventures among masterpieces, and the ultimate aim of the critic should be to create a work of art from works of art; to give an intimate and expressive interpretation of the immanent features of the creations of genius; and to be a keen, suggestive, imaginative, and finished writer in the manner of Walter Pater and George Moore.

Romanticism, however, was by no means the only cultural force affecting criticism in the late eighteenth, nineteenth, and early twentieth centuries. There was the enormous expansion of science, especially the extension of exact science to living and growing things, as in biology, under the unifying concept of evolution. This development stimulated the use of the genetic or historical method in every field, and the critical study of the arts was no exception. One of the first results in art criticism was to produce well-documented and increasingly accurate scholarly records of the outer facts about artists and works of art, an enormous historical erudition.[10] In addition, there were the attempts,

---

[10] Germany was the center of this new industry, of which American academic studies in literature by the professoriat and graduate scholars of the universities constitute one of numerous later by-products.

by Taine and the Marxists among others, to explain these facts by various genetic or historical principles. With the growth of psychology and the appearance of psychoanalysis, the genetic emphasis was extended by a more inward approach to art and artists. The result was the numerous case histories and psychoanalytic biographical studies that are the commonplaces of recent criticism.

There is no doubt that the very best criticism of these hundred and fifty years has had very great merits. The genetic approach has immensely increased the exactness of our knowledge of the sources and historical conditions of works of art and has immensely broadened our conception of the motivation of artists. If, sometimes, the outer facts turned up have seemed trivial and the inner divinations far-fetched, this approach has nevertheless yielded considerable subtle commentary and illuminating exegesis to our understanding of the backgrounds of art. The immanent approach at its best has had equal merits. It has resulted in numerous excellent expositions and elucidations of the aesthetic values of specific works of art and has stressed the importance of basing criticism on firsthand personal experience. It has also set a high standard of literary excellence for criticism and has kept alive, in the face of the scientific avalanche, the similarities of criticism to art.

Nevertheless, both these modern developments have had a serious defect. They have failed to provide an adequate canon of judgment to replace the discredited criteria of the classicist. The chief canon of many leading romanticists, for example, was personal feeling. A critical judgment is describing one's personal feelings, one's pleasure in, or repugnance for, the public object. A critical judgment is simply a statement of an honest prejudice and rests upon nothing more solid or objective than the spontaneous sentiments that occur to one in the contemplation of the object.[11] The difficulty with this canon is that personal feelings about objects are conditioned by one's sensitivity and imagination, one's interest and knowledge. And, no matter how exuber-

---

[11] Cf. Anatole France, *La Vie Littéraire* (Paris: Calmann-Lévy, 1889–92). Preface; see also H. L. Mencken, *Prejudices* (New York: A. A. Knopf, 1919–27).

antly or gracefully one may state these feelings, criticism will be blind, tangential, irrelevant, or erroneous if one is deficient in sensitivity, imagination, interest, or knowledge. Much more than strong feeling is needed as a basis for a judicious estimate of the values in a work of art, and this "more" is a knowledge of the value possibilities which it is proper to require of a work of art and an awareness of a work's intrinsic aspects and of the actual stature of these aspects in relation to the value possibilities.

The geneticist often tried to dodge the whole problem of standards. He made no judgments, he said; he described facts. He merely showed the soil from which certain works of art sprang. And, of course, this was his chief contribution and his main task. But his work usually employed or involved standards of judgment. Otherwise, it would have ceased to be art criticism, as so much latter-day scholarship derived from the genetic outlook has. Moreover, geneticists whose orientation to art was through history, psychology, or genetic philosophy rather than through natural science, often stated these standards explicitly. The most characteristic of these standards were two: the intention of the artist and the standards and needs of the time of the artist. A work of art is good if it fulfils the intention of the artist, the motives of the individual behind it. And a work of art is good if it fulfils the standards and needs of its time or of the society from which it springs. Neither of these criteria is very impressive.

In judging works of art in terms of the intention of the artist, the geneticist was, of course, accepting the romanticist's general premise, which elevates the creative artist above any "objective" rules. This league with romanticism, however, did not greatly strengthen the geneticist's hand. Indeed, the criterion of intention is inherently defective on many counts. The intentions of artists are often difficult to determine and, once determined, are often multiple—e.g., the artist was aiming to make money, to amuse himself, to pay off in satire a long-standing grudge, to add to the list of his works. The criterion of intention leaves us in some cases with no basis for judgment and in other cases with too many bases, unless we limit it in these cases to the specific aesthetic intention that the artist obviously had in fashioning the particular work. Even with this limitation and supposing that the aesthetic intention of artists is always knowable, difficulties arise. Many works of art have undertones and overtones not contained in the specific aesthetic intention that the artist obviously had in fashioning a given work, and sometimes these undertones and overtones are much more interesting than what the artist actually intended. Should these be excluded from an estimate of what the work is for critical judgment? The criterion of intention, strictly interpreted, implies that they should, since these undertones and overtones are not part of the intention or of the fulfilment of the intention of the artist. But in that case criticism would necessarily be an inadequate judgment of what there is in the public object for aesthetic perception. Furthermore, the specific aesthetic intention of an artist may be trivial, e.g., gracefully to say as little as possible as long as possible, and the artist may succeed perfectly in this intention, saying nothing gracefully for a very long time. The criterion of intention would imply that the result is as perfect a work of art as possible, since it completely fulfils the intention behind it. But, obviously, such a work falls far short of what a work of art can be as an aesthetic object.

Similar remarks apply to the second criterion—fulfilment of the standards and needs of the time of the artist. There is the great difficulty of determining what these standards and needs are and, since they are usually multiple, which ones should be chosen as bases of judgment. And, once this is settled, if it can be settled, other difficulties arise. Many works of art that are considered masterpieces today violated prevailing standards of their day and, instead of serving prevailing needs, lay relatively neglected until later epochs. Moreover, a work of art may fulfil prevailing standards and needs perfectly. But, if these standards and needs are superficial and ephemeral, the work will be superficial and ephemeral, although it should be as perfect as a work of art can be and hence the very opposite of superficial and ephemeral, if this second criterion were right. In general, the standards and needs of an era supply only a very limited basis for the judgment of artistic excellence. In some cases they may be important. For example, they may help in judging the social expressiveness of a work, as the intention of the artist may help in judging a work's personal expressiveness. But, as a canon for judging a work completely or perennially, the standards and needs of its era provide a hopelessly provincial criterion, which in many ways is much less useful than either the romantic or the genetic criterion previously criticized.

VIII. SUMMARY AND CONCLUSIONS

Art criticism, then, consists of exegesis, immanent description, and judgment with a view to rendering a documented and suggestive estimate of the aesthetic values of works of art. Its most basic task is judgment or relating the aesthetic properties of a work to a scheme of possible aesthetic values relevant to artistic creations. Exegesis relates the aesthetic properties of a work to the work's causal origin and setting; description relates these properties to the actualities of a work's being. Judgment, however, relates them to the best possible relevant values and is therefore the definitive element in an estimate of the aesthetic excellence of the properties.

Judgment of works of art has two major tasks. The first is to evaluate the interrelation of the dimensions of a work of art, to detect incongruities, inconsistencies, and failures of implementation, to attend to a work to determine whether its dimensions combine with and amplify one another, e.g., whether the form, the function, the expressive spirit, the materials and site of a building, co-operate in a voluminous and harmonious effect. The basic criterion of judgment here is integrity, the union of all aspects of a work of art into an integral ensemble with densely interior relational values. This principle of interdimensional integrity replaces the traditional classical criteria of form in our account.

The second task of judgment is to appraise the terminal features of a work of art. These termini—materials, form, expression, and function—exist outside art, which is merely a particular integrated realization of them within a larger relational setting. How far are these termini, as realized in a work of art, adequate to the aesthetic possibilities of art? How far are they the refined and clarified aesthetic foci that art at its best can provide? Besides dealing with a different question, this second task of judgment differs from the first in another respect. It cannot be performed entirely in abstraction from the temperament of the critic. One can estimate whether a given dimension fits in with and reinforces another, independent of one's temperamental affinity for either dimension. But in any wide and searching estimate of the adequacy of termini as refined and clarified foci of intrinsic perception, temperamental affinities—a preference for one type of refinement or clarification over another—are bound to enter. It is the individual values of works of art—what makes Bach not Ravel and Ravel not Bach—as well as the universal values that make art worth while, and these individual values are bound to tinge one's experience of the termini and elicit different responses from differently tempered individuals and different estimates of the termini.

This circumstance does not bar the way to the discernment and enunciation of terminal values of universal scope. Considerable agreement on the comparative refinement and clarification attained by diverse works of art—the comparative width and depth and coherence of their termini for perception—still remains possible. But it does make untenable the common conception of art criticism as concerned exclusively with the formulation of judgments which are all universally valid as they stand. The view we have urged is that the aim of art criticism in the region of terminal values is to formulate estimates that, if not universally valid as they stand, will lead diverse percipients to a discovery of the exact stature of the terminal values for their own experience. The main function of criticism is to be suggestive, not legislative here. This recognition of temperament as a limitation upon terminal universality takes the place in our theory of the traditional romantic recognition of personal feeling as a vehicle for projection of the evaluations of the critic.

We may say, then, that the judgmental phase of art criticism has two tasks—to measure the *integrity* in perception and to suggest the *richness* for perception of a work of art, communicating

these findings in such a way that the informed and qualified percipient can learn the interdimensional values of the work and is
led to discover more completely the exact terminal values of the
work for his own experience. In brief, the aim of art criticism is
to evaluate a work of art for perception generally, in so far as
this can be done successfully by a given temperament.

In concluding this account of art criticism, I should like to
comment on a conception of it that critics sometimes offer in explanation of its current shortcomings. A great deal of art criticism today is contained in newspaper and magazine reviews,
which for most people are "previews" of works of art. Some critics have complained that properly to fulfil their function of giving a foretaste or preview they would have to reproduce the actual work of art, which is impossible in most cases. The music
critic of a daily newspaper cannot by words which are his medium literally reproduce a concert that he heard today and his
readers may hear tomorrow. To do that he would have to employ means utterly different from those available to him. Hence
his criticism is foredoomed to failure.

This conception of art criticism as literal reproduction of
works of art seems a rather odd interpretation of its nature. Literal reproduction of works of art, in whole or in part, it has
usually been thought, is the business of the manufacturer of
phonograph records, the copyist, the photographer, and the
printer and has only an incidental illustrative role in art criticism. The main business of the art critic who writes for a reader
who has not yet experienced a given work would rather seem to
be to formulate his reactions to the work in terms useful to his
reader. Not to reproduce the work of art, but to reproduce or
give his observations and judgments of it: this would seem to be
the critic's primary business. That this is difficult to do well in
words—that, in general, it is difficult to communicate well any
thought or experience in words—is, of course, not to be denied.
But that the critic should aim primarily to reproduce a work of
art itself, instead of to communicate his understanding and judgment of it, seems a rather naïve misconception of the business of
art criticism.

IX

ART AND SOCIAL LIFE

I. THE PROBLEM

FINE art is much more than a subject for expert analysis by art critics. Indeed, one of the better reasons for art critics and criticism, if conceptions in the preceding chapter are correct, is that fine art has a large public life, in the service of which art critics and criticism at their best can play a useful role. In a sense, criticism of art is a social agency that delineates the aesthetic values of works past and present so that these values are more clear and available in their precise stature in a literate society. It is a clarification—if not for the creator, then for others of the social group—of the levels of intrinsic perceptual experience opened up by particular artistic creations.

We turn now explicitly to the topic of fine art in human society. Our chief question here will be this: What does fine art imply for human living generally? Or, since human living generally means living in society, what importance has fine art for society, for our society and the good society? In discussing the creative process, we described something of the importance of society for fine art, and we shall say more on this topic as we proceed. But now we shall be concerned mainly with what fine art has to contribute to the larger system that conditions and nourishes its existence and, in particular, what it can contribute to the good society as far as this seems possible within the circumstances of the twentieth century.

In discussing this topic we pass to a consideration of fine art in its total nature and to a completion of the theory of art implied in the relational standpoint. Our topic is the total ramification of fine art in human life. This topic is of considerable magnitude, and we shall divide our treatment of it into several

201

parts. In the present chapter we shall be concerned mainly with
assessing the social importance of the central or distinctive nature of fine art, viz., its nature as the construction of objects for
aesthetic experience. In the next chapter we shall consider the
social importance of the nonaesthetic aspects of fine art, then
seek to come to some comprehensive resolution of the question
now before us.

II. ART AS A SPIRITUAL ASSET

The first importance of the arts for a society, I think, lies in the
wealth of immediate value with which they enrich it. The arts
are means to many ends. But, first and foremost, they are themselves ends and creative of works that are ends. Both as an activity and as a product, fine art at its best is, indeed, one of the great
immediate and self-rewarding goods available to human energy,
bringing the self directly and completely to fulfilment on a certain level of its being and forming a spiritual good in the sense of
something unquestionably good simply for what there is in the
"spirit" of the experience of it.

As a spiritual good, fine art has considerable magnitude,
actually and potentially. In concerts, operas, dramas, books,
dancing, painting, statuary, and buildings the arts for centuries
all over the world have claimed the attention of untold millions
of creators and appreciators. That all this attention has been of
the highest spiritual quality or that it has been rewarded by the
finest possible array of spiritual values cannot be maintained.
But that a great deal of it has been attention to intrinsic values is
clear from the accelerated growth of the arts over the centuries
from handmaidens to other pursuits toward more purely aesthetic agencies; and that a great deal of the attention to art has
been rewarded amply is plain from the great number of masterpieces of art that have come down to us from the past. And as the
past of art as a source of superior immediate values has been great,
so the potentialities of art as a spiritual asset are equally great.
What these potentialities are we have sought to point out in the
preceding discussions. To the creative artist fine art can be the release of the whole self into a complex and intrinsically worth-
while activity. To the percipient, including the artist as per-

cipient, fine art can offer an object with a wealth of immanent values (the sixteen types of intrinsic values outlined in Part II) and a vision of immanent values probably unparalleled anywhere else in its perceptual clarity and immediate vividness.

In reckoning the social values of art it is customary to consider merely the consequences of the arts in society—the arts as means. The arts are means, for they do have consequences, and great ones, as we shall see. But to consider these mediate values as the sole social values of the arts seems a great mistake. In themselves alone and apart from their consequences, the arts have values of the greatest social importance. The intrinsic values of art occur within society and are direct enrichments of the life of the society. Moreover, they are among the peak values occurring there. The most obvious justification of living is found in moments that are immediately self-justifying, that have in themselves so much clear good that they are their own reward and warrant for being. It is to moments of this sort in a peculiarly eminent degree that the arts at their best are a substantial and direct addition. Indeed, the fine arts in themselves, as ends and apart from consequences, might be considered one of the better reasons for the existence of society and social life, so great are the actual and potential intrinsic values contained within them. Nor is this an esoteric opinion plausible only after an expert historical study and an elaborate philosophical survey of the intrinsic values of the arts. It is to some extent a part of common wisdom. One of the common ways used to appraise the stature of a society is to measure the stature of its arts. When people ask whether this civilization or that was great, good, or inferior, they answer in part by considering and estimating the artistic achievement of the civilization. This achievement, it is felt, constitutes a definitive point reached by the society, a mark of its internal power and a symbol of the worth of the life that went on within it. That this criterion is incomplete and misleading if overemphasized must be admitted. But that it is some clue to the level of the good life attained in the society and one decisive mark of the quality and value of the society itself is taken as axiomatic in the common appraisal of human civilizations.

III. ART AS A SOCIAL FORCE: ITS METHODS

As social assets, however, the arts are more than spiritual goods consumed in the moment of their goodness. They are also social forces with consequences that appear and have a social effect after the great immediate good they offer has been consumed. This is true of fine art as a purely aesthetic enterprise. The point here may be stated as follows: Both in creation and in appreciation the arts are internally connected with the springs of social action. They employ and affect the senses, feelings, imagination, and intellect. They employ and affect one's knowledge and will, and one's value attitudes and value insights. But in the greatest degree the deeds of people, at work and at play, are a function of these resources. They are a function of a person's sensory observations and imaginative appreciations of situations, of what a person feels, thinks, knows, wills, and prizes. They are a function of his value attitudes and value insights, of his cultivated capacities and enhanced background. In short, fine art transforms what social action everywhere embodies and is thus implicitly a social force in the very creation and appreciation of an object which serves purely aesthetic purposes.

A more complete and detailed statement of the various ways in which fine art as an aesthetic enterprise is a social force will be given in succeeding sections of this chapter. But, before we proceed to this, it may be instructive to note the range of methods employed by the arts in exerting social influence.

These methods range from the most "unconscious" and unobtrusive to the most explicit and outspoken. This latter method, of which preachment and open incitement have frequently been features, has been employed in Western art from the days of the Hebrew prophets and has produced the most diverse works, from the Bible to "Yankee Doodle," from *De rerum natura* to *Uncle Tom's Cabin*, from early Christian painting to the very latest propaganda art. In all ages, however, the method has had one steadfast purpose—to convince people, often including the artist himself, of the validity of a certain social direction or redirection —political, religious, economic, and the like. Hence all its creations might be called works of "directive art."

This forthright explicit method of influencing social change labors under serious handicaps. First, its maximum effect usually depends on fortuitous external circumstances over which the artist has practically no control. Unless a work of directive art is bulwarked by pressures and terrors from elsewhere, by a critical situation such as a war, a national calamity, an economic or moral crisis, its message is likely to seem artificial and labored and its point irrelevant. And even where it is bulwarked in this way, the work is likely to have only short-range effectiveness, since such supporting agents are invariably short-lived. Furthermore, the need to propagate explicit beliefs clearly and to reach large masses instantly usually requires the sacrifice of almost all the subtler and novel possibilities of fine art. The social point must be made very palpable and very plain, and to do this the artist customarily must forego the unusual and less obvious possibilities of his craft and employ the more elementary and conventional and hackneyed.

As a result of these serious handicaps, the overwhelming majority of works of directive art, including even the most successful in their day, come to seem to a later generation "almost completely valueless" and their authors "manifestly second-rate."[1] Nevertheless, in the heat of battle an artist may accept enthusiastically the risks of this method and be able to surmount its hazards and handicaps to a surprising degree. The very urgency of his undertaking may drive him to penetrate deeply and to image vividly the subject of his work and to create an effect that continues to have extraordinary interest long after the smoke of the battle has passed away. He is unlikely, however, to escape with a whole skin. There is antiquated science in Lucretius, antiquated cosmology and petty politics in Dante, antiquated sociology in Tolstoy. But from these men and from many others—Swift, Hogarth, Goya, Daumier, and the like—have come works possessing a great and lasting power that surmounts their limitations.

Whether the effort was always worth the candle in social or aesthetic terms is a highly controversial question. Undoubtedly, in some cases it was. Had certain artists not been inspired by the

---

[1] Aldous Huxley, *The Olive Tree* (New York: Harper & Bros., 1937), p. 17.

desire explicitly to direct their fellows, they probably would have created works much inferior in aesthetic quality as well as in social influence to the best that they have left, as the mediocrity of the early nondirective works of certain directive artists suggests. On the other hand, the reverse seems equally probable in other cases, e.g., Tolstoy, the majority of whose greatest and most widely respected works preceded his later messianic period. In any event, two things seem clear. Directive art does not seem to be a perfect method to exert the immanent social influence that fine art can effect, and it does not exhaust the list of methods available to the arts for this end.

Indeed, there is a much more usual method of achieving this end which is employed to some extent by all the arts. This is to make the scheme of values sponsored by a work, including the intellectual convictions and social attitudes of the artist, implicit instead of explicit, burying them in the perceptual texture of the creation so that they form a kind of framework within which its subject is articulated. To cite a crude example, instead of declaring explicity that capitalism fosters violence and corrupts character, this method would simply show incident and character in three-dimensional fulness under a capitalistic economic system. Intentionally or not, Shakespeare's tragedies are good examples of works that simply show the course of events and the plight of character when certain motives—incautious generosity, overleaping ambition, excessive jealousy, procrastination—are released and allowed to operate under a certain set of feudal social conditions. The larger ethical and social implications are implicit and come out chiefly in the way they serve to shape events and fix the climax and fate of the characters.

This implicit or imaginative method is the only major method of social influence available to nonrepresentational arts, such as music and architecture, which cannot formulate or transmit explicit social messages. These arts must rely on abstract presentational accents to crystallize or insinuate attitudes or scales of value. They cannot "teach," although there may be sermons in stones and ordered tones for him who shapes or perceives with imagination the presentational content of such creations.

In all the arts, including the representational, the implicit method lacks the pointedness and immediate brute force of the more blunt directive method. In particular, the social doctrine is more vague and indeterminate just because it is implicit. But this disadvantage, if it is a disadvantage—and it is always possible that a percipient will be as quick to seize a suggestion as to follow an explicit direction—is offset by several advantages.

Since the social implications of the work of art are part of its artistic structure, they need not rely for their force mainly upon fortuitous extra-artistic circumstances or for their continued life chiefly on the continuance of these circumstances. Their force and vitality can be based upon the force and vitality of the art itself. Indeed, these suggestions can be insinuated into the percipient with all the power of the art. There is no need to sacrifice artistic subtlety for doctrinal explicitness. The art can become saturated with the outlook of the artist, and this outlook can be empowered by all the subtleties and devices of the art.

Moreover, inasmuch as the social implications of these works are aways implicit, the apprehension of them in the aesthetic experience can give rise to a subtler use of intellect there. It can also frequently be turned into the apprehension of a universal with a generality of applications. For example, the apprehension of one of the more obvious general social implications of *Macbeth*—the ultimate futility of murder as a tool of selfish political ambition—is the apprehension of a universal, carrying with it application to an indeterminate number of other instances besides the case of Macbeth. Furthermore, because the social implications are now imbedded in perceptual images instead of enunciated in abstract concepts and because the artist is naturally more adept at formulating perceptual images than at expounding abstract concepts, the social implications of his work are likely to be more true to his subject, more telling and right, when he uses the more implicit and imaginative method.

Even where his outlook is clearly wrong in a "realistic" sense, the error need not rest like a dead weight upon the work, as do such errors in directive works. Being part of the framework of the creation, this outlook may be taken as an artistic instrument or convention. And such is the desire of the human being to hear the tale of the poet or to see the concrete scenes of the painter or dramatist that he easily acquiesces in taking the outlook in this way. In the *Rime of the Ancient Mariner*, for example, upon the shooting of the albatross, two hundred sailors drop dead and the mariner is doomed to endless life. "The punishment, measured by the standards of a world of balanced penalties, palpably does not fit the crime." But, if the ethical implications of *The Ancient Mariner* are in one sense absurd, they can retain an instrumental dramatic role and with an easy adjustment of attitude can be taken simply in this light. Indeed, "the function of the ethical background of 'The Ancient Mariner,' as Coleridge employs it," says Lowes, "is to give the illusion of inevitable sequence to that superb inconsequence,"[2] viz., the amazing fate of the sailors and the mariner. Thus, though absurd as explicit doctrine, an implicit social tenet may be energizing as artistic means. If to find it so requires us to discount it in one respect, it can be, within the allowances made, a very effective feature of the perceptual object in this other respect.

The implicit or imaginative method of social influence, then, may not give a work of art the blunt relevance and explicit timeliness that the directive method can. But it involves a more "natural," complete, effective, and enduring fusion of fine art and social doctrine; it permits the articulation of outlooks that are more subtle in aesthetic appeal and more elastic and general in social application; it is more favorable to the creation of objects less marred by intellectual distraction and gross error; and it employs the doctrinal element in such a way that, erroneous or not, it can be of permanent usefulness as an artistic instrument.

Independent of method and considering art merely as an aesthetic enterprise, what does it contribute as a social force? The main contributions of the arts here, I believe, are of two types, specific and broad.

IV. SPECIFIC CONTRIBUTIONS

The specific social contributions of art taken aesthetically are almost endless, even if we include only the specific influences of

---

[2] J. L. Lowes, *The Road to Xanadu* (Boston: Houghton Mifflin Co., 1927), p. 300.

works of art on percipients other than the artists who created them. Through aesthetic experience of it, a work of art may incidentally illumine for such percipients a particular type of character and career. The character and career may be those of an Oedipus or a Socrates, a Paul III or a Werther, a Babbitt or a Master Builder. And the illumination may be sympathetic, unsympathetic, neutral, or to some extent all three. Similarly, a work of art may incidentally illumine particular social ideals. These may be the specific ideals that the Greeks drew from Homer and Hesiod or the specific ideals that a twentieth-century Englishman or American draws from the novels of Aldous Huxley or Ernest Hemingway. Literature has devoted much energy to the delineation of human character, action, and ideals, and its contributions here for diverse readers have been frequently described. Thus Chandler writes: "For young readers literature is in part a rehearsal of life. By its aid they form their ideas of love and honor, adventure, success and failure, comradeship, parenthood, and death. It has for them the fascination of depicting the manifold paths which they are soon to explore for themselves. . . . . For the most attentive and thoughtful readers literature is an interpretation of life. They seek enlightenment amongst essayists and philosophers; they derive from the great novelists and dramatists a sense of penetrating into the inner truth of human character and life. Such readers are the better for reading great literature, not in the sense of renewing their allegiance to the Ten Commandments, but in the sense that they are rendered more sensitive to the varied spectacle of nature and life, and are enabled to understand their neighbors more sympathetically and to meet their fate more serenely."[3]

Literature, however, is not alone or even paramount among the arts in the illuminating presentation of specific human characters, actions, and ideals. Painting and sculpture often present trenchant portraits of historical characters or mythical, but possible, individuals and suggest modes of life in glowing or caustic

[3] A. R. Chandler, *Beauty and Human Nature* (New York: D. Appleton–Century Co., 1934), p. 295. Matthew Arnold's description of poetry as the "criticism" of life is, of course, a classic statement of this point.

light. Music often distils magnificently the diverse qualities of actions and ideal attitudes—striving, resignation, defiance, grace, resolution, ruthlessness, heroism, verve, confidence. Moreover, to experience sympathetically and deeply the music of Beethoven, Wagner, or Mozart, for example, is to become momentarily identified with three very different personalities and to take into one's self something of the character and aspiration of each personality. It may be the heroic quality of Beethoven, the tenacity or swelling longing of Wagner, the darting vividness or graceful melancholy of Mozart, or any number of other qualities. But anyone who submits sensitively and wholeheartedly to the powers of great music is unlikely not to be affected by its emotional levels and personal emphases; and to some persons, indeed, it is creative musicians rather than figures in literature or in the graphic arts who embody the specific ideal tendencies and perspectives on life that they most unreservedly admire.

The specific contributions just mentioned emanate largely from the expressive side of art. Especially important here, besides the specific human characters, actions, and ideals it illumines, is the endless variety of specific feelings that this side of art can vivify. The expressive side of art can bring home to percipients the feelings of innumerable peoples of innumerable ages about all the major concerns of human life. At least, it can do so in its total scope. Indeed, this capacity of the arts to vivify specific feelings is so great and its utility to percipients so vast that some thinkers, defining art simply as the transmission of feeling—which is certainly one of the incidental powers of art in aesthetic perception—have argued that the arts are an indispensable condition of civilization or of the adjustment of one individual to what is basic in the lives of other individuals and an indispensable foundation of congruity of feeling or social solidarity between individuals and peoples.

The specific contributions of the arts, however, are not limited to the expressive side of art. Equal contributions can arise from the other dimensions, especially from materials and form. A new movement in painting may emphasize a certain purity of colors or certain types of shape or line, and this may alter the taste of innumerable people and even be adopted in public displays, in home decoration, in dress style, and in advertising. A new type of drama or prose fiction may introduce a characteristic vocabulary, tone, and mode of speech; and these may permanently alter to some extent the vocabulary, tone, and mode of ordinary speech and communication. The materials and form of an inherited architecture may shape in endless ways the everyday habits of the people who adapt themselves to it, while the dance, the stage, and the screen may be equally profuse in similar specific effects. A new movement in the dance may start a widespread trend in bodily carriage and posture, just as stage and screen may originate endless specific styles in personal appearance and social manners.

There is one very important general point to recognize regarding the specific social influences of the arts. This concerns their value quality. A great majority of these influences, I believe, have been for good, but certainly not all. Indeed, these influences range from inspiring a noble way of life or adding a permanent enrichment to culture to inspiring a rather foolish way of life or starting a senseless fad or craze. Nevertheless, this seems to be the case: The more fine a work is as art—the more choice its material; the more complex and universal its forms; the more vivid, accurate, and illuminating its expression of character, incident, ideals, and feelings; the more useful its functions—the finer its particular social influences are. The values of the dimensions of works of art are merely the values of life, clarified, intensified, and raised to full aesthetic stature. And, although a work of art may be very good in certain respects—e.g., as a formal or technical achievement—and yet very bad in its specific cultural influences owing to some dimensional feature, such as the craven ideals or crass personality expressed through it, a work of art that is very good in all respects, in all its termini and in the interrelation of these termini, will inevitably exert, on those who can take it for what it is, good particular influences.

When we turn to the broad cultural contributions of the arts, this value correlation between fine art and social influence is even more evident. The finer the art, the finer are the broad cultural contributions that it makes possible; and works that are finest as art are also the finest sources of art's broad cultural influences.

V. BROAD CONTRIBUTIONS

The first of these broad contributions of art as art is the development of certain capacities in individuals, and the fostering of maturity of personality. Art can heighten the capacity for experience. Writing about the visual arts, Berenson says, art "must give us not the mere reproductions of things but a quickened sense of capacity for realizing them."[4] In a similar context, Munro has pointed out that after the study of a group of paintings one may find "that all the visible world outside of art has become a little more interesting. We now notice in nature, in the fields and in crowds of people, forms like those to which the artist has called our attention. There is endless interest in observing, selecting and rearranging them into imaginary pictures of our own."[5] This enhancement of personal capacity is more than a cultivation of exquisite sensations. It extends to the imagination, feeling, and intellect; and the fine arts, to the extent that they are fine, can refine these powers and strengthen imaginativeness, delicacy of feeling, and incisiveness of intellect. Art can make the mind more flexible, receptive, discriminate, and responsive. "The poets are failing us, or we them, if after reading them we do not find ourselves changed: not with a temporary change, such as a luncheon or slumber will produce, from which we inevitably work back to the *status quo ante*, but with a permanent alteration of our possibilities as responsive individuals in good or bad adjustments to an all but overwhelming concourse of stimulations."[6] In addition, the fine arts can cultivate in individuals innumerable other valuable qualities—vitality, originality, spontaneity, humaneness of outlook, creativity, independence, increased freedom from possessiveness. And all such

[4] B. Berenson, *The Italian Painters of the Renaissance* (London: Oxford University Press, 1930), p. 88.

[5] T. Munro, *Great Pictures of Europe* (New York: Coward-McCann, Inc., 1930), p. xxi. The original publisher of Munro's *Great Pictures* is Brentano's (New York, 1930).

[6] I. A. Richards, *Science and Poetry* (New York: W. W. Norton & Co., 1926), p. 53; cf. also *Life and Letters of Charles Darwin*, ed. Francis Darwin (New York: D. Appleton & Co., 1896), I, 101–2.

qualities also expand and refine the capacities of the individual, and make for maturity of personality.

It is true, of course, that all the potential riches of the arts available in creation and appreciation may be spread before a barbarian, and he may still remain in many ways a crude and greedy soul, i.e., a barbarian. And some who cultivate the arts— creators, appreciators, and interpreters alike—remain callow and uncouth in certain personal respects. But this is simply an instance of the general fact, illustrated in all education, that if you start with material inferior in certain basic ways or subject to powerful external influences contrary to the goal of the education, you work within ineradicable limitations, and the education is likely to have far less than the desired effect. It is still a superstition to believe that by some single piece of magic everything can be turned into gold. And the arts certainly cannot do that.

Still, given passable material and not unfavorable circumstances, the arts can go a long way. In creation and appreciation they can increase the range of our sensory and imaginative grasp, enlarge the scope and subtlety of our feelings and insights, preserve and strengthen a large sheaf of the finer and rarer values of human existence—creativity,[7] originality, spontaneity, and others previously mentioned. And all this makes for increased capacity and maturity of personality and a richer personal life. In addition, it makes for decent social action; for we act largely on the basis of what we sense and imagine, on what we feel and think, on what we value and cherish. And if the fine arts at their best refine these bases of behavior, making our capacities more able and our values more wide and discriminate, they constitute a discipline in decency and a modification of character from which decent social action can spring.[8]

[7] Cf. Milton Nahm, *Aesthetic Experience and Its Presuppositions* (New York: Harper & Bros., 1946), p. 78.

[8] Cf. Sidney Hook, *The Hero in History* (New York: John Day Co., 1943), pp. 237 ff., on the importance of the artist as well as the man of ideas in developing persons capable of mature social action, although earlier in this work Hook refuses to give the title of "hero" to either the artist or the man of ideas and limits its use to the statesman and similar direct determiners of decisive public events in political and social history.

Second, fine art can cultivate a sense of human worth and dignity. The great works of art of the world are usually products of intense devotion, great fertility, and immense skill. They are monuments to the enormous strength and resourcefulness of which the human being is capable. Viewed from some superhuman standpoint, they may not seem very significant; but, compared with the more commonplace and everyday human achievements, the best of art reminds us of a strain of grandeur and limitless value potential to man. Sometimes the sense of human worth and dignity vivified by the arts seems exaggerated in the artist himself, especially the romantic artist, who abounds in colossal egotism. But it need not be excessive in the artist, and often it is not. And it is certainly capable of acquisition in true proportion by the appreciative and active percipient. Any amateur who has tried his hand at an art, who has tried to compose music, for example, will return from his trials, if he is honest and intelligent enough to realize the comparative value of his results, with a very high regard for the Mozarts and Beethovens who have achieved masterpieces in the field of music. Deep familiarity with the greater achievements of an art and with one's own capacities in it usually breeds the greatest respect for the miracles of man that have been wrought in the art in question. And certainly today, when a sense of human worth is radically dimmed by the standardization and insistent routine of commercial and industrial life, by war and social conflict, and by the leveling power of mass custom and pressure, some reminder of the heights of creative freedom and initiative of which man is capable and of the great potential for extraordinary accomplishment of the human being, which fine art at its best exemplifies, is more than ever relevant and worthy of every emphasis.

Third, fine art can suggest a generalized model for human living in all its forms. This fact has been widely recognized by those who have reflected critically on the relation between art and human life, from the greater Greeks to such recent thinkers as Havelock Ellis and John Dewey. In certain dialogues, notably the *Phaedrus* and the *Symposium*, Plato describes the artist as seeking in his peculiar medium a realization of the principles of harmony, proportion, and self-sufficiency, which, according to Plato, are the foundations of the good life generally. In the *Nicomachean Ethics*, Aristotle's conception of the good man as feeling and acting in accordance with the Mean is frankly based on the analogy of the good artist, who, according to Aristotle, follows a similar Mean principle in the tuning of his instrument. Havelock Ellis in *The Dance of Life* has tried to show how the forms of art, typified by dance forms, may recur in social life, which itself may be modeled on the dance and shaped in the manner of an art. Dewey in *Experience and Nature* has argued that fine art at its best exhibits a model solution of the basic conflicts and dualisms of human existence and that its union of means and ends, the instrumental and the terminal, the physical and the spiritual, presents in the most vivid terms the goal toward which all personal conduct and social life should be directed. "Yesterday," to requote Nietzsche, "I heard for the twentieth time—will you believe it? —Bizet's masterpiece. . . . . How such a work perfects a person! He becomes a masterpiece himself." In the best works of art one catches a glimpse of a total perfection; and captivation and impregnation by it may, as Santayana says, "refine the mind and make it familiar with perfection. By analogy an ideal form comes to be conceived and desiderated in other regions, where it is not produced so readily, and the music heard, as the Pythagoreans hoped, makes the soul also musical."[9]

We may put this thought more specifically in our own terms. Fine art, we have said, is the ordering of an area of the perceptual world so as to bring to pass vivid intrinsic values within it. Its aim is to change things into the intrinsically interesting and intrinsically fine, and in its greatest achievements it does this with immense skill and resourcefulness. In great art, experience and thought and energy and purpose are employed with precision,

[9] G. Santayana, *Reason in Art* (New York: Charles Scribner's Sons, 1905), p. 53; see also Irwin Edman, *Arts and the Man* (New York: W. W. Norton & Co., 1939), pp. 130 ff.; Van Meter Ames, *Introduction to Beauty* (New York: Harper & Bros., 1931), chap. xvi. Cf. also Cézanne's advice to Charles Camoin. After exhorting Camoin to work hard at his art, Cézanne writes: "For this is what you must strive to do, not slackly without backbone, but steadily and quietly which will not fail to give you exceptional insight, very useful to guide you firmly in life" (*Letters*, Eng. trans. [1941], p. 220).

tact, and a fine sense of form to bring forth a product radiant with immanent values. Now something of this sort is equally possible in all the major activities of living. All these activities can be purposively shaped so that they yield an intrinsic good and possess an immanent value. Some acts seem so trivial—sweeping a room, taking a walk—that to conduct them after the analogy of fine art may seem a misdirection of energy. But certainly in the greater concerns, especially in professional undertakings and personal relations, something of the aim of fine art is clearly relevant. The sense of being a free agent or an originative cause of value and, above all, the effort conscientiously to magnify immanent values can enter here; and life, instead of being a mere treadmill of routine and habit or a nervous concern for results and consequences, may blossom into experiences and situations which are vivid with immanent values.

Nor need the ideal foreshadowed by art be limited in application to the personal conduct and professional life of individuals. It can serve equally as a model for the state—the national and the world state. The Greeks saw a suggestive analogy between the construction of a work of art and the ruling of a state. The true ruler or statesman, they held, was concerned with the good of the whole state and sought to treat each class and member in such a way as to allow them that individual fulfilment which was compatible with a comparable fulfilment of the other classes and members. The true ruler sought a maximum of immanent values within a harmonious whole. And something of this aim the Greeks saw already vividly realized in great art. Whether the artist was constructing a statue, a lyric, a temple, or a drama, he sought to make each detail intrinsically valuable, yet not so overfavored that it rendered other details ineffective and void of intrinsic value. The great artist was concerned with the whole and with each part as an individual and as a member of the whole. This view of art, as concerned, like government, with the harmonious ordering of a developed diversity, has a clear parallel in our own theory. Thus we have described the canon of art as the ideal of a diversity of dimensions, each with its own terminal values, integrated with one another into a complex public object

—an individuated diversity governed by integrity or harmony. This conception is clearly similar to the Greek view of the ideal of art, and its application to the political state has a similar possibility.[10]

VI. RECAPITULATION

In society, then, fine art has at least two central values. It is a spiritual asset, yielding to the members of society a large variety of immediate goods which in themselves have a justification that is positive and decisive. It is also a civilizing force, capable of exerting a social influence along two different lines. It can make innumerable specific contributions to an enlightened social life, as our list of art's specific offerings to percipients has indicated, and it can make at least three major broad contributions—developing the capacities, the value range, and personality of the individual; fostering a sense of human dignity; and providing a vision of human purpose in ideal embodiment that can serve as a guide for both personal and group life.

These two central values—the spiritual and the cultural—flow from art as an aesthetic enterprise. Taken simply as a perceptual spectacle, art offers the wealth of immediate goods and exerts the specific and broad social influences—in fineness varying with the fineness of the art—which we have described. Fine art, however, is more than an aesthetic enterprise. It has numerous nonaesthetic functions. Before completing our account of the values of art to society, it is therefore important to note briefly the values to society in these nonaesthetic functions.

[10] Cf. E. Jordan, *Theory of Legislation* (Indianapolis: Progress Pub. Co., 1930), p. 175. In many ways, of course, our view of art is very different from the Greek. Thus the principle of interdimensional integrity is not the Greek principle of harmony or form, which is only one dimension of the public object. The similarity between our own and the Greek conception consists merely in the ideal of art as the achievement of a developed and well-ordered diversity, whose principle is applicable and fruitful in other domains, such as personal life and politics.

X

ART AND SOCIAL LIVING

I. VALUES IN THE NONAESTHETIC FUNCTIONS

VERY prominent among the numerous values in the nonaesthetic uses of fine art is its recreational value. Fine art can be play, pastime, relaxation, entertainment, a way of having fun. Of course, it can be all of these to some incidental extent in being an aesthetic enterprise, and it often is, both to the serious artist and to the serious percipient. But fine art can be pleasure-giving and time-filling, independent of its aesthetic power, through creating factitious excitement, stimulating reverie or agreeable reminiscence, or providing diverting information. There are, indeed, many ways in which fine art can be a means of recreation and relaxation independent of the aesthetic aim; and perhaps the enjoyment that a great many people derive from the arts, as we suggested in our discussion of naïve aesthetic experience, is only in small part aesthetic and is in larger part a pleasure arising from some nonaesthetic source, such as those just mentioned.

Closely connected with the recreational value of the arts is the medicinal value. The fine arts can provide a tonic, lift, or restorative, especially in times of anxiety, irritation, and profound dislocation. They can be morale-builders, giving solace and inspiring strength, courage, and hope. They can bring repose and relief from the restlessness of life and can effect a catharsis of disturbing emotions, both for percipient and for creative artist. Some people have a need for music or poetry, similar to the need of others for a stimulant or strong drug, and life is sick and desolate when the enjoyment of such arts is unavailable. Moreover, the arts can serve as muscular, as well as mental, therapeutics, enabling persons to regain certain elementary manual powers lost in accidents and wars. Here again, the arts can have at least

218

some of these values, especially the catharsis of disturbing emotions, as aesthetic enterprises, as Aristotle noted long ago. But they can also have these values when taken primarily as means to ends different from the aesthetic end, for example, when taken self-indulgently, as we shall note again later on.

Fine art can have extensive educational value. From works of art one can glean much history, biography, psychology, and sociology—endless information about human beings past and present. Wise statesmen have used the arts to teach peoples about their past and to focus their purposes for the future. The priest has used the arts, particularly sculpture, painting, and poetry, to present in vivid form the chief figures and beliefs of his religion. The arts can also have religious values additional to their value as instruments of religious education. They can provide shrines for religious worship and icons for religious meditation. In dance and sculpture they can be efforts at homage, propitiation and veneration of deities. Music and poetry can garnish the religious service and become part of the ritual of the religion. There is no aspect of religion with which the arts cannot entwine themselves.

Fine art can have considerable commercial value. Indeed, fine art is today a vast professionalized activity, by which countless persons—musicians, novelists, painters, actors, sculptors, architects, and the like, not to mention publishers, managers, and impresarios—earn a livelihood. Its products are commodities with a market and a price. Its established masterpieces are often looked upon as choice investments, and its latest ventures are often judged as commercial enterprises and given a standing in terms of their merit as such. Indeed, fine art today is a big business, as well as lending itself, in architecture, advertising, and commercial illustration, to the purposes of business generally. Fine art can also be the gateway to fame, prestige, and favor, as well as to money—in some cases even more so than most professions—in contemporary society.

Fine art can have considerable value as an instrument of commemoration. Odes, elegies, statues, portrait paintings, buildings, overtures, and symphonies have all been composed in honor of some great event or hero. Commemorative work is often not very memorable as artistic accomplishment, although innumerable exceptions—Shelley's "Adonaïs," Beethoven's *Third Symphony*, Velasquez's "The Lances"—instantly spring to mind. But the commemoration of the distinguished present and past is nevertheless a social value that works of fine art can have, independently of whether these works are very valuable on any other grounds. Fine art can also have considerable value as a source of physical utilities—bridges, buildings, centers for traffic circles—as we mentioned in the discussion of the functions of art in chapter vii.

Finally, fine art can have immense historical value. Not only do its works often record the public events and the outer appearance of illustrious personages of the past, but they often are eloquent indexes of the modes of feeling, the inner aspirations, and the spirit of peoples long vanished. The character of Greek civilization can be read in its philosophical discourses and historical tracts. But we see a good deal of it more concretely and intimately if we turn to Greek sculpture, architecture, ceramics, lyrics, epics, and drama. A Greek temple is a record symbolizing one type of group aspiration, a Gothic cathedral another type. And, besides documenting the traits of a civilization, outer and inner, fine art often provides a peculiar type of documentation. Its works, frequently part of the major historic substance of a civilization, often continue into later epochs intact. Kings, battles, and economic and political systems vanish in the holocaust of historical change, but works of art often survive the tidal shock of events and remain as living surrogates of civilizations no longer existent in most other major respects.

Fine art, then, can have a large number of social values in addition to the spiritual and cultural values it has as an aesthetic enterprise: viz., recreational, medicinal, educational, religious, commercial, memorial, utilitarian, and historical. In recent times these nonaesthetic values, or at least some of them, have frequently been considered the chief or sole values of art, much to the confusion of philosophical theory and of thinking generally about the arts. Our account aims to place these values in proper perspective. These values differ in two fundamental ways from the other social values of art—i.e., from the spiritual values and the cultural values flowing from the spiritual.

First, although some of them, as I have mentioned—e.g., the recreational and medicinal—can be obtained by taking fine art as an aesthetic enterprise, all of them can be obtained by ignoring or subordinating the aesthetic side of fine art. For example, one can obtain recreation from the arts by taking them self-indulgently, e.g., in the manner of the dilettante whose aim is not so much the creation or appreciation of a flawless perceptual whole as the indulgence of his whims and his itch to be clever. One can equally obtain therapeutic value from the arts by taking them self-indulgently, e.g., as a means by which one is carried off into a cheery dream-world largely of one's own manufacture. And it is fairly obvious that educational, religious, commercial, memorial, utilitarian, and historical values can be derived from works of art without any central concern for aesthetic values. Educators, priests, businessmen, public administrators, and historians, although often learned in many respects, are sometimes very ignorant of aesthetic values. But this does not deter them from using works of art in a great many of the ways in which works of art are useful for educational, religious, commercial, memorial, utilitarian, and historical purposes. Of course, as I say, one may obtain at least some of these additional social values from the arts as a consequence of having taken them aesthetically. But this is not necessary, whereas it is necessary to take art aesthetically, if one is to obtain the spiritual values of art or the cultural values that are consequent upon the spiritual.

A second basic difference between these additional social values and the others is that there is no direct correlation between the fineness of art of a work and these additional social values, as there is between this fineness and the spiritual and consequent cultural values. Very great art—great both in its intrinsic aesthetic values and in the specific and broad cultural effects consequent upon adequate aesthetic apprehension of these values— may be inferior so far as the amount of pure fun or druglike forgetfulness it provides. Froth is often much more entertaining to people than serious art, and many a cheaply made topical creation may relieve from boredom and even provide emotional stimulation and uplift far more extensively than penetrating and profoundly original artistic work. And this noncorrelation of the recreational and therapeutic values of art with artistic excellence holds for all the other additional social values here under discussion. A great work of art may, of course, have great religious, commercial, educative, commemorative, utilitarian, and historical values and also great recreational and therapeutic values. But an inferior work of art—a deft religious melodrama, a huge ostentatious building, an agreeable didactic poem, a mediocre statue, a sturdy but ugly bridge, a heavy sociological novel—may have, respectively, greater religious, commercial, educative, commemorative, utilitarian, and historical value than innumerable works of art that are immeasurably finer as aesthetic creations but not particularly suited for religious, commercial, didactic, commemorative, utilitarian, or historical purposes.

These remarks are not meant as disparagements of the additional social values here under discussion. Without doubt, these values are important adjuncts of the arts. Indeed, in some societies, such as a fanatically religious society, these values, or some of them, may be crucial for the life and death of fine art. But it is equally important not to confuse issues. These additional social values *are* additional and are often obtainable without any concern at all for the central nature of art. And, although some of these values exist to some extent in most art and all of them often exist to a very great extent in very great art and although these values are very important in any adequate estimation of the arts as social phenomena, they are not the values most distinctive of art, and they should not be substituted for the central or distinctive values, as they often are in popular thought and superficial philosophical analyses.

II. THE IDEAL OF ART

In the light of the present and preceding chapters, we might say that fine art in its total nature possesses for society a complex set of central values and a complex set of peripheral values.

The central are the spiritual and cultural values described in the preceding chapter. The peripheral are the values in the nonaesthetic functions of art just described. Two questions arise regarding these two sets of values. First, what would be the ideal or optimum realization of these values in a society? Second, what are the conditions required for the realization of this ideal?

In most general terms, I believe, the ideal realization of these values would be the achievement of a maximum of each type of value with a minimum of conflict and contradiction between them. More accurately, it would be the realization of a maximum of central values, together with that maximum of peripheral values that can be combined with such a realization without detriment to it. Such a combination would achieve in proper proportion the fullest actualization of the values which we have said fine art can possess for society and so be the limit of the possibilities, or the ideal, relevant to art in the circumstances. Great art would be art that approached this limit or ideal. What would this mean in more detail?

Great art would involve a high level of interdimensional values—high, that is, in comparison with what has been achieved and might easily be achieved in the interdimensional structure of works in the art in question. Equally, great art would involve an effective solicitude for all the termini of the work of art and a high level of terminal values—high again in the comparative sense. Interdimensional excellence, we have seen, is measured by the degree in which the dimensions of works of art combine to implement and reinforce one another, i.e., by the degree of their inner amplifying harmony. Terminal excellence is measured by the degree of perceptual refinement and clarification that the personal vision of the artist has brought into the dimensions of works of art, the comparative incisiveness and inclusiveness and coherence that his original and peculiar terminal realizations possess. Great art is terminally original and profound, as well as interdimensionally harmonious and sound. It combines richness with integrity, or complexity with simplicity.

So-called "primitive" art is an approach to great art by way of simplicity. Simplicity tends to dominate over complexity.

The works of such art exhibit a vivid, but limited, interdimensional implementation; and they employ standardized and stylized materials, forms, expressions, and functions, clearing out dimensional complexity for the sake of an insistent depersonalized purity and regularity. Decadent art is a retreat from great art by way of complexity. Complexity tends to dominate over simplicity. The art is overluxuriant. The interdimensional instrumentation is so vehement that it exaggerates all the termini of the work of art, or so tenuous that it diminishes none of the slackness of the dimensions. The terminal realizations themselves are riotous or lax, substituting melodramatics for incisive clarity or looseness for refinement and restraint. Decadent art is an overstatement of the central possibilities of art, just as primitive art is their understatement.

Great art possesses the virtues of primitive and decadent art without the excesses that tend to nullify even the virtues of each. It is simple, like primitive art. But it has more subtle interdimensional instrumentations and more voluminous terminal realizations. It has fineness without the slightness of primitive achievement. Great art is thus complex, like decadent art. But it avoids the decadent's sacrifice of refinement and clarity for the sake of a dissolute largeness or dazzle and melodramatics. It has fineness without the extravagance of decadent achievement. In sum, great art possesses a simplicity compatible with complexity and a complexity compatible with simplicity and so achieves the main values of primitive and decadent art without the defects that limit the achievement of each.

We might state this in another way, in relation to classicism and romanticism. Greatness in art can be reached from either a classical or a romantic orientation. You may have it in a Bach or a Beethoven. But where you have it from a classical orientation, it possesses subtlety and richness as well as solidity and simplicity. It is not the facile, empty art of neoclassic effort. And where you have it from a romantic orientation, it abounds in powerful form and integral strength. It is not the fragmentary overluxuriant art of the typical romantic. In its central nature, great art is at once romantic and classical, yet characteristically neither. It has the virtues of each, while avoiding the excesses and deficiencies that tend to cancel out even the virtues of typical romantic and ordinary classical achievement.

Fine art, however, can attain a greatness beyond mere centrally or focally great achievement. This occurs when art that is focally great is effectively combined with some great extra-aesthetic enterprise. In the West this combination has probably been most signally achieved in religious art. At least, the examples of the combination that will probably occur most immediately to the Western mind as approximations of this ideal are such works as fifth-century Greek temple sculpture and architecture, Hagia Sophia and Amiens Cathedral, and, perhaps to a lesser degree, the Giotto frescoes at Assisi and Padua and Bach's *St. Matthew Passion* and *B Minor Mass*. All these are works of very considerable focal excellence, so considerable as likely to surmount purely temperamental demurrers to a very high degree. But they are also works that were parts of extra-aesthetic enterprises fundamental in their cultural epochs, and they made substantial contributions to these enterprises. They served basic nonaesthetic ends of their times in a marked degree.

Obviously, however, the ideal here in question is not restricted in its particular extra-aesthetic occasion to the religious undertakings of a society. Any extra-aesthetic enterprise is relevant, provided that it has crucial value for the society and that artistic work, focally excellent, can contribute effectively to it. An educative, political, economic, commemorative, or recreational venture might be such an occasion; and in our day, if greatness of this sort is to be achieved by art at all, it is most likely to be achieved in relation to such occasions as these. In the main, such occasions should have two properties: first, they should be socially of the first importance, i.e., valuable to the whole society in question; and, second, they should be such that focally great art can contribute to them, and not occasions, such as an urgent council of state, where great art might rather get in the way.

This combination of great extra-aesthetic usefulness and great focal or central excellence would seem to constitute the fullest genuine value possibilities open to art, its total ideal; for, with such a combination, art would be a spiritual asset, a cultural force, and a nonaesthetic utility; and, assuming the art to be focally great and equally effective in an extra-aesthetic enterprise socially great, it would necessarily contain at a maximum the types of values for human beings which we have seen to be potential to artistic achievement.

To turn, then, to our second question: Under what conditions can the arts reach this total ideal or, if that is not possible, approach it? I believe there are two sets of necessary conditions, the first pertaining to the artist, the second to the society.

III. CONDITIONS OF THE REALIZATION OF THE IDEAL

Clearly, the artist must have the technical capacity to attain superior focal excellence in his art. Without this, no great art is possible. But technical capacity, while necessary, is not sufficient. A certain broad value outlook must guide this capacity.

What is chiefly required here, I think, is that the artist reach an attitude toward the difficulties confronting his times that is truly coherent with himself as an artist. As an artist, we have said, he can be an agent of a spiritual, cultural, and nonaesthetic good. What value attitude toward the difficulties of his times will make it possible for him to be to the fullest extent an agent of a spiritual, cultural, and nonaesthetic good? This is, I believe, the basic question for the artist.[1] And only in the degree in which the artist is successful in answering this question and finds a value outlook that in practice makes it possible for his art to be to the fullest extent a spiritual and cultural and nonaesthetic good will he fulfil what is required of him by the ideal of art.

What, specifically, this value outlook will be depends on the specific contemporary difficulties of the artist's world. In very

[1] Cf. Thomas Mann, "The Coming Humanism," *Nation*, Vol. CXLVII (December 10, 1938), 618: "For everybody, but most particularly for the artist, it is a matter of spiritual life or spiritual death; it is, to use the religious terminology, a matter of salvation. I am convinced that that writer is a lost man who betrays the things of the spirit by refusing to face and decide for himself the human problem put, as it is to-day, in political terms. He will inevitably be stunted. . . . . His work will suffer, his talent decline, until he is incapable of giving life to anything he produces."

different specific circumstances it will presumably be very different, e.g., as different as the value outlook of a Phidias and that of a medieval French craftsman. How the artist will hold the outlook, e.g., as a set of explicit beliefs or as a set of tacit presuppositions, may also vary considerably. Certainly, he need not cast it into the form of militant "social-message" art. The purely imaginative method should be entirely adequate. In any case the value outlook would be no empty allegiance to a set of abstract and conventional ideals—courage, justice, and the like. It would be entertained and would function in terms of the specific needs of the times, and the basic requirement would be that it guide the work of the artist successfully. More precisely, the basic requirement of the outlook would be that it be effective in his specific art, that it communicate range and depth and coherence to his art as a spiritual and cultural force and a nonaesthetic utility. Its essential character would be disclosed not by lofty pretensions but by effective action and would be verified not by official claims but by the actual effects it had on the artist's specific creations.

Besides this major requirement of an effective value outlook in the artist, there is a major requirement of art, viz., that it have available for the artist the materials and technical traditions which are a sufficient foundation for an effective realization of his capacities and vision. This requirement of art is usually met abundantly by all thriving arts that have had a history, as all of the more vigorous major arts of our day have had. Yet even here this requirement is not always met sufficiently to make great art immediately possible in certain directions, as we shall see in the discussions of Section VI of this chapter.

The second set of conditions required for the realization of the ideal of art concerns society. In general, we might define a society as good to the extent that it puts paramount the welfare of all its citizens and is ready to favor any agency in so far as it contributes to the attainment of this welfare. Such a society, as sponsoring the good of society, would be itself good or adequate to its purpose. In particular, this means that a society would be good to the extent that it recognized its responsibility to such agents as artists who, as we have seen, can be productive of a complex social good. What, specifically, would such a recognition require on the part of society?

First, the society would be required to recognize the difficulties to the good confronting itself and to have attained a unity of belief, enshrined in laws, customs, institutions, and social practices and, above all, in a set of ongoing social enterprises, which had resolved these difficulties to the good, at last to such an extent that an approximation of a general welfare was diffused throughout the society. This unity of belief would not have to be expressed in a particular public document, although it might be. But it would have to be embodied in a set of active agencies operating within the society in such a way as that just mentioned. Second, the society would be required to increase and multiply, as far as harmonious with the general welfare, the extra-aesthetic occasions of art: commemorative, economic, educative, and similar occasions. Third, the society would be required to seek, rather than to force, the co-operation of the artist. It would have to recognize that coercion, bullying, and a callow external censorship produce a timid, not a robust, art; and it would have to treat the artist as a responsible adult, to be allowed the fullest autonomy and freedom compatible with his responsibility. Fourth and finally, the society would be required to stimulate alert, informed, and critical attention to the works of the artist. It would be necessary for it to recognize that these works must be widely seen and heard; that their value realizations must be compared with the best value realizations in the arts and the best value insights of the society; and that, where the artist has slipped below the best that was in him or lost himself in some dubious dream, this should be discovered and understood quite clearly. It would have to recognize not only that the good of art should be shared as widely as possible but that the artist should live up to the potentialities of good in his art as fully as possible; for, as Santayana has said: "An architect or a sculptor, ... or a public performer of any sort, that thrusts before us a spectacle justified only in his inner consciousness, makes himself a nuisance. A social standard of taste must assert itself here, or else no efficacious and cumulative art can exist at all.''[2]

These four requirements of a society—a beneficent unity of belief, a great spread of extra-aesthetic occasions for artistic collaboration, the maximum of freedom to the artist compatible with his responsibilities, and a wide and critical alertness in society to hold the artist to his responsibilities as well as to secure the diffusion through the society as far as possible of the maximum of good that art can bring—are, of course, ideal requirements of a society. But they are minimum requirements for the ideal of art, I believe, since, if any one were removed, there is no certainty that art could attain its maximum effect. Remove a beneficent unity of belief from society, replace it by a malignant, sinister unity of belief or by disunity, and the artist becomes either a collaborator in a mirage or a broken reed whose influence is limited by opposition or fragmentated by disunion. Remove a suitable spread of extra-aesthetic occasions, and the artist's possibilities on the nonaesthetic level are equally diminished or negated. The other two requirements—freedom for the artist; widespread and enlightened critical attention from the society—are particularly necessary for maximum focal excellence. Limit the artist's freedom below that necessary for optimum focal excellence, and the result, if any, will be a cowed or insincere art. Remove energetic and widespread enlightened critical attention to art from society, and the result will be either a lax art or an art likely to be undeveloped in certain directions.

Probably no society has ever actually fulfilled all four of these requirements. Nevertheless, there have been approximations. Fifth-century Athens, thirteenth-century medieval France, the Venetian Republic of the Renaissance, Elizabethan England—all commonly recognized as societies harboring high artistic accomplishment—had to some extent the unity of belief and the goodly variety of extra-aesthetic opportunities required. To a lesser extent, some of these societies possessed the requisite freedom from doctrinaire imposition ideally desirable, while others,

[2] George Santayana, *Reason in Art* (New York: Charles Scribner's Sons, 1905), p. 202.

such as the Elizabethan, lacked that searching and fastidious criticism necessary to save the artist from a laxity inimical to his best achievement.

IV. RECENT ART UP TO 1929

In any case it certainly cannot be said that, in the Western world during the fifty years preceding 1929, there was even a close approximation, either in society or in the artist himself, to the requirements necessary for the ideal of art. Indeed, quite the opposite. In the decades immediately preceding and following the beginning of the twentieth century, the irresponsibility of the artist to society and of society to the artist was probably as complete as at any time in the history of Western culture. The industrial, commercial society of rugged individualistic capitalism, which Carlyle, Ruskin, Dickens, William Morris, and numerous others scolded, ruthlessly drove the artist to the fringes of the social scene, and the artist himself blithely turned his back upon the dynamic forces of his time. "The master," Whistler asserted, "stands in no relation to the moment at which he occurs . . . . having no part in the progress of his fellowmen."[3] "The good artist," wrote Herbert Read later, "is very rarely interested in anything but his art."[4] These statements, uttered at the times roughly bounding the period here referred to, reflect the majority opinion and practice of that era. Read continues: "Is our outer world, in its state of political, economic and spiritual chaos, one which man can face with 'universal piety,' sensuous satisfaction, spiritual aplomb? Is it not rather a world from which the sensitive soul, be he painter or poet, will flee to some spiritual refuge, some sense of stability?" This retreat from the larger social world into the stable ivory tower of the artist's "own states of subjectivity,"[5] to some extent characteristic of the whole modern romantic tradition from 1789, became aggressively and excessively characteristic of the artist in the twentieth century. "Why should artists bother about the fate of humanity?" asks

[3] James McNeill Whistler, *Ten O'Clock* (Boston: Houghton Mifflin Co., 1884).
[4] Herbert Reed, *Art Now* (London: Faber & Faber, 1933), p. 13.
[5] *Ibid.*, pp. 116, 117.

Bell. "If art does not justify itself, aesthetic rapture does. . . . . Rapture suffices. The artist has no more call to look forward than the lover in the arms of his mistress. There are moments in life that are ends to which the whole history of humanity would not be an extravagant means; of such are the moments of aesthetic ecstasy."[6] In the sooty, dynamic, gargantuan hurly-burly of the industrial commercial society of the times, the artist hid his head like the proverbial ostrich in "the realm of his subjective fancies,"[7] and society at large considered him an odd, eccentric, and definitely irrelevant bird. The result was the manifold types of esoteric art, highly individualistic, obscure, rebellious, restless, bizarre, anarchic, which created innumerable tiny eddies of mystic interest on the fringes of society.

Of the development of this esoteric, highly subjectivistic, anarchical art—the art of expressionism, dadaism, imagism, vorticism, futurism, constructivism, stream-of-consciousness, surrealism, and the other tail-ends of romanticism[8]—what was the cause? Clearly, neither the artist nor the society but both. "Perhaps one reason that painting and sculpture of the twentieth century have been restless and bizarre is that modern society, unlike the Catholic Middle Ages and the humanist Renaissance, offers no compelling themes to stabilize the artist's mind and elicit his best work."[9] "In a society with no solidarity of purpose, with no unifying religion and no general idealism; in a world which encourages pretense and factitious achievement—anything, in fact, that looks important—it is to be expected that art too should be polluted by snobbery, inanity, and commercial cunning."[10] But it seems an exaggeration to put the whole blame on society. To be sure, the most evident demand of recent society from the arts

[6] Clive Bell, *Art* (London: Chatto & Windus, 1914), p. 241.

[7] Read, *op. cit.*, p. 125.

[8] Cf. Randall Jarrell, "The End of the Line," *Nation*, CLIV (February 21, 1942), 222 ff.; on recent poetry; cf. also Eric Bentley, *A Century of Hero Worship* (Philadelphia: J. B. Lippincott Co., 1944), p. 261: "Surrealism marks the point at which the individual cuts the last rope that binds him to society and leaps into unabashed irresponsibility."

[9] A. R. Chandler, *Beauty and Human Nature* (New York: D. Appleton–Century Co., 1934), p. 362.

[10] Thomas Craven, *Modern Art* (New York: Simon & Schuster, 1934, 1940), p. 233.

was not the evocation of a driving, generous vision integrated with a driving, generous vision of its own, for the society did not have or want any such vision. Its most evident demand of art was for easy or startling entertainment to cajole it upward and onward to bigger and better mass production, competition, aggrandizement, conquest, and disaster. It lacked basically a humane orientation in economics, politics, or anything else, and it was quite complacent that the arts should have none. But the artist himself was also at fault. Nominally, at least, society kept open all the outlets of artistic endeavor. It did lack a beneficent unity of belief. And it was indifferent. It did not give a serious place in its scheme of things to the artist; it would rather not be bothered. But the society did not curb the artist in any ruthless manner. It was, indeed, immensely tolerant, and the great expansion of communication systems in the period theoretically enlarged many times the scope and the social potentialities of art.

But the artist made the great refusal. He turned his back on society. Its clamorous forces, its difficulties, its strident contradictions seemed to him a purely external spectacle. He regarded society with indifference, or as merely appropriate "material" for "realism" and ridicule. He felt that its larger issues were not his particular business. He laughed or sighed and retreated into his own little world of private observation and reverie, or he became absorbed in the methods and experimental techniques of his craft. Those who place the whole blame on society forget that even in the greatest epochs of art the society of the times was far from ideal in all respects. It had marked shortcomings, if not the same shortcomings as recent Western society. Had the artist of those periods been as indifferent and negative as recent artists, the art of such epochs might easily have been as ingrown, disillusioned, and negative as recent art.

Although the creative art and the society of the times (1880–1929) had, on the whole, no healthy, mutually invigorating connections such as the ideal of art requires, connections remained. Such connections are inevitable, if our view of the internal connectivity of art and society is correct. People of Europe and America who felt that there was something ignoble and perverse in their society were corroborated by its creative art. The vacuity, anarchism, cynicism, and defeatism of much of this art found a ready and happy acceptance in these people and strengthened their convictions and fostered similar convictions in others. At the same time, it helped to discredit the arts themselves. So many people found in the new works nothing but a childish play with materials, a barbaric whoop, or an unintelligible sigh. The critical intellectual, impressed by the cycles of history or flush with new psychological and sociological theory, was prompted to formulate the numerous recent "nihilist" conceptions of art that we have previously mentioned. He plied one or the other of two themes, and sometimes both: that art is basically infantile or that in a scientific world art is no longer relevant and is reaching the end of its years. In the meantime, the common man who paid any attention to the matter was greatly puzzled and, receiving no helpful illumination from on high, shrugged his shoulders and returned to his ordinary task, ready to serve without the solace of the new arts in his usual role of pawn in society's monumental game of plunder.

Thus the arts of the period, although widely publicized, failed to have any large-scale fortunate effect. Often they won the attention and patronage of the more clever of the rich, dilettantes liberated by family wealth from the pressing aims and clamors of the bourgeois society of the day. But they failed to penetrate effectively the more massive currents of the society, and they failed to invigorate innumerable keener minds. Indeed, voicing the bewilderment, disillusion, inner spiritual poverty, and indifference of the artist, they infected with their spirit many of the leaders of action and belief. This infection of leading minds, together with failure to have a fortunate effect or any effect at all upon the mass mind, was one of the tragic elements of the recent history of the West. The social effect was to encourage an attitude of futility, ineffectuality, triviality, and despair among many who should have been resolute, strong, and unyielding. The rapacity and greed of capitalistic enterprise in the active sphere, the olympian neutrality of science in the intellectual sphere, and calamities, such as 1914, were themselves sufficient to try the most sen-

sitive and resolute. These called for combative energy, strong
will, and great humaneness of vision. And here the arts failed
lamentably. They celebrated indifference, their own technical
self-sufficiency, and purity, i.e., emptiness and hollowness. They
celebrated weariness, cynicism, or despair. All this simply
opened wider the gateway for the barbarians. When men despair,
they grow desperate. When men of capacity and intelligence sit
down and weep, the man of cruder stuff jumps up and starts
swinging. The failure of the arts to relieve the cloudy vision of
the times, their encouragement of bitterness or indifference, and
their dimming of any conception of what is humanely grand did
their bit toward preparing the way for the rise of snarling im-
patience and violent action. Of course, recent art with its esoteric content and weak mass appeal did not cause the recent widespread resurgence of violence. To say that would be absurd. But
recent art did not help to stem it, and it did help to weaken the
fiber of enlightened minds who might have helped more vigorously to stem it. In this sense the greater body of recent creative
art takes its place with a great number of other factors—political, economic, intellectual, and the like—as one element in the
social tragedy of the last fifty years.

Is the image of a withering skeleton in a social wasteland, suggested by the preceding discussion, a complete picture of recent
art? I believe it is a broadly correct picture of certain more obvious and spectacular aspects of recent art up to 1929. But it is far
from a complete picture. For one thing, recent art has had, at a
minimum, a great many "minor" masters who have produced a
large number of at least "minor" masterpieces. One thinks at
once of the work of Ravel, Stravinsky, Eliot, Gide, Matisse,
Picasso, Meštrović, and Wright, to mention only a few figures.
Recent art has also been highly inventive and has brought forth
in its freedom numerous experiments that mark lasting acces-
sions to the technical resources of the artist's craft. No one who
has paid the slightest serious attention to the arts of the first
three decades of the twentieth century, for instance, could fail to
be impressed by the ingenuity and novelty of its highly varie-
gated creations, as well as by the subtlety and technical fastidi-

ousness of its more definitive achievements. And, besides considerable accomplishment both permanent and experimental, the arts of recent times and the society in which they have existed have exhibited tendencies that augur well for the future of art, if these tendencies become increasingly dominant. This is particularly true, I think, if we enlarge the span of "recent times" beyond 1929 to include the art and society of the last eighteen years. I should like now to say something about these tendencies in recent art and society, understanding "recent" in the enlarged sense. That these tendencies are not and have not been unencumbered and all-dominant, that they still face formidable obstruction and opposition, is perhaps all the more reason for setting them forth sharply and in the highest possible relief. In what follows, I shall describe them in this way, noting especially the significance of the tendencies for the future of the arts and their relation to the ideal of art and to the conditions required for the realization of this ideal that we have been describing in this chapter.

V. THE FUTURE OF ART: NATIONAL ART

In the society of recent times, the first of these significant tendencies has been a trend toward a new type of nationalism. In the last two decades particularly, there has grown up within the nations of the world a new sense of the interdependence of the citizenry upon one another. Almost everywhere laissez faire conceptions of social organization have been in retreat. Either by edict from a few central mentors or by a ground swell from the masses, a general realignment of social agencies has been under way in the direction of a more planned economy and a wider diffusion of goods over the whole economy. The conception of a general-welfare state operated in the interests of the community instead of in the interest of the profit-first capitalist has been taking shape, and numerous decisive steps have been taken in most of the leading nations of the world to put such a conception into concrete action. That this general conception has been used by Fascist states as a cloak for the continuation of the minority greed and power politics of the past is a tribute to the great persuasiveness and appeal of the conception among people in recent decades rather than an illustration of its falsity and error.

Now such a conception of a nation or state is one with which the whole ideal of great art which we have described is, I believe, fundamentally consonant. A laissez faire economy such as was dominant in the recent past is basically hostile to great art. "As in economics, so in art: laissez-faire within a capitalist economy (or within any economy) merely abandons art to the chances of unrestricted competition, and the devil take the hindmost. It means that art becomes one more commodity on the free market, and that to succeed it must practice all the wiles of salesmanship—mass appeal, sex appeal, adulteration, and the sacrifice of quality to cheapness."[11] On the other hand, a general-welfare society, such as has been lately envisioned widely is, I believe, in principle, fertile soil for the realization of the ideal of art. It would have to follow out the imperatives implied in its principles. It would have to establish in concrete institutions the beneficent unity of belief that its principles imply. It would have to support extra-aesthetic occasions which were consonant with great art and which allowed art to flow into channels permitting its maximum entrance into the life of the people. It would have to allow the artist the liberty requisite for the exercise of his fullest capacities in his tasks. And it would have to promote a program in art education, a training of people in the fullest and freest use of their perceptual powers, with a view to making the bounty of art as widely diffused as possible and as liberally appreciated as possible no less than with a view to holding the artist to the highest level of achievement. But these imperatives are

---

[11] Herbert Read, "Culture and Liberty," *Nation*, CLII (April 2, 1941), 438. (Parenthesis mine.) Berlioz (*Autobiography of Hector Berlioz, 1803–1865*, Eng. trans. Rachel and Eleanor Holmes [London: Macmillan & Co., Ltd., 1884], II, 337 ff.) describes stifling a symphony, nearly the whole first movement of which he had already composed in a dream, at the thought of the great expense, the certain financial loss to himself, and the considerable aggravation of his already distressed economic and personal situation, which would have resulted if he had worked out the symphony and secured its production in the artistically indifferent bourgeois Paris of his later days. This happened nearly one hundred years ago (1852), but it typifies the often desperate dilemma of the original creative artist with his unwanted "children" in the laissez faire economy dominant throughout most of the following century.

all clearly and completely compatible with a state genuinely dedicated to the diffusion of a maximum of welfare over the whole of it.

The imperatives necessary to realize the ideal of art in such a society, however, would not all be on the side of society. The artist would have his share of them. The artist would have to live up to the possibilities of social good inherent in his task. This means that he would not only have to exercise his talents to fullest capacity but also have to face the issues of his day and attain a value outlook that permitted him to co-operate with all the tendencies in the society that favored the possibilities of great art and allowed him to make the contributions to social good that, ideally, art can make.

Something of this sort, a beginning at least in certain directions, seems to have happened in Russia as it has struggled to its feet, following revolution, in recent decades. The arts there have had a position not unlike that in the best "organic" societies. They have been integrated with institutions enshrining a widely supported unity of belief. They have had not only official but immense popular support. The artist has been held in the highest esteem. His training has been anxiously attended to. He himself has enjoyed great respect and prestige. He has dedicated himself to the enrichment of the life of all the people. Commercialism between artist and audience has been eliminated, and the disposition toward official interference, although certainly far from nonexistent, has been felt adversely far less than is commonly believed. The arts have been carried to the factories and farms and the remotest villages, and the great figures of art, such as the Pushkins and the Gorkys, are among the greatest national heroes. Nor have the arts been made into a tool of merely "nationalistic" interests, although the relation of the arts to the life of the people has been kept immediate and evident. Traveling historical museums and theaters have penetrated into all parts of the country, the arts of all mankind have been displayed and studied, and sometimes a non-Russian artist has become as great a hero as the greatest of Russians, e.g., Shakespeare as great as Pushkin.[12] Not only has the result of all this been a tremendous development of interest in the arts all over the country and a great burst of fresh artistic activity of considerable promise, but, together with other basic factors—economic, political, and sociological—it has helped to develop a new type of Russian national—alert, informed, vigorous, courageous—and a national society of great spirit and strength and energy and power.

How far Russia after World War II will continue from these beginnings toward a fuller realization of the conditions of great art as we have described them, especially toward greater freedom for the individual artist, remains to be seen. How far the other nations of the world will parallel the condition of Russia is equally uncertain. As this is written, the less dormant nations of the Orient and the whole of Europe are under a cloud resulting from the appalling destruction of gigantic warfare. It seems likely, however, from present indications, that many nations of Europe will follow or parallel the example of Russia in many respects. Of oriental nations, particularly China and Japan, one can speak with even less certainty. As to the United States, it has already had some very small beginnings in a publicly sponsored art. But these beginnings have not rested on a firm foundation. The United States has always been a place of relative bounty for the individual. It has had a less pressing need than most nations to think and act in terms of a centrally organized diffusion of the good. In recent years, however, American society has witnessed a revolution in this regard, and, combined with other factors, this revolution has implications for the future.

The United States has many of the essentials of a fertile social

[12] Sidney and Beatrice Webb, *Soviet Communism: A New Civilization* (London, New York: Longmans, Green & Co., Ltd., 1937), chaps. x, xi; Edmund Wilson, *Travels in Two Democracies* (New York: Harcourt, Brace & Co., 1936), pp. 211–16; Frankwood E. Williams, *Russia, Youth, and the Present-Day World* (New York: Farrar & Rinehart, Inc., 1934); Harry Ward, *In Place of Profit* (New York: Charles Scribner's Sons, 1933), pp. 418–25; Max Lerner, *It is Later than You Think* (New York: Viking Press, 1938), chap. ix; Norris Houghton, *Moscow Rehearsals* (New York: Harcourt, Brace & Co., 1936); Serge Eisenstein, *The Film Sense*, trans. Jav Leyda (New York: Harcourt, Brace & Co., 1942), Introd. Lion Feuchtwanger, *Moscow, 1937*, trans. Irene Josephy (New York: Viking Press, 1937). These remarks on Russia refer mainly to the decades prior to the German invasion of 1941, and especially to the 1930's.

soil for the arts. It has, in the first place, a very vigorous latent idealism, a good will toward the good in great abundance. Its material wealth is such that it could easily provide innumerable extra-aesthetic occasions—recreative, educative, commemorative, utilitarian—in which the arts at their very best could participate. Its traditions of tolerance are far more sturdy than the provincial intolerance that frequently breaks out over its surface. It has developed to the maximum the instruments of communication and diffusion—press, radio, and the like—and its people have shown an eagerness to learn and a capacity to learn that, in the arts at least, is rapidly advancing them toward a very remarkable maturity. Moreover, traits that Americans manifest as a people—vigor, energy, enormous productive and organizing capacity, keen intelligence, and good humor—are not only deeply characteristic elements of American individuality, but, so far as they go, highly desirable characteristics of artists.

On the other hand, American society has many traits that make it unpromising soil for realization of the ideal of art. Its public offices have only rarely attracted the more imaginative, sensitive, versatilely trained, and enlightened individuals who might provide the leadership to secure the proper place in the national economy for the arts. Its society has been dominantly a middle-class business society, which is to say a society that puts material values and profits first and considers aesthetic values and spiritual goods as dispensable trimmings, except where they involve serious material interests. Indeed, the United States has been one of the shining examples of a dominantly laissez-faire society, which, as we have noted, is basically hostile to great art, abandoning art for enterprises with more immediate tangible advantages. Above all, the United States has lacked a deep sense of the potential importance of the arts for its life, a sense comparable to that of Russia or China, for example, where the social potential of the arts has been known by long experience from ancient times. In a peculiar sense, America is a young society, young not only physically and mentally, as the new Russia and China are, but young spiritually, lacking a spiritual and cultural depth indigenous to it that these other new societies have to draw upon.

Were this a static world, these characteristics of American society, the first set favoring and the second set not favoring the ideal of art, would cancel each other, and America would retain its rather undistinguished place among nations as a soil for the growth of creative art. But the world today is on the move, and in recent times the American mind has been stirred by impulses in the direction in which the world is moving, a direction more favorable to the first set of characteristics than to the second. Thus it is possible that the miracle may happen in America. But the obstacles are enormous and the prospects far from clear. The forces of inertia and reaction, as the last two years show, are still immensely strong and vigorous in this rich and thoughtless land. Yet this seems true and a sound reason for hope regarding the future: in so far as America reaches more surely in the direction of a genuine general-welfare state, as conditions may force it to do, the latent resources in it favorable to the realization of the ideal of art will assert themselves not only more vigorously but with mountingly successful effect.

VI. THE FUTURE OF ART: WORLD ART

The second tendency in recent society which possesses promising possibilities for the future of the arts is more broad in scope. It is a tendency toward a new internationalism. There is today all over the world a profound sense of the awful horror and tragedy that will be unloosed by another war and a yearning for peace rarely, if ever, equaled in human history. To be sure, for some people this yearning is a desire for the *status quo ante* when "peace," so-called, seemed to rule. But with most intelligent people this is not the case. The desire is for some sort of common understanding and agreement between the peoples of the world to end the bloody business once and for all and to act with some regard for the welfare of one another rather than for the welfare of one at the expense of the others. The desire is for a world society of mutually valuable members, so ordered that a genuine welfare exists throughout the whole community of nations approaching in character that within a single general-welfare state and all excuse for war is excluded. This new community of nations, outlawing war and with sovereign power to enforce its will, is still largely theoretical; and whether it will prevail practically in the years immediately ahead or whether the politics of nationalism and "realism" will continue indefinitely the era of international fear, distrust, greed, imperialism, and disorder cannot now be asserted with certainty. But this new world society embodies a conception so widely held and deeply felt and a tendency so strong and inevitable in the modern world that the probability of its actualization in some substantial form in the future seems of a very high order.

Now such a world society is clearly one with which the whole ideal of great art which we have described is also fundamentally consonant. Being simply a general-welfare state remodeled in form and adopted to serve international purposes, it would possess in principle all the excellent qualifications for the realization of the ideal of art that we have seen are possessed in principle by the general-welfare state. It would have to carry out the imperatives of its principles, as must the general-welfare state on a national scale. But the imperatives in its case would be the same as in the other and would require merely the same sort of provisions and actions from it. The chief difference at present between such a world society and the general-welfare state on a national scale is its far greater remoteness from actuality. This world society today is only in process of formation, while the general-welfare state on a national scale is already in operation to some extent in a number of the leading nations. This fact makes the availability of the new world society as a scene for realization of the ideal of art far less immediate and imminent. But this fact is less important at present than it might otherwise be, when one realizes what is required of the arts today before they will be ready at all for such a world society as an arena of operations.

The requirements here consist of much more than the attainment by artists of a new value outlook enabling them to realize the full social potential of art in the new circumstances. Such a revolutionary value outlook is, of course, necessary. But an even more rudimentary requirement is a revolution in the material and technical equipment of the arts, which will probably be a long time in coming. The arts will have to speak a new "language." They will have to attain a material and technical re-orientation. By and large, they do not have at their disposal at present the objective basis required for a new and distinctively international art, as they already have for an effectively national art. And they will have to find and develop this objective basis; for only when the arts are part of the new world, objectively as well as subjectively, in their peculiar material and technical processes as well as in their general outlook, can they hope to bring forth in this world that realization of good peculiarly pertinent to it of which they are capable.

Up to now the arts of our world have been international only in a superficial sense and basically provincial. Their works have sometimes circled the globe. But they have not been works of world art. They have been works of French, Chinese, Russian, Italian, Japanese, American, German, Indian, and English art and, at the maximum, Western and Eastern art. They have originated under national or regional conditions to serve national or regional needs, and they have been phrased in the peculiar "vocabulary," "grammar," and "syntax," of the nation or region. Up to now the arts of our society have belonged primarily to a nationalistic or provincial world. Their first task in preparing themselves for the requirements of art in the new international society will have to be to change this direction and to shake off this provincialism.

This elementary task by and large remains to be done. But to some extent it is already in the process of being done. Perhaps the most vital art of the last thirty years, and the one that could be most vital in the decades ahead, is architecture. And in it a new international "language" and style have already appeared. In Japan and Asiatic Russia, no less than in France, Germany, England, Italy, and the United States, a new type of steel-concrete structure has arisen in the past decades. The numerous examples of this new type of work exhibit marked similarities in form, manner, and accent, as well as in material. On the non-aesthetic side, these works have often been connected with international commerce, which, with the abridgments and accelerations of life produced by scientific inventions for war and peace, has done most to cause people to think in terms of a new world society. The new works here have been built to serve as trim, efficient instruments of some phase of international commerce: manufacture, including plant and workers' quarters; storage; transportation; exchange; and so forth.

That architecture should be the first art to exhibit such a development is not surprising, since it is the most closely connected of all the fine arts with those needs of peoples that propel them most vigorously to discard old ways and invent new ones, namely, urgent physicosocial necessities. We have often been reminded by writers that vital art has a folk basis,[13] but the architect is reminded of this by the folk and the workaday world themselves, and this direct spur has accelerated his activity and given architecture a definite head-start. There is, however, no visible reason why this awakening in the arts to the emergent realities of today should be confined to architecture and why the other arts should not have a parallel internationalist development arising from the realization of common conditions and needs throughout the whole modern world.

The major requirement of the arts here, apart from the reorientation of the artist, would be, as I have suggested, the discovery of new materials—materials as new today as steel and plastics were decades ago in architecture and materials dissociated from the provincial past and distinctive of the new international era. Thus the diatonic materials of Western music and the pentatonic of Eastern music, being languages characteristic of provincial traditions, would have to be transcended, and a new musical material would have to be introduced to which the older diatonic and pentatonic materials would be related in the way in which the masonry architecture of the West and the wood architecture of the East are related to the new steel-concrete architec-

13 E.g., Constance Rourke, *The Roots of American Culture* (New York: Harcourt, Brace & Co., 1942).

ture. In this connection the proposed supra-diatonic musical system of Yasser, based on the most general principles of the pentatonic and the diatonic systems, yet transcending both, is of extraordinary interest.[14] Similarly, the easel painting of the West and the screen painting of the East and the heavy, inflexible stone and metal materials of the sculpture of both East and West probably would have to undergo parallel replacement by fresh materials involving novel and far-reaching technical processes. And, obviously, all the provincial tongues traditionally employed in the literatures of the various nations would be ill-adapted to serve the purposes of a literary art distinctive of a new world society and would have to be supplanted by a new language, if such a world literary art were to become possible.[15]

In the meantime, the regional arts with us today which employ the older materials would retain their current character and glory. Indeed, if the tendencies outlined in the previous section come to fruition, these arts would continue to develop important new works for many years, as organic parts of general-welfare states on national lines. Certainly, they would not be scrapped. But, as the new international arts developed, these older arts would acquire more and more the status possessed today by traditional European and American folk arts, a local vintage transcended by works of wider relevance and appeal. At the same time, these newer works, for all their fundamental breadth and novelty, would not be required to sacrifice regional overtones for a bald global style. Regional individuality would certainly still be part of their basic texture. Just as the music of Germany and Italy of the nineteenth century, for example, shows regional differences although it is formulated in the common diatonic musi-

---

[14] Joseph Yasser, *A Theory of Evolving Tonality* (New York: American Library of Musicology, 1932).

[15] Frederick Bodmer, *The Loom of Language* (New York: W. W. Norton & Co., Inc., 1944), discusses the considerable work that has already been done by experts toward the development of a new international language for pragmatic purposes. Such a language could well serve as the basis of a future art language, as the history of literary beginnings frequently illustrates. The language of literature usually has been a refinement of materials already extensively in use for pragmatic and other nonaesthetic purposes. In its material basis, literature is one of the more conservative of the arts, and the howls of the current literati at the suggestion of a new world literary art should surprise no one.

cal language of the West, so works of the new arts originating in New York and Chungking would be different in various ways although employing the same international musical or other language. The individual values of works of art are as precious in certain respects and as ineradicable as the universal, as we have seen, and they would appear as vigorously in the new arts as in the old, provided, of course, that these new arts were as powerful and as vigorous as the old.

It is important to note that gropings toward such a radical material reorientation as architecture to a substantial extent already enjoys, have not been totally absent from the other arts. These gropings include such experiments as the atonal musical "system" of Schoenberg and others; sculpturing in terms of steel wires and glass rods; painting by adding bits of colored material, such as cloth, to canvas; the invention of novel word-combinations by Joyce and others. Being divorced from larger social requirements, such experiments have been rather artificial, blind, and sterile in the sense of leading to little except imitations. But they do show a vigorous striving for a new material basis for artistic creation. The way to this new basis is opened up fully for the first time by the simple realization that necessity or need in art also is the mother of invention and that today there is slowly emerging for the artist a new set of needs implying a fundamental reorientation of his material means, as well as of his value outlook, namely, the needs of a new international society. In art the greatest advances have usually first come from without, from the whole social matrix or system of stimuli bearing in upon the artist and releasing new possibilities, as a radical change of climate and soil makes possible new types of flowers. Once the new stimuli have been felt and inner adjustments to them have been made by artists and once new material means have been discovered exactly appropriate to the full and distinctive realization of the needs which the new stimuli embody, the beginnings of a great art have been laid, whether it be the art of ancient Greek sculpture, medieval French architecture, or Italian Renaissance painting. And the new world art herein envisaged, being predicated on new social necessities and being assumed to involve new materials and a new outlook consonant with the new necessities, seems equally to contain the possibility and promise of a future of artistic greatness and, in its proper setting, should come into its own as artists are nurtured from the ground up, as current artists are not, to fulfil its requirements.

Such, then, are two important tendencies in recent society and art favorable to a future in which a progressive approximation to the ideal of art that we have described might be achieved— one national, the other international. That these trends will speedily and completely prevail in the future is not at all maintained. The trends are unequal in strength, but, whatever their strength, they are still less powerful and intrenched in many places than those opposite tendencies hostile to the efflorescence of a great art or society that have prevailed in our culture for many years. Being new and implying far-reaching consequences, both tendencies have met and will continue to meet determined and vehement opposition. In relation to the society and art dominant during the last fifty years, they mean either a material reorientation at the bottom or a displacement of enormous vested interests at the top, or both. In view of this alone, it would be mere wishful thinking to predict with certainty the triumph of either tendency. Still, as our survey of recent events shows, such a triumph remains a possibility. Moreover, it contains, I believe, the promise of a state of affairs in art and society, at home and abroad, that is far superior to any that this century so far has seen. Without it, numerous artists here and there will doubtless continue to do good work. But neither art nor society will attain the full measure of good that is potential to them. The two tendencies, therefore, are worthy of every allegiance. And while, doubtless, the emergence of either tendency into dominance depends on many factors, not the least of these, I believe, is the way in which intelligent people use their intelligence, whether for carping and sharp practice in the interest of ends that make less and less sense in the increasingly interconnective pattern of modern life or for the realization of pertinent, far-reaching, and fundamentally beneficent ideas.

INDEX

INDEX

[PRINTED
IN U·S·A·]

5 2 0 0